The Best of
Holidays & Seasonal Celebrations

Grades 1-3
Issues 13-17

Teaching & Learning Company

1204 Buchanan St., P.O. Box 10
Carthage, IL 62321-0010

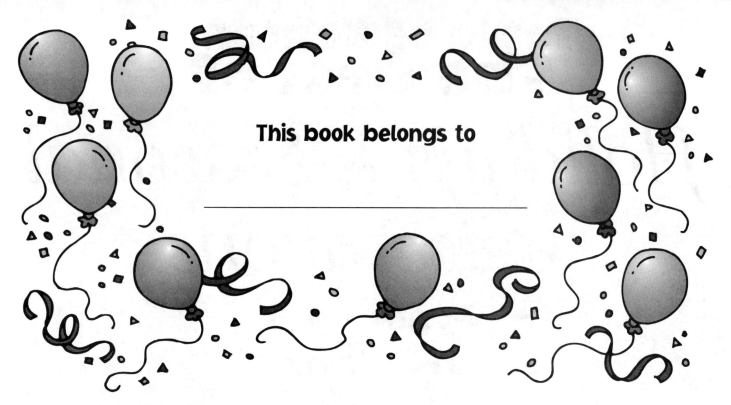

This book belongs to

_____

Edited and compiled by Donna Borst

Cover photos by Images and More Photography

Cover designed by Kelly Harl

Illustrations by

Janet Armbrust	Shelly Rasche
Cara Bradshaw	Vanessa Schwab
Marilee Harrald-Pilz	Luda Stekol
Gary Hoover	Veronica Terrill
Kathryn Marlin	Gayle Vella
Becky Radtke	

Copyright © 1999, Teaching & Learning Company

ISBN No. 1-57310-198-2

Printing No. 987654321

Teaching & Learning Company
1204 Buchanan St., P.O. Box 10
Carthage, IL 62321-0010

At the time of publication every effort was made to insure the accuracy of the information included in this book. However, we cannot guarantee that agencies and organizations mentioned will continue to operate or to maintain these current locations.

Table of Contents

Fall 7

Winter 63

Spring and Summer 201

Dear Teacher or Parent,

Welcome to our latest compilation of the best of the best, the cream of the crop, the piece de resistance—*The Best of Holidays & Seasonal Celebrations* (Issues 13-17). This latest addition to our popular series is packed with the most creative and most fun ideas, as well as the best skill-based reproducibles we could find.

As in the past, the criteria was the same—take the very best materials from the past year's issues of the magazine and turn them into a single, easy-to-use classroom resource. We think you will be quite pleased with what we've come up with, and we want to thank every author, illustrator and teacher who contributed to our success. Without you, none of this would be possible.

On a different note, the process for compiling this book has been a little different, as we had to do it without the guidance and input from our leader and publisher, Don Mitchell. Sadly, Don passed away in February. Don, and his wife, Judy, started the Teaching & Learning Company five years ago with the creation of *Holidays & Seasonal Celebrations*. They wanted very badly to come up with a magazine that was a little different and a little better, and after many long meetings and discussions, *Holidays & Seasonal Celebrations* was born. Those meetings and discussions were ongoing over the years as we strived to make each issue a little more creative and a lot more useful. Don will be missed every time an issue of the magazine is put together and every time we start discussing another "Best Of." However, his legacy continues as his guidance and knowledge will shine through in every issue. He taught us well, and although we miss him every day, he will always be with us and with all of you whenever you use a product from the Teaching & Learning Company in your classroom.

Thank you for allowing us to be a part of your day.

Donna

Donna Borst

If you would like to contribute to future issues of *Holidays & Seasonal Celebrations*, please direct your submissions to:

Teaching & Learning Company
Holidays & Seasonal Celebrations
1204 Buchanan St., P.O. Box 10
Carthage, IL 62321-0010

It's Autumn!

Summer's past! It's fall at last,
And we're all back in school.
Apples round drop to the ground,
And nights are crisp and cool.

The trees all bend in rain and wind,
And sometimes even sleet.
Leaves gold and red hang overhead
And rustle under feet.

The year is old. The air is cold
And almost smells like snow.
But how I praise these autumn days—
The loveliest I know!

by Bonnie Compton Hanson

FALL SENSATIONS

Celebrate the fall season with this exciting array of book favorites. Your students are sure to enjoy the motivating activities that follow each book review. Happy reading!

Perk up the autumn holidays with seasonal cards for your family and friends. Just use the easy-to-follow directions in *How to Make Holiday Pop-Ups* by Joan Irvine, illustrated by Linda Hendry (Morrow Junior Books, 1996). This handy book features holidays from all over the world, including Rosh Hashanah, Diwali, Halloween, Veterans Day, and Thanksgiving.

Treat your class to some delicious pumpkin "surprises" using the recipes from *The Pumpkin Cookbook,* edited by Nicola Hill (Hamlyn, 1996). Some of the recipes included are Halloween pumpkin cookies, pumpkin and raisin muffins, and candied pumpkin. Did you know that pumpkins are one of the oldest known vegetables? Fascinate your students with the interesting pumpkin trivia and folklore that are also featured in this book.

Curtain call, everyone! Your budding young actors will love performing in *Plays Around the Year,* compiled and edited by Liza Schafer and Mary Beth Spann (Scholastic Professional Books, 1994). Some perfect plays for fall include "Planting Seeds," "Spreading Sunshine," "The Ugly Pumpkin," and "A Native American Welcome." A teacher's guide is included with each thematic play and features background information, book suggestions, and cross-curricular activities.

TOO MANY PUMPKINS

by Linda White
illustrated by Megan Lloyd
Holiday House, 1996

There was an old woman who hated pumpkins . . . or that's how the story goes! However, when a gigantic pumpkin falls off a truck into her yard, the seeds scatter everywhere. The old woman soon gets an autumn surprise—a yard full of pumpkins. What will she do with all the pumpkins? The wise woman whips up pumpkin goodies galore for a feast her neighbors will never forget.

- Pretend that you had "too many" pumpkins in your yard. Tell what you would do with them.

- Extra! Extra! Read all about it! You have just grown the biggest pumpkin in the world. Write a news story telling everyone about your amazing pumpkin. Don't forget to answer the "five Ws" in your story: Who? What? When? Where? and Why? Draw a picture of your prize pumpkin.

- It's dessert time! Think of a delicious dessert using pumpkins. Draw a picture of your special treat. What would you name your new creation?

BOOK NOOK

RED LEAF, YELLOW LEAF

by Lois Ehlert
Harcourt Brace Jovanovich, 1991

Follow the life cycle of a majestic maple tree through the eyes of a child. The vibrant collage illustrations showing the growth and development of a tree will appeal to any young audience. A section featuring information on seeds, leaves, and other parts of a tree is included.

- Be a leaf detective! Hunt for interesting facts about leaves and trees. Make a "Be'leaf' It or Not" trivia game with questions and answers about trees.

- Draw a picture and label all the parts of a tree.

- Pretend you find a magic leaf that can talk. Tell what happens next.

CLASS TRIP TO THE SPOOKY MUSEUM

by Buster Yablonsky and Sarah Albee
illustrated by Margeaux Lucas
Little Simon, 1997

All aboard the school bus for the spookiest field trip ever. Join Miss Match's class as they visit an unusual museum and are given a tour by a mysterious guide called Mr. Blood. The Hall of Dinosaurs, an Ancient Egypt display, and the Hall of Dark Ages are all part of this unforgettable tour. Also included in the book is a fold-out Mystery Museum Tour Game.

- What was your favorite exhibit at the museum? Tell why.

- Design a thank-you card that Miss Match's class could have sent to the tour guide.

- Fantastic field trip! Pretend your class could visit any museum in the country. Which museum would you visit? Draw a picture showing one of the exhibits you would see there.

CRANBERRY HALLOWEEN

by Wende and Harry Devlin
Four Winds Press, 1982

When the people of Cranberryport decide to raise money for a new dock, the mayor chooses none other than Mr. Whiskers to be the treasurer. While on his way to the Halloween party to celebrate the fund-raising, Mr. Whiskers is confronted by two "pirates" who try to steal his money box. Never fear, our clever and courageous Mr. Whiskers outwits the two robbers. The delighted townspeople are soon having their best Halloween party ever.

- Draw pictures of two ways the people of Cranberryport earned money to build the new port. What are two other ways they could have earned money?

- Challenge yourself! How many words can you make using the letters in *Cranberry Halloween?*

WINNIE THE POOH AND THE BLUSTERY DAY

by Teddy Slater
illustrated by Bill Langley and Diana Wakeman
Scholastic, 1993

Winnie the Pooh and his endearing friends are back just in time for a blustery new adventure. A strong wind seems to be stirring up trouble in Hundred-Acre Wood—first the leaves are blowing all over the place, and then Owl's house comes crashing down. There's even more trouble when a rainstorm causes a flood, but Winnie the Pooh manages to rescue Piglet from the raging water with the help of his trusty honey-pot.

- Who is your favorite character in the book? Tell why.

- Be an author! Write a story about Winnie the Pooh and his friends on a snowy day.

- Draw a picture of your favorite scene in this story.

WHO CAN BOO THE LOUDEST?

by Harriet Ziefert
illustrated by Claire Schumacher
Harper & Row, 1990

One night two ghosts conduct a booing contest and decide the one who scares the moon will be declared the winner. After much huffing and puffing, and no winner, the two devise the perfect plan—they will work together to scare the moon. Will they succeed?

- Create your own *Amazing Moon* picture book. Include pictures and facts about the moon on each page. Use an encyclopedia or book about the moon to help in your research.

- 5...4...3...2...1... Blast off! Pretend you are the first kid to visit the moon. Design the space suit you will wear. Make a list of three things you will do on the moon.

COMPUTER CORNER

SOFTWARE

Go batty with bats this Halloween! Set the stage with Broderbund's Living Book version of *Stellaluna* by Janell Cannon. This charming interactive story tells about a baby bat's experiences when she falls in a bird's nest and is raised by these new feathered friends. The bat is later reunited with her mother. Now it's time to explore the fascinating world of bats using the handy Bat Quiz full of information about these creatures of the night.
Broderbund, P.O. Box 6125, Novato, CA 94948. Windows, 3.1, Windows 95, or Macintosh on CD-ROM.

SURF THE WEB

Here's a holiday web site you won't want to miss! For holiday information and activities galore, go to http://www.holidays.net. Some of the holidays featured include Halloween, Thanksgiving, Hanukkah, and Christmas.
Looking for seasonal crafts for Halloween? Take a trip to Aunt Annie's Craft Page (http://ww.auntannie.com/pumpkin/pumpkin.html). Everyone will enjoy making these paper crafts with a jack-o'-lantern theme, such as pop-up cards, envelopes, decorations, and masks.

BY MARY ELLEN SWITZER

Autumn

Kid Space is an ever-changing, fascinating place where children can connect with the natural world and learn all kinds of things. It is a space where kids can explore freely, embark on adventures, and make learning discoveries all on their own. Allow your group of children to appreciate all of Earth's beauty as it comes to life this fall.

Nature Breaks

You can always take a break in nature, whether it's a three-minute romp or an all-day excursion, a tramp through the woods or an organized outdoor activity—you're sure to have an enthusiastic group of little learners.

Take Your Imagination for a Walk

Take your imagination for a walk, observe, and be creative.

Look at rocks, twigs, hills, paths, and trees as if they were works of art—sculptures, maybe. Sometimes nature seems to play a trick and something looks like something else. Take photographs of nature's sculptures—clouds that look like horses, trees that look like giraffes, rocks that look like hearts, and so on.

Fall Nature Hikes

Outdoor hikes offer children many exciting learning opportunities and they need not cover much territory—just many experiences! Fall is an exciting, bug-free time to take a close look at your natural environment.

Take your keen senses on a hike in search of these autumn treasures:

- migrating birds
- colorful leaves
- touch-me-not flowers: these orange wildflowers will delight all when the seed pods are gently squeezed (or merely touched) to release seeds in a small explosion.
- nuts, fruits, and seeds hanging on their trees and plants or fallen on the ground
- creatures preparing for winter
- varieties of dried grasses

Leaf Walk

You can't visit your Kid Space at this time of year without being awestruck by the leaves!

Take a walk into the leaves on various occasions during this season. Record observations about the leaves on each venture. How do you feel? What colors do you see? What fraction of the leaves do you think have fallen? Describe the shapes you see. In what ways has the landscape been transformed?

On later ventures you will notice changes in the landscape, the trees, and the leaves. Draw children's attention to these changes.

Leaf Collection

Take a walk to collect a variety of leaves—about three for each student. Remind children that we normally leave the natural environment undisturbed—but in this case, a few falling leaves won't affect the forest too much.

Leaf Creations

Take your collection of leaves back to the classroom for this seasonal craft activity.

Materials
- leaves
- glue and glue brush
- construction paper
- drawing tools

Procedure
1. Have students choose an interesting leaf that suggests another object or creature to their imagination.
2. Have children paste the leaf to the construction paper and then draw beyond the leaf to turn it into something else.

Roll the Pumpkin

This simple exercise will enhance fitness and offer a little fun for the school yard.

Have children roll a very large pumpkin around the school yard along a path designated by markers of any sort. Can they do it?

Save Our Seeds!

You can save and plant vegetable seeds from tomatoes, peas, beans, cucumbers, and squash, as well as flower seeds from marigolds, zinnias, snapdragons, poppies, and sunflowers. Save the seeds from the most hardy plants in the garden.

Materials
- seeds from your own plants
- cookie sheets
- envelopes
- shoe box
- pens for labeling

Procedure
1. Pick seeds from the vegetables or flowers.
2. Rinse the seeds in water and spread them out to dry on a cookie sheet.
3. Store seeds in labeled envelopes. Record the seed name, the year, and other information.
4. Store the seed packets in a box in a cool, dry place.

Try This

Obtain permission to take a few seeds from some special plants in your area, from historical sites, beautiful gardens, experimental farms, or very old gardens. Plants that you grow from these seeds will not only be beautiful, they will carry memories and history with them.

Help preserve our plant heritage by saving and replanting the seeds of important plants.

Apples, Apples, Apples

Cooperative Apple Relay

Materials
- one small apple
- stopwatch
- group of children
- running track, field, or walking path
- whistle or other signal to begin the race

Procedure
1. Position students equal distances apart along the running track. If the same path will be used repeatedly, new runners can join the relay from the position where previous runners begin their leg of the race.
2. Give the apple to the first child and prepare to give the "On your marks, get set, go!" call, and to start the stopwatch.
3. On the signal, the first runner will carry the apple to the second runner, who will run and pass it off to the third child and so on until all students have had the opportunity to run.
4. Using the stopwatch, determine how much time it takes for the apple to travel through the entire class and across the finish line.
5. Throughout the season, your group may decide to challenge their previous time record. Time them as they run the relay again, and see if they can do it faster this time.

Fill the Bushel Basket

Materials
- one bushel basket filled with apples
- one empty bushel basket
- starting line

Procedure
1. Students will line up along the starting line so they can cheer for their teammates while awaiting their turn.
2. In turn, children will run to the full apple basket, remove one apple, and carry it to the empty basket.
3. When an apple has been added to the empty basket, the next runner takes his turn and so on until the empty basket is filled and the full basket is emptied.

Try This
Add to the excitement by timing this event. Have children estimate how long they think it will take to empty the full basket in this manner.

Plant a Sock

Materials
- one pair of large, old socks for each child
- overgrown, densely vegetated field or forest
- wooden stakes or craft sticks
- indelible markers
- garden trowels
- plot of overturned earth

Procedure
1. Have children prepare for a short hike.
2. Each child should pull a pair of old socks over their footwear. Rubber bands may be used at the top of the socks to keep them safely in place.
3. Have children walk through a densely vegetated area.
4. When the hike is over, have children remove the seedy socks.
5. Use a magnifying glass to help study the seeds that hooked on for a ride.
6. Have each child prepare a marker to label the location of their sock.
7. Dig a hole about 2" (5 cm) deep, and long enough for the stretched-out sock to fit into.
8. Cover the sock with loose earth and then pat lightly.
9. Place the marker firmly in the earth to mark the sock's location.
10. Wait patiently for spring to show you what seeds were picked up along the way.

Discussion
Why do seeds hitch a ride like this? If we had not walked through this area, how might the seeds have traveled to another area?

Respect the Environment

Encourage children to respect the natural environment; its powers and dangers as well as its fragile beauty.

Children should be taught (through word and example) to tread lightly upon the earth. Try to leave as little trace of yourself as you can when you venture into nature.

Remind children that the outdoors is the home of many living things—including ourselves.

Up in the Treetops

To the tune of "Down in the Valley"

Up in the treetops,
The treetops so high,
Red leaves are stirring;
Soon they must fly.
Twisting and twirling,
Tossed by the breeze,
'Til they lay silent
Under the trees.

Discussion

1. The poem mentions red leaves. What other colors are leaves in autumn?

2. Autumn is the only season with two names. Why do we also call it *fall?*

3. What makes leaves turn color? Two autumn colors, yellow and orange-red, are present in leaves all the time but are hidden by the green color called *chlorophyll.* Chlorophyll and sunshine make food for the tree. As the days shorten and the nights become cooler, the green chlorophyll breaks down, allowing autumn colors to appear. Red and purple colors form in the dying leaf. The color of the autumn leaf is determined by which color is most plentiful.

4. Why do leaves fall? After the food-producing chlorophyll breaks down, the attachment of the leaf to the twig becomes weak and the wind blows the leaf free.

Dance of the Leaves

Instruct children to stand still. Sing "Up in the Treetops." When the song begins, have children sway and wave their hands gently back and forth. On "twisting and twirling," have children twist and twirl their bodies around, then sink to the ground at the end of the song. Sing the song slowly to give time for the actions, or pause after every two lines.

Leaf People

Place leaves under sheets of white paper. Rub the sides of red, orange, and yellow crayons on paper over leaves until leaf shapes appear. Cut out leaf shapes and paste them to background paper. Add heads, arms, and legs. Encourage students to have the leaf people engaged in some activity. Display some of the leaf shapes with the names of their trees.

Name _____

Season of Colors

Look for autumn words diagonally, up, down, forward, and backward.

acorn	apple	aster	brown	chilly
cider	crisp	fall	football	frost
grapes	harvest	Halloween	leaves	October
orange	pinecone	pumpkin	rake	red
season	squash	trees	trick or treat	yellow

```
                    X
            A Q T Y     G
        S V F R O S T
            B D I E Z
        T P S C R   I S P
        O D R K V E C H
B S E L W E C E H R O N U M T P V R U C B S
G E C M K B J O I P R A E T Q O W E R Z
D V E I C H V B U O T Y B M D J F V B J A
S A C A S C W M C J R H U L H S A U Q S B
    E G N A R O A N E E W O L L A H I T U Q
    L A W X O L M K J A H G A F T A E P C
    F S B B L L A B T O O F N T R E E S
        B O C E R F R T G Z H U I V C D
    F B T X N Y Z V O F K R L K U E L P P A
    S A E C C I V B Y W N G R A P E S U C T
    B C E C R A K E X L N B Y E F X Z T F U I W S
    H C E W E F P H B L I Y T B C R V X V O W
    W O P D D M D P I N E C O N E V R T J K S C
    O I D V B U L T H X Y U T I N T F H B T U M
    U T D A S C P D E C C D T C I D E R C P E N B
    T G V B Y N J E M F U T O F M G O F R D I Y T
```

by Jean Powis

Welcome Back to School

Use this bulletin board to welcome students in the fall. The recycled look is very appealing to students and can lead to a worthwhile discussion on the environment.

Directions

- Cover the entire bulletin board with brown paper. If paper is not available, brown paper bags can be cut open and stapled together.

- Paint the words *Welcome "Bag" to School*, in forest green.

- Staple brown paper lunch bags all over the board. Make sure they are open and that there is one for each child.

- Staple name tags in the shapes of trees on the lunch bags.

- Explain to students that they will receive special rewards such as stickers or pencils for demonstrating proper behavior. Use the bags to hold the rewards during a specified amount of time. At the end of that time, send the bags home with the children. The number of stickers and rewards in the bag will be a true indication of the way the school year is beginning for each student.

by Jo Jo Cavalline and Jo Anne O'Donnell

Back-to-School Bulletin Boards

Grab the attention of your students with this three-dimensional reminder of some basic back-to-school rules.

Materials
> one large fold-out tissue apple
> one small fold-out tissue apple
> one large fold-out tissue pencil
> any color poster board for books

The fold-out tissue pieces are a great way to give your bulletin board a three-dimensional look.

Laminate poster board pieces for protection and longer use. The size of pieces will vary according to bulletin board size.

This surefooted creature reminds students of some of the basic steps needed to become good learners.

Materials
> brightly colored poster board for body segments and shoes
> black pipe cleaners for antenna
> footprints cut from black felt or poster board
> cut-out letters for title

Laminate poster board pieces for protection and longer use. The size of pieces will vary according to bulletin board size.

by Marcia Jeffries

After-School Activities

Abby, Ben, Chaundra, and Devin each signed up for after-school activities of soccer, cheerleading, gymnastics, and piano lessons. Find out what each of them did.

1. Abby told the boy cheerleader that she planned to take lessons to learn handstands before joining the squad.

2. Learning to play an instrument was important to Devin.

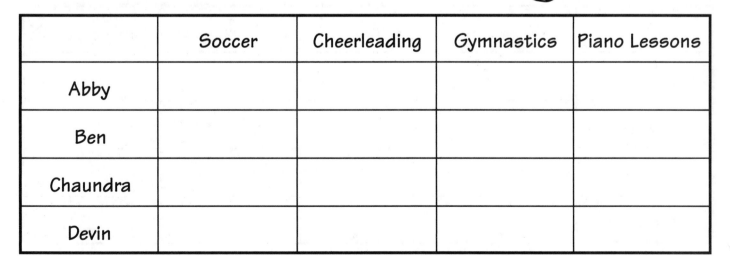

	Soccer	Cheerleading	Gymnastics	Piano Lessons
Abby				
Ben				
Chaundra				
Devin				

Name _____

Open House

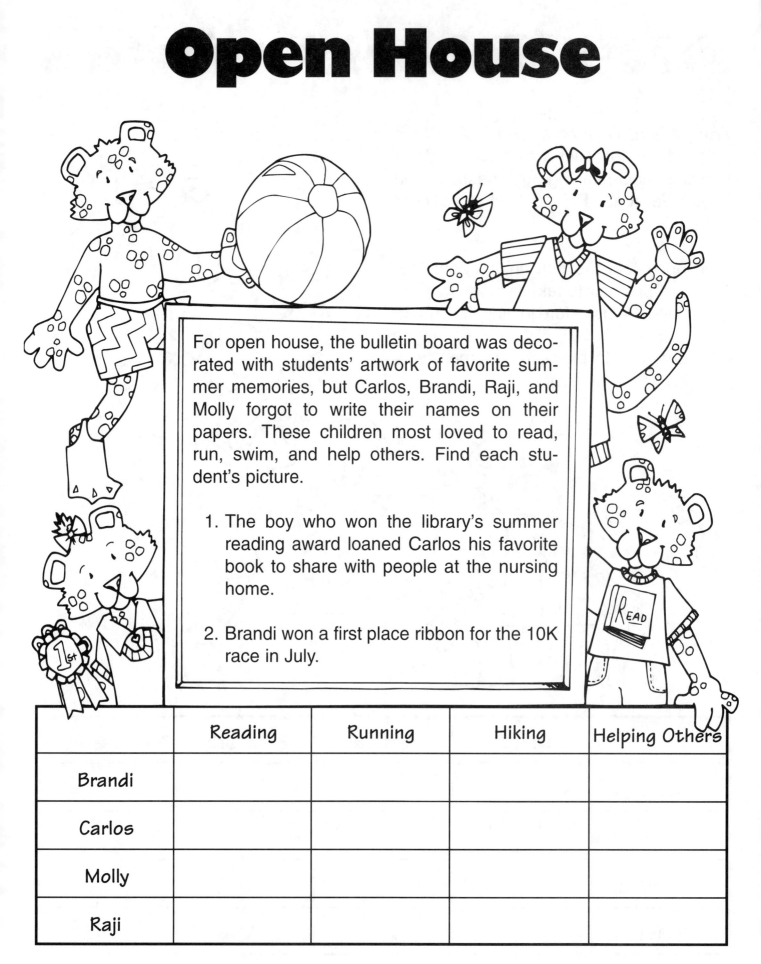

For open house, the bulletin board was decorated with students' artwork of favorite summer memories, but Carlos, Brandi, Raji, and Molly forgot to write their names on their papers. These children most loved to read, run, swim, and help others. Find each student's picture.

1. The boy who won the library's summer reading award loaned Carlos his favorite book to share with people at the nursing home.

2. Brandi won a first place ribbon for the 10K race in July.

	Reading	Running	Hiking	Helping Others
Brandi				
Carlos				
Molly				
Raji				

by Millie Harris

5-A-Day Month

September is National 5-A-Day Month. This is a nationwide nutrition campaign to encourage Americans to eat five or more servings of fruits and vegetables every day for better health. The program is jointly sponsored by the National Cancer Institute (NCI) and the Produce for Better Health Foundation (PBH).

The annual 5-A-Day Week (the second week in September) provides a special time for the agencies to spread messages through logos on banners, bags, and boxes, and through educational materials, TV, and radio ads. The governors of nearly all 50 states are supporting this important health program. Only in its third year, the goal of this program is to increase the daily consumption of fruits and vegetables to at least five per person each day by the year 2000.

To get involved in your state program, call your state health agency "5-A-Day" coordinator.

For the free brochures, "Time to Take Five: Eat 5 Fruits and Vegetables a Day," and "Eat 5 Fruits and Vegetables Every Day," call 1-800-4-Cancer.

On-line—visit the "5-A-Day" web site: http://www.dcpc.nci.nih.gov/5 a day

Dole Food Company has become involved with educational and fun ideas to get children interested in this campaign. Dole will provide booklets, posters, and a CD-ROM for your school. Mail or fax your request on school stationery to:

> Dole Nutrition Program
> 155 Bovet, Suite 476
> San Mateo, CA 94402
> FAX: (415) 570-5250

Visit their web site: http://www.dole5aday.com

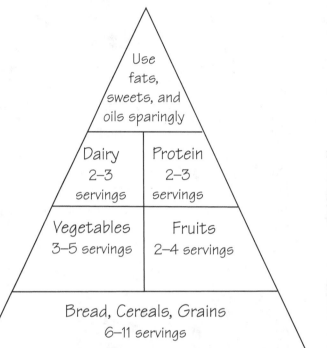

Use fats, sweets, and oils sparingly

Dairy 2–3 servings	Protein 2–3 servings
Vegetables 3–5 servings	Fruits 2–4 servings

Bread, Cereals, Grains
6–11 servings

by Tania K. Cowling

Food Construction

Plan "edible construction" projects as snacks. Let students dream up some ideas, too!

Funny Faces

Cut a whole orange horizontally into ¼" thick circles. Create a funny face using raisins, cherries, apple slices, banana circles, strips of orange peel, and so on. Let the children share their creations with the class, then enjoy! If a camera is available, take photos to preserve the memory of this project.

Bugs on a Branch

Fill a length of celery with peanut butter. Place raisins on the branch as "bugs."

Party Parfait

In a clear plastic cup, layer different fruits between vanilla yogurt. Sprinkle the top with chopped nuts and a maraschino cherry.

Tossed Salad Puppet

Convert a lunch bag into a tossed salad puppet. Have children place the bag with the open end towards them and draw a salad bowl full of lettuce for the body of the puppet. Include arms, legs, and shoes. On the top flap, have children cover the puppet's "lid" with vegetable enhancements such as cherry tomatoes, radish circles, carrot rounds, broccoli florets, and so on. These enhancements can be drawn and colored or cut from construction paper or magazines. Have children glue them onto the flaps. Instruct children to put their hands inside the puppets and flip their lids to "toss the salad."

Send for:
Dole's Fun with Fruits & Vegetables Kids' Cookbook

Another good resource:
Disney's Family Cookbook by Deanna F. Cook & Family Fun Magazine, Hyperion, 1996.

Activities for the Classroom

Creative Writing

Have students get their families involved by writing a paragraph or illustrating an idea using the following topics:
- My family's favorite fruits and vegetables are . . . .
- It's important for everyone in my family to eat five fruits and vegetables daily because . . . .
- My family could eat more fruits and vegetables at our meals by . . . .
- My family could eat more fruits and vegetables as snacks by . . . .
- Lunch box ideas that include more fruits and veggies are . . . .

5-A-Day Calendars

Create individual fruit and vegetable calendars. Make a copy of September from a calendar for each child. Have each child fill in the fruits and vegetables he or she has eaten for breakfast, lunch, and dinner each day. (Check craft and education stores for inexpensive stickers.)

Create a Colorful Collage

Collect magazines, food ads, and brochures. Have children cut out pictures of their favorite fruits and vegetables. Glue the pictures onto a paper plate. Label each plate with the student's name and display them in the classroom. Print copies of the whimsical Dole fruit and vegetable characters from the internet web site (www.dole5aday.com) or from the Dole "5 A Day Adventures" CD-ROM disk available from the company.

Study Groups

Assign groups of students a specific fruit or vegetable to research. Have each group give an oral presentation to the class, including facts like how and where it is grown, why it's good for you (vitamin content and fiber), and what it looks like (show pictures or bring samples in for a taste test). Use the senses—taste, smell, and touch. Try unusual produce such as mango, kiwi, jicama, pomegranate, star fruit, and so on.

Supermarket Tour

Arrange a tour at your local supermarket. A field trip is a visual and hands-on learning experience. There are many kinds of fruits and vegetables, as well as different varieties of specific fruits and vegetables. Apples come in many varieties, and so does lettuce. Prior to the trip, decide on a recipe to make. Purchase the necessary produce for the project. Here is one example.

Fruit Kabobs

skewer sticks
chunks of fruits in season (apples, oranges, grapes)
Clean and prepare the fruit by cutting it into chunks.
Arrange the fruit in a sequence on wooden skewers.

It is important to be aware of any food allergies or restrictions before tasting.

Seasonal Science

Science experiences help children learn about cause-and-effect relationships. Things happen for a reason. This enables children to improve such skills as observation, problem solving, and predicting, which they will use in other academic areas, as well as in social interactions. Science is not an isolated concept. It is an exciting part of the total learning experience. Integrate the following activities and follow-up projects throughout your fall program.

Pet Nutrition

Dog Week

Activity

Dog Week is in September. As every pet owner knows, animals must be cared for and fed properly to ensure a long, healthy life. Bring in several examples of dog food, both canned and dry, for children to observe and compare. Have them read the labels and note the ingredients. First, open several cans and compare the list of ingredients with what they actually see. (Stew contains peas and carrots!) Discuss the different scents and textures. Which would they rather feed to their dog? Next, open several bags of dry food. Why do the pieces come in different sizes? (Smaller dogs can better eat smaller pieces.) Experiment with the "makes its own gravy" kind. Does it? Carefully replace lids on cans, seal in a plastic bag, and send home with dog owners or donate to a local shelter.

Project

Let the children make posters for Dog Week. Have them write a slogan for each poster. Hang the posters throughout the school and collect pet food donations for the local animal shelter. Also, write to the American Kennel Club for its "Best Friends" elementary school program. It contains a video, teacher's guide, student activities, and more to help children learn about pet care responsibility, as well as some of the wonderful things dogs do for people. The address is:

American Kennel Club
Public Education Dept., 51 Madison Ave.
New York, NY, 10010

by Marie E. Cecchini

Name _____

Dog Week

Elizabeth, Ashley, Quintan, and David are learning about the different breeds of dogs during Dog Week in September. For extra points, they may choose a particular breed and write a report about a dog they would like to own. They could choose from the following dogs: collie, Great Dane, poodle, or Pomeranian.

Clues
- Elizabeth and Ashley did not want a large dog.
- Quintan was allergic to animals with long hair.
- Ashley did not like dogs with curly hair.
- David's dad wanted a dog for the farm.

What dog would each of the four students choose if they could have their own pet?

Directions
Make a line graph to help students understand how to solve a logic puzzle.

	Elizabeth	Ashley	Quintan	David
Collie				
Great Dane				
Poodle				
Pomeranian				

Grandparents' Day!

Septem

Celebrate National Grandparents' Day with your class. The first Sunday after Labor Day has been set aside to honor grandmothers and grandfathers. Bring together the love and experience of an older generation with the enthusiasm of your students.

Begin the unit by sending a letter. The letter will ask parents or guardians to provide information about each child's grandparents, as well as an address. If a student doesn't have a grandparent, ask the parent or guardian to help you contact an older family friend or staff member to act as an adopted grandparent. By reading the activities below and on the following pages, you will find what types of information should be asked for in the letter.

A Grandparent by Any Other Name Still Loves the Same

On the board, list the different names children use for their grandparents. Combine similar ones into categories such as Grandma or Grandpa used with a last name. As a class, create a bar graph. Find the most commonly used name for grandparents, as well as the most unusual.

Grand Activities

List and discuss favorite activities grandparents do with their grandchildren. During class discussion, ask students to help combine any similar activities into categories. For example, playing checkers or a board game would go together into a single category. As a class, make a large bar graph displaying the categories and the number responding to each.

by Terry Healy

Reading Together

Write the titles of books that grandparents enjoy sharing with their grandchildren. If any titles are given more than once, put a tally mark beside that title. Ask students to look at the titles and decide which book was the favorite for grandparents and grandchildren.

Grandparent Geography

Use large maps of the United States and the world to identify where grandparents live. Help each student locate the city where his or her grandparents live and label it with a removable dot. If a student brings a picture of himself or herself with a grandparent, place the picture along the edge of the map and run a string from the picture to the location on the map. During the week before Grandparents' Day, review the different locations on the map and discuss city and state names, special attractions at the cities, and landforms at that location.

Silhouettes for Grandparents

Have children draw their profiles to give to grandparents on Grandparents' Day—the first Sunday in September after Labor Day.

Materials

    10" x 12" lightweight white paper
    masking tape
    high intensity flashlight or desk lamp
    pencil and eraser
    scissors
    black construction paper
    12" x l4" mounting paper;
        heavy white paper or tagboard

Setup

Prepare pencil, masking tape, and pre-cut paper at craft center. Place a chair sideways approximately 4' from the wall. Mark the wall with chalk or tape to indicate where papers should be fastened. Tape the first paper to the wall in the position required. Dim the lights in the room where the activity will occur.

Discussion

Everyone's face has its own unique shape and characteristics. Some traits run in families. Do you look like anyone in your family? What do artists look for when painting a portrait? What makes one face different from another? Do you think that your face will change much over the course of this school year?

Let's Make It

1. Choose a partner and visit the craft center.
2. Tape a paper to the wall inside the marked area.
3. Choose one partner to sit in the chair and face straight ahead. Move the chair closer to the wall or farther away to make the shadow fit on the paper.
4. The model must sit absolutely still and the artist will trace the shadow very carefully with a pencil. Try not to miss any details.
5. Partners exchange places and repeat the process.
6. When both tracings have been made, partners will securely tape their profile over a piece of black construction paper and cut out the shadow profile.
7. The shadow portrait can be centered and glued to sturdy white mounting paper.
8. Record the date and your name on the back or bottom of your silhouette.

Try This

- Repeat this exercise at the end of the school year. Compare the two profiles. What differences are noted?
- Reduce the profiles on the photocopier and compile a class portrait. Keep a master list to identify the profiles. Can children recognize their classmates?

"Write" on, Grandparents

Grandparents' Day Cards

Set aside some time early in the week for students to make special cards for grandparents. Using markers, colored pencils, or paints, instruct students to fold and then illustrate these special cards. Ask students to copy one of the following verses on the cards or write one of their own.

North, South, East, or West,
Grandpa (Grandma), you're just the best!

Roses are red; violets are blue!
Grandma (Grandpa), I love you!

After the cards are completed, have students copy their grandparents' address to complete the envelope. Mail the cards to each grandparent. Parents might donate envelopes or stamps to help defray mailing costs.

When I Was Your Age!

How was school different when Grandma was a kid? Did they have TVs when Grandpa was growing up? Encourage students to learn more about their grandparents by developing a list of questions. Direct students to think up one or two questions they would like to ask their grandparents about growing up. List these questions on the board. If a grandparent has been invited to visit to the class, ask if he or she would answer four or five of the questions. Older children may write a letter with their card or interview a grandparent by phone. On the last day of the unit, discuss what the students learned about life when Grandma and Grandpa were young. Assign older students to write a short story about growing up in that era.

Grandparent Quilt

Stitch together students' best memories of grandparents by creating a paper quilt. Give each student a 6" square of white paper. Instruct them to draw a favorite memory or occasion they experienced with their grandparents. Ask older students to write about the memory when the square is done. To make the classroom quilt, mount each white square in the middle of a 7" x 7" square of colored construction paper. Punch a hole about every inch along each side of the square. Next, lay out the squares on the floor and arrange them in rows until the pictures, colors, and patterns are pleasing. If there is an uneven row, fill it in with one to three squares giving the title of the quilt, class name, and year. Take a length of yarn and lace the squares together. Display your quilt on a wall of the school.

Literature Link

Link literature with the celebration of National Grandparents' Day with some of the following books. Invite a grandparent to read and share any of the following books. Extend the books with some follow-up activities.

Watch Out for the Chicken Feet in Your Soup

by Tomie de Paola (Prentice-Hall, 1974) is about a fun-filled visit to Joey's grandmother. Joey and his friend, Eugene, go to see Joey's grandmother. Joey is not sure how Eugene will feel about his grandmother and her unusual ways. Eugene finds many special things about Joey's grandma and learns to appreciate her unique foods. Read this colorful book about an original grandmother.

Activity: Ask each student to name and illustrate a picture of a favorite food his or her grandmother prepares.

Our Granny by Margaret Woods (Ticknor and Fields, 1994). Celebrate grandmothers by reading this book. Grannies are special whether your granny is soft, blows you kisses, or tucks you into bed every night.

Activity: After reading the book, find several phrases used to describe grannies. Direct each student to write five describing words about his special granny.

The Wooden Doll by Susan Bonners (Lothrop, Lee, and Shepard Books, 1991). Stephanie wants to be grown-up enough for Grandpa to trust her to handle a very special doll. The wooden doll leads Stephanie to learn many new things about her grandfather's past and brings the two closer together.

Activity: Ask students about toys that are special to them. Ask younger students to draw a picture of the toy. Older students may write and illustrate a story about how they came to receive the toy and why it is so important to them.

Grandpa's Garden Lunch by Judith Caseley (Greenwillow Books, 1990) is an easy-to-read book. Sarah and her grandpa plant and care for a garden. The garden provides them not only with beauty, but also the food for a very special lunch.

Activity: Play a game of "In my garden I grow. . ." Begin by arranging your class in a circle. To start the game, say, "In my garden I grow . . ." and list a fruit, vegetable, or flower. The next person in the circle must repeat "In my garden I grow" and give the first food or plant listed, then add one of his or her own. The game continues as consecutive students repeat all the responses given before and add one more. The game ends when someone misses repeating the sequence of foods or plants.

POPCORN PROJECTS

October Is Popcorn Month

Turn a snack time favorite into a learning experience.
Pop plenty of corn and get ready for some new project ideas.

Puff Patterns

Make use of both cooked (puffs) and uncooked (kernels) popcorn for patterning practice. Prepare cards or paper strips with various patterns, perhaps using dots to represent kernels and circles to represent puffs. Provide the children with these patterns and containers of both kernels and puffs. Challenge them to re-create the patterns on a separate sheet of paper by gluing the puffs and kernels to the paper in the appropriate sequence.

Shapes

Let your children invent their own creations with this sticky mixture. Keep a bucket of warm, soapy water and a roll of paper towels nearby for easy cleanup.

10 c. popped corn
1/2 c. raisins
1/4 c. margarine
1 c. toasted oat cereal
1 (10 oz.) pkg. marshmallows

Melt the margarine in a large saucepan. Add the marshmallows. Cook and stir over low heat until a syrup consistency is reached. Remove from heat. Add the popped corn, raisins, and oat cereal. Stir to coat. Let mixture cool to the touch, then shape as desired. **Note:** For a large class, you may need to make two batches.

crunchy   hard   white

Descriptive Signs

For a hands-on vocabulary lesson, observe and describe popped and unpopped corn. Invite children to touch and smell both corn variations. Have them observe both under a magnifying glass. As a group, brainstorm a list of words (crunchy, hard, white, and so on) that describe either variety. Write the list on chart paper. Review the completed list and ask each child to choose one word. Have the children write their words in large letters on a cardboard or paper strip, helping as necessary. Let them trace their words with glue; then have them place kernels, puffs, or both into the glue. Allow the glue to dry, then punch two holes at the top of each sign. Insert a yarn length through the holes, and knot the ends, creating a hanger for each descriptive sign.

by Marie E. Cecchini

Ghostly Creations

Fill your classroom with ghostly puff creations made with popped corn. First, have the children cut ghostly shapes from cereal box cardboard. Make a hole at the top of each and thread with string for hanging. Next, provide the children with plastic lids to hold glue and popped corn. Have them dip each piece of popped corn into the glue; then stick the popcorn onto one side of their shapes, covering the cardboard. Allow the glue to dry, then proceed in the same manner to cover the back side of the shapes. Have children cut black eye and mouth shapes and glue them on one side. When dry, suspend the ghostly creations from the ceiling, or bring in a small branch from the playground and create a Halloween tree.

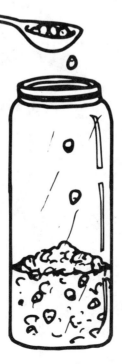

Geometric Coasters

Use a bag of uncooked popcorn to help children learn shapes. Cut a variety of coaster-sized geometric shapes from cardboard. Provide children with glue and a container of popcorn kernels to use along with the shapes. Demonstrate how to spread glue over half of the shape, then set the kernels into the glue. Have them proceed in the same manner to cover the rest of the shape. Invite them to make a set of coasters, one of each shape, to give as a gift.

Math Pictures

Reinforce basic math skills using flash cards, popcorn puffs and/or kernels, glue, markers, and wide paper strips. Have children model a flash card math problem by gluing two sets of popcorn to their paper strips in place of numbers. Have them add a plus or minus, and an equal sign with a marker. Next have them glue on the correct number of popcorn for the answer. Finally, have them write the numerical equation next to their popcorn version.

$$4 + 3 = 7$$

Mark the Page

Encourage interest in reading by having your class create clever bookmarks. Supply students with poster board strips, glue, markers, and popcorn kernels. Have them use markers to draw a simple line design or write their initials on the poster board strips. Have them trace these lines with glue. Next, they can set popcorn kernels into their glue designs. Allow the glue to dry. Now, what good is a great bookmark without a great book? Take a trip to the library and help them choose seasonal reading material. All you have to do is plant the seeds to watch reading pleasure grow.

About How Many?

Popcorn can also be used to help children begin to understand the process of estimation. As a class, measure out a teaspoon of popcorn kernels, estimate how many kernels the teaspoon contains; then count the actual number. Proceed in the same manner using a tablespoon. Next, fill a small jar with kernels. Allow children several days to speculate on the number of kernels the jar holds. Provide children access to measuring spoons and kernels to work with. Finally, ask each child to estimate the amount of kernels held in the jar. Count them out as a group and compare the results.

Sukkot

October 4th, 1998, marks the beginning of Sukkot, a Jewish holiday where families give thanks for gifts that come from the land. It is a "thanksgiving for the harvest" that lasts for eight days. You can mark this holiday each year by counting five days after Yom Kippur. During the holiday, it is a custom to build a booth called a sukkah. It commemorates the place where the farmers from Palestine ate and slept during the days of the harvest when returning home to the village was difficult, and also the place where wandering Jews rested during the exodus from slavery.

The sukkah is made using green branches which are decorated with fruit and flowers. It can be built in a garden or on a porch. During this festival, families eat all their meals in the sukkah. There are four symbolic plants chosen for the sukkah; the "etrog" (citrus fruit), the "lulav" (branch of a date palm), the "hadassim" (myrtle), and the "aravot" (willow). During the festival, these plants are bound together and carried around the synagogue in a prayer procession.

The day after Sukkot is called Simhat Torah. It is a happy day dedicated to the Torah, which is the Five Books of Moses. *Simhat Torah* means "rejoicing in the law." It's celebrated in the synagogue with readings from the Torah, and by carrying the scrolls and flags around. Fruits and sweets are consumed.

Paper Plate Mobile

Materials

    crayons, markers, colored pencil, and so on
    coat hangers
    paper plates
    glue
    magazine pictures of fruits
        and/or vegetables
    colored construction paper
    scissors
    pipe cleaners

Poke holes in three paper plates. Draw pictures of fruits and vegetables on the paper plates. Or paste magazine pictures of fruit and vegetables, and/or cut out construction paper in the shapes and paste to the plate. Decorate both sides of the plates. Poke pipe cleaners through each of the paper plates then attach the plates to a hanger. Hang the mobile in the succah.

by Devorah Stone

Classroom Decorations

To celebrate this holiday in the classroom, make a sukkah by decorating a corner of the room with green crepe paper streamers. Hang paper flowers and fruits from the streamers. Use the area to eat snacks and lunch. Colorful tissue paper makes beautiful flowers. If you have children of the Jewish faith in your class, invite them and their parents to speak about how they celebrate Sukkot in their home.

An individual sukkah can be made using a green plastic berry container. Take children on a nature walk to gather leaves and grass. Weave the greens inside the squares of the basket. Back in the classroom, cut out colorful fruits and flowers from construction paper to brighten up the sukkah. Glue these inside and out.

Make mini Torah scrolls using paper and craft sticks. Cut a strip of white paper about 4" wide. Have the children color a picture on the paper. Glue a craft stick to each end of the paper. When dry, roll the two sticks to form a scroll.

Let each student decorate their desk chair with a fruit and flower swag. Tie a green crepe paper streamer across the back of the chair. Have children cut out pictures of fruits and vegetables from magazines or design them on construction paper. Glue them onto the streamer.

Shipshape

These ships may be a little like the ones Columbus sailed on when he discovered America in 1492. Look carefully at the shapes used to build each ship. Color the two ships made with exactly the same set of shapes.

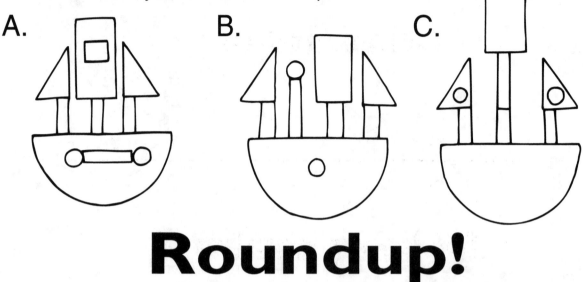

A.   B.   C.

Roundup!

Christopher Columbus was a brave explorer who believed the world was round. We know now that he was right—the world *is* round! What other things are round? The names of six round objects are hidden in the circles below. For each one, start at one of the letters and read around either in a clockwise or counterclockwise direction. Write the words in the blanks. Can you think of five other things that are round?

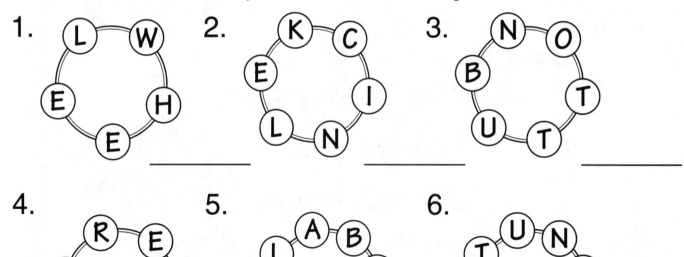

1.   2.   3.

4.   5.   6.

by Ann Richmond Fisher

Awarded to

_____

name

for being number 1 in learning fire safety rules

Spot, the fire safety dog, gives you two tail wags.

Name _____

Safety Scramble

Rewrite each fire safety rule, putting the words in the correct order. Remember these important safety tips if there is a fire in your building.

1. open it if Never a door feels hot

_____

2. to floor Stay the your low and cover nose mouth and

_____

3. under in Don't a hide bed or closet a

_____

4. out house quickly Get of the burning

_____

5. into a house burning go Never back

_____

6. place Go and your to meeting there stay

_____

If your clothes catch fire, don't run. Instead STOP, DROP, and ROLL. Practice this with a family helper.

by Ann Richmond Fisher

Autumn Craft

Kids of all ages like to combine their thoughts and skills in active learning projects. This craft offers children the opportunity to visit a craft center to put their creative thoughts, problem-solving abilities, and fine-motor skills into action with a simple craft that takes only minutes to complete. This craft is a perfect follow-up to a lesson, can be combined with a center task program, or can offer a productive between-task activity for those who complete work before others.

United Nations Day Flag

October 24 is a day to celebrate peace and reflect on the diversity of the many people of the world.

Materials

    straws
    11" x 17" white paper
    writing and/or painting instruments
    stapler and staples

Setup

Prepare a blank sample flag to illustrate how the flag is made. Prepare a center providing the materials listed above.

Discussion

The United Nations organization was founded on October 24, 1945. This group of nations works together to promote peace around the world. Today over 150 nations are members of this organization. Is your country a member? What harm is caused by violent conflicts between nations? How might nations resolve conflicts? How does it make you feel to know that many nations have united together to try to achieve worldwide peace?

Let's Make It

1. Use the sample to help you explain how the paper is wrapped around the straw and folded in half.

2. Staple the folded side of the paper, anchoring the paper to the straw.

3. Run cellophane tape around the edges of the flag to secure the two sides together.

4. Decorate both sides of the flag to represent world peace.

Try This

Display the flags on a bulletin board or along a border with a background of blue skies and white clouds. Center your display around the words *United Nations for Worldwide Peace.*

FINGERPRINT DAY

Activity

On Fingerprint Day in October, police units in many areas offer free fingerprinting services to parents for their children. Have children observe themselves and those around them; then ask them to name characteristics that distinguish one person from another. Guide the discussion toward characteristics that may not be as visible as others, such as teeth and fingerprints. Help the children conclude that just as two people have many traits that help to differentiate between them, so too, no two people have the same fingerprints. Have them look at their fingertips through a magnifying glass, then provide washable ink pads and paper for them to stamp their own fingerprints. Encourage them to compare their fingerprints with others in the class. Let them experiment with dusting for fingerprints by having them press their fingers on a black piece of paper, sifting cornstarch over their papers, then lightly dusting the cornstarch off with a soft paintbrush. The cornstarch can also be removed by holding the paper up and gently tapping on the back of it. Because skin contains oil, the cornstarch should adhere to the oily fingerprint but not the surrounding area.

Project

Provide the children with white paper, brown markers, and washable stamp pads in fall colors. Have then draw a tree trunk and branches with the marker; then add fingerprint leaves.

Make a Difference Day

The fourth Saturday in October is a special day that was specially named in the '90s, although the idea behind it has been in people's hearts and minds for ages. It's Make a Difference Day.

Across the country, groups and individuals will take part in this national day of doing good, each in their own way. That's the great part of this special day —there are no specific rules or regulations. All ideas are good ones, all ways are good ways. The only requirement is that whatever is done makes life better for someone else.

Last year a group of senior citizens donated a snow blower to a day-care facility. A group of adults repaired and painted homes for some elderly neighbors. A group of college students cleaned up a run-down lot in their neighborhood. A group of high school students visited and read to children in a pediatric hospital ward. Each group made a difference to the people they helped.

While these projects are beyond the realm of students in grades 1-3, these children need to know that they, too, are valuable links in the "making a difference" chain. Talk with them about the many ways in which they can help others. Elicit from them the names of groups that could benefit from their help: people in senior citizens' homes, children in day-care centers, old and young alike who don't have adequate food or clothing or who lack money for health care necessities, students in poor school districts, families who are needy because of unemployment, even animals in shelters. Discuss what could make a difference in their lives.

If started at the beginning of the school year, a successful drive could net a supply of clothing for the needy; blankets for a shelter; toys for a day-care center; nonperishable foods for a food bank; art and writing supplies for needy school children; basic hygiene items such as toothbrushes and toothpaste, soap, shampoo, and deodorant for people in a shelter; money for a family that needs medicine or eyeglasses; even newspaper for animal cages or "treats" (like dog biscuits) for animals in a shelter.

Participation in each project for Make a Difference Day could be by a single classroom, a grade level, a group of grades together, or school-wide. If projects like those mentioned above are not feasible, there are many other ways young children can make a difference right at school, or in their own homes or neighborhoods.

Think of all the non-teaching staff who make the school better. Secretaries always appreciate a friendly smile or a "please" or "thank you" when you ask for something. Custodians would have an easier job if they didn't have to pick up bits of paper, pencils, erasers, and crayons or clean muddy shoe prints left on the floor. Cafeteria workers like to see smiles and hear polite words as well as to know the food they prepare is eaten and not wasted. Health care personnel should be thanked for the aid they give. Bus drivers (as well as their passengers) benefit from orderly, quiet riders. The school grounds might need leaves raked or litter picked up.

At home there may be younger siblings to read to or play with, small chores to do around the house, parents or older siblings to express your thanks to. Elderly neighbors may need small errands run or help with simple jobs around the house, or they might just appreciate a few minutes spent visiting with them. There's no end to what a child can do once he or she starts to think about it.

Whatever the Make a Difference Day activity is—be it large or small, involving many people or just a few—one thing is certain: when you help someone, you make them feel better about themselves. That, in turn, will make each of you feel better about yourself, too. Best of all, it's an action that can become habit forming, enriching your life and that of others forever!

by Elaine Hansen Cleary

Choose a classroom project to help a group or organization.

- Invite someone from the group to speak to the students, explaining exactly what the group or organization does and what its needs are.
- In language arts class, write letters to parents explaining the project.
- In art class, make a banner or poster to remind students to bring in contributions.
- In math class, make graphs indicating amounts contributed.
- In music class, think of appropriate new words for an old tune to encourage school spirit for the drive. For example, revise "On Top of Old Smokey" with verse that says, "We will make a difference. We'll help (insert name of group), We'll (insert what actions will be taken), And (insert the result)."
- Make thank-you cards to be given to staff members who help make your school safer and nicer to attend.
- If any students belong to Girl/Boy Scouts, they might ask their leaders to help these groups plan an activity of their own.

Discuss ways students could help the following:

- people in a nursing home
- children in a day-care facility
- animals in a shelter
- people who are hungry
- unemployed families
- the homeless
- students in poor school districts

Ask them to think of others who might need help.

- Role-play situations in which one child could make a difference.

Character(s)	Prop	Situation
Student	paper scraps	tiny bits of paper are scattered under the desk
Student	cafeteria tray	going through the lunch line
Student/Neighbor	bag of garbage	elderly neighbor has difficulty walking
Student/Child	broken toy	child needs someone to help fix toy

Ask students to make up others scenarios.

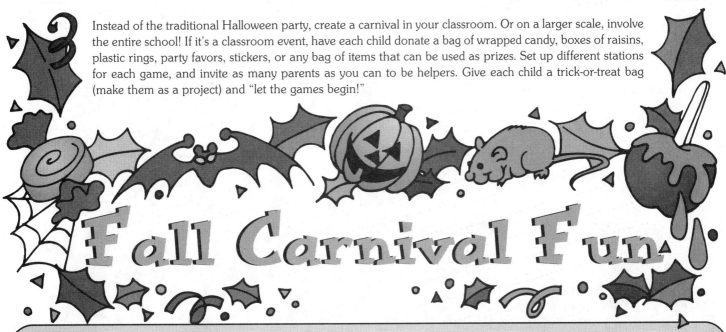

Instead of the traditional Halloween party, create a carnival in your classroom. Or on a larger scale, involve the entire school! If it's a classroom event, have each child donate a bag of wrapped candy, boxes of raisins, plastic rings, party favors, stickers, or any bag of items that can be used as prizes. Set up different stations for each game, and invite as many parents as you can to be helpers. Give each child a trick-or-treat bag (make them as a project) and "let the games begin!"

Fall Carnival Fun

Knock-Knock

An adult stands behind a door. A child knocks and the adult opens the door. Instruct the child to say "Trick-or-treat." The adult commands a trick first, such as hop on one foot, make an animal noise, sing a short song, count to 10, and so on. Reward each trick with a treat (prize).

Mouse in the House

Have each child kneel on a low chair with a small basket placed behind it. Have each child drop rubber mice (or clothespins) into the basket. Hand out one treat for every mouse that lands in his house. Rubber mice can be found in most pet stores.

Squirt Jack

Place a sheet of plastic behind and underneath a real jack-o'-lantern. Place a real candle inside the pumpkin. Have an adult light the candle. Allow each child to extinguish the flame using a squirt gun filled with water. Instruct children to squirt the water through the jack-o'-lantern's face to extinguish the flame. Give each child a prize.

Shave Jack

Inflate and tie off the end of an orange balloon. Draw a jack-o'-lantern's face with a black permanent marker on the balloon. Cover the balloon with shaving cream. Instruct children to shave "Jack" using a "razor" such as a plastic spoon or plastic knife. Give a treat if "Jack" is cleanly shaven and does not break!

by Tania K. Cowling

Mystery Maze

Design an obstacle course. Have children walk a balance beam, climb steps, crawl through a tunnel of boxes, walk around a line of chairs, and so on. Give each child a treat after completing the "mystery maze"!

Ring Around the Pumpkin

Write a point value on each of four pumpkins with a permanent marker. Arrange them in order, having the highest point-value pumpkin the farthest from the starting line. Instruct each child to stand on the starting line and toss a Hula-Hoop™ around a pumpkin. Give each child three tries, then total his or her score. Award a treat to each child. You might give an extra prize to the child with the highest score.

Counting Worms

Place a small amount of water in a large kettle. This is a "witch's brew." Color the water with a small amount of black tempera paint. Place several handfuls of rubber worms into the brew. These worms can be bought at sporting goods stores. (You could use large colored rubber bands.) Instruct children to reach into the "witch's brew" and grab a handful of worms. Have children count the worms, and give a treat for each worm. Have a container of clean water and a towel available for hand washing afterwards.

Catch a Ghost

Inflate a white balloon for the ghost, but do not tie the end. Release the balloon and let each child try to catch the ghost before it touches the ground. Award a prize for catching the ghost, or just for giving it a good try!

Pumpkin Push

Place an inflated round, orange balloon at a starting line. At the signal, instruct each child to kick the balloon and guide it to the finish line. This is a tough game, so every child should receive a prize after crossing the finish line.

42

Flying Bats

Make a fishing pole by attaching string to a wooden dowel. Tie a magnet to the end of the string. Cut bats from heavy black paper. Attach a large paper clip to each bat. Place the bats inside a box that has been painted to look like a "bat house." Have each child guide the "fishing line" inside the box and fish for bats. Set a timer for one minute. See how many bats can be retrieved in the allotted time. Give a prize for each bat.

How Much Does the Pumpkin Weigh?

Have a pumpkin at this station. Let each child handle the pumpkin and guess its weight. Then have them check their guesses by weighing the pumpkin on a scale. Estimating weight is not an easy skill to master. Give everyone a prize!

Feed the Jack-O'-Lantern

Paint or draw a jack-o'-lantern on the outside of a cardboard carton. Cut out a large mouth area. Provide about five beanbags. Have children stand on a line and toss the bags into the jack-o'-lantern's mouth. Give a treat for each beanbag that goes in the mouth.

Pumpkin Catch

Inflate a round, orange balloon. Set the balloon on a large kitchen funnel. Instruct children to hold the funnel and toss the balloon into the air and catch it again with the funnel as it floats down. Give prizes for playing this game!

Tricky Treats for Halloween

Your children will love to tickle their tummies with these tasty treats. They are easy to make, and so much fun to eat, they will seem to disappear. It must be magic!

Monster Pockets

Ingredients

pita bread
sandwich spread of choice
carrots
celery

cheese slices
cream cheese, softened
fruit and vegetable chunks

Cut off one edge of several pieces of pita bread. Gently open each pita to form a pocket. Fill the pocket with sandwich spread. To make monster hair, place celery, carrot, and cheese strips into the filling at the opening. Use soft cream cheese for "glue" and add slices or chunks of fruits and vegetables to create a scary monster face on the front of each pocket.

Superhero Celery

Ingredients

celery
raisins
carrot slices

toothpicks
lettuce leaves
peanut butter

Fill a stalk of celery with peanut butter. Using the wide end of the celery as the top, place two raisins in the peanut butter for eyes; then add a raisin nose. Cut a carrot slice in half and set in the peanut butter as the mouth. Wrap a lettuce leaf cape around the celery stalk just below the mouth and secure it with a toothpick. Remind the children to remove the toothpick before eating.

Finger Sandwiches

Ingredients

French/Italian bread
cheese slices

pepperoni slices
tomato sauce

Slice the bread and toast lightly under a conventional or toaster oven broiler. Set cheese pieces on each individual bread slice, and place a piece of pepperoni at one end to resemble a fingernail. Dribble a small amount of sauce over each "finger." Broil to melt the cheese.

Spooky Spider Salad

Ingredients

lettuce, shredded
tomato slices
green olives

cheese slices
corn

Sprinkle a shredded lettuce spiderweb on a plate. Set a tomato slice spider body on top of the lettuce. Top the tomato with olive slice eyes, a pimento nose, and a corn kernel mouth. Cut or tear the cheese slice into curvy strips. Place eight curved cheese strip legs around the tomato spider.

Count Dracula Drink

Combine 1 cup strawberries, 2 tablespoons honey, 4 cups milk, and a few drops of red food coloring in a blender. Cover tightly and blend until smooth.

Halloween
Art Idea

Here is a Halloween art project that students love to make! Use the "haunted houses" for a seasonal display in the hallway or your classroom.

Using chalk, draw an outline of a haunted house or mansion on black construction paper. A pattern is provided on page 47. The bigger the house, the better! Next create windows with shutters by drawing a capital *I* in every spot a window is desired. A capital *T* can be drawn for a double door entry at ground level, or an upside down *L* for a single door. After doors and windows are placed, have children cut on the chalk lines to make the windows and doors open. It is important to "open" all windows and doors before continuing. Have children cut out the entire house. Instruct them to carefully apply glue to the house, avoiding the openings. Glue the house onto a contrasting piece of uncut construction paper of the same or larger size.

Next instruct children to draw and cut out seasonal things to place behind the doors and windows. When the shutters are opened, the spooky surprises are revealed. Some suggestions for surprises to place behind the shutters are jack-o'-lanterns, bats, skeletons, witches, owls, monsters, ghosts, and black cats. Clip art is provided on the following page.

Finally create an outdoor scene around the house. Children could draw graveyards, a moon, dead trees, and so on.

Simplify this project for younger children by making only the shutters. Use a contrasting background paper and black or brown paper for the shutters to make a spooky window. Cut one piece of 9" x 12" paper in half for the shutters. Glue to the right and left edges of contrasting background paper. Instruct children to make a jack-o'-lantern or other spooky item to place inside the shutters.

Display the following poem with the completed project and encourage interaction.

If you're afraid of monsters
That growl and grin,
Don't open our shutters!
Don't look in!

by Karen K. Bjork

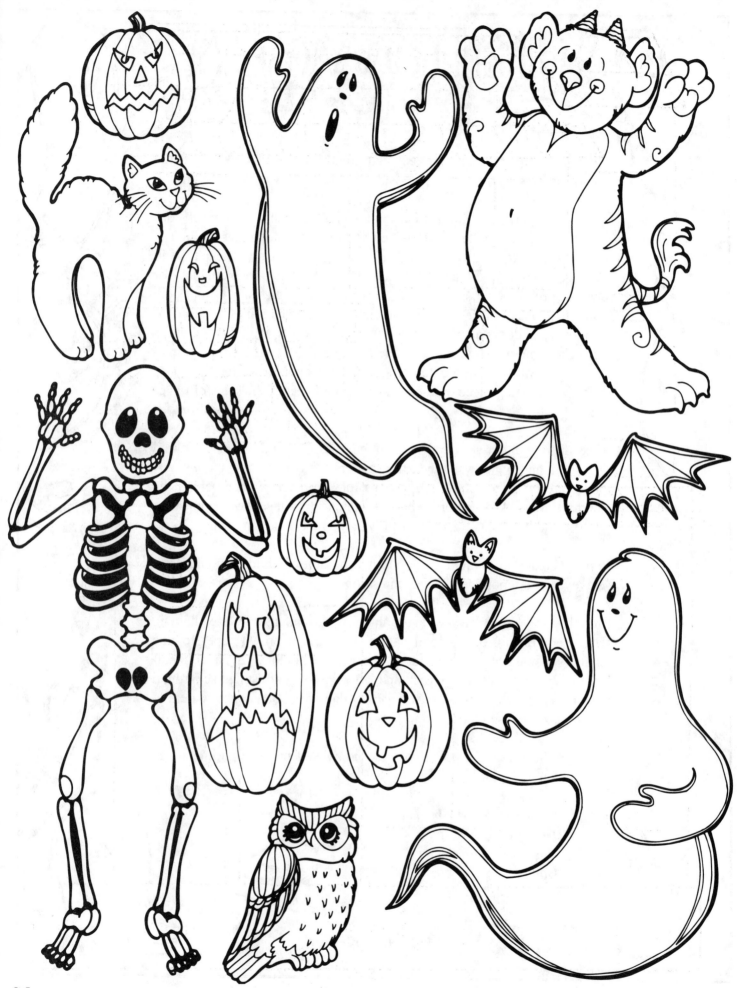

46

Little Lost Ghost

A newborn ghost crept up the hill
To try his newborn haunting skill.
But weary from his expedition,
He found himself in sad condition.
Although he studied all the stones,
He could not find his earthly bones.

A wise old spirit passing through
Asked newborn ghost, "What's wrong with you?"
"There's nothing that I recognize,"
The small one said with teary eyes.
"I don't remember how I came,
And all these tombstones look the same."

The wise old ghost began to laugh.
"Why don't you find your epitaph?"
The small one raised his head and sighed.
"I don't know how to read," he cried.
"And no one I can ask," he said,
"'Cause all the folks in here are dead."

by Ruth Winne Roberts

Directions for Little Lost Ghost

1. Reproduce patterns on white construction paper and cut out.
2. Apply glue to the shaded lines on Figure 1.
3. Align the top of Figure 2 to the shaded area and glue together.
4. Place a small amount of glue on the pointed ends of parts 3a and 3b. Attach to the top of Figure 2.
5. Print name at the bottom of Figure 2.

Figure 1

Figure 2

Little Lost Ghost may be stood up to use as a party place card or spread open and inserted between pages of a book and used as a bookmark.

Jack-O'-Lantern and Jill-O'-Lantern

Jack-O'-Lantern sat beside
The window, on a shelf,
Grinning like a Cheshire cat
And talking to himself.

He didn't feel like smiling.
He was just cut out that way.
He wished that he could frighten kids.
Oh, that would make his day!

"I'd love to SCARE the little monsters,
See them turn and run!
Drop their pillowcase of candy.
Man! Would that be fun!"

Across the room, Jill-O'-Lantern
Sat there looking mad.
They'd carved her mouth all turning down,
Which left her feeling sad.

She wore some lipstick, cherry red,
With magic marker hair.
The way her mouth was turning down
Was more than she could bear.

Jack couldn't see what Jill could see.
The TV pointed south.
But Jill was watching exercises
All for face and mouth.

The voice was saying, "Stretch your face,
Your mouth and chin the most,
To keep you looking young and gorgeous.
Otherwise, you're toast!"

by Irene Livingston

50

Jill stretched and stretched her pumpkin face
To pull the corners up.
At last, although a little crooked,
Jill was smiling. Yup!

The folks were out and, as you know,
All things can move around,
As long as they get back in place
And not a trace is found.

So Jack he rolled around to see.
He grinned some more and said,
"If this can work for curving up,
I'll curve it down instead."

Then Jack began to stretch his mouth,
To turn the corners down,
Which pulled the corners of his eyes
And made a crabby frown.

He pulled and stretched a little more.
Jack really was a sight—
A kooky, cockeyed character
As day turned into night.

Now Jack, he sat before the window,
Awful scowl in place.
But darkness brought reflections,
And he saw his goofy face!

At that, he burst out laughing,
And his howl became a roar.
He truly laughed his head off,
For his lid, it hit the floor.

Then Jill got laughing wildly
And she held her "tummy-face."
They laughed so hard they couldn't stop
And rolled around the place.

Then Jack, he saw his face again.
He laughed, "I just can't win!"
He'd laughed so hard, he'd made himself
An even bigger grin!

"I think I like you better now,"
Said Jill and cuddled near.
"You, too," said Jack "I like your smile.
There Coming! Sit Right Here!"

The Haunted House

A Storytelling Activity

Looking for a way to engage your students in storytelling?
Try this exciting and fun creative thinking activity!

1. First brainstorm ideas! Talk about a setting for a haunted house. Describe what you might see, hear, smell, and touch.

2. Have all students sit in a circle and assign each a number. The first student will have one or two minutes to begin telling the haunted house story. Student two will add on to the story of student one and so on, until everyone in the circle has had a chance to add onto the story.

3. Tape the oral story and replay it over and over again. Students can transcribe the story or draw pictures to illustrate the tale.

4. Give students a new number and tell a different haunted house story.

5. Remind students to tell about the characters, sights, and sounds. Go wild with descriptions, and have a "ghoul" time!

by Donna L. Clovis

A Halloween Costume for Johnny

Characters

Scarecrow
1st Tree
2nd Tree
Johnny Jones
Anne, dressed as a fairy princess
Jane, dressed as a cheerleader
Rob, dressed in a karate outfit
Joe, dressed in a Batman outfit
Tim, dressed as a lion
Rabbits*
Snails*
Kittens*
Mice*
Owl
Fox
Pumpkins*
*Indicates need for more than one character

Production Notes

Playing time: About 20 minutes.

Costumes: Animals wear makeup and appropriate attachments (ears, lion mane, tails, shells, mittens, glasses for the owl, limbs). Pumpkins wear paper pumpkin outfits. Friends dress as noted in list of characters. Scarecrow wears jacket and hat. Johnny wears street clothes.

Props: Pom-poms, wand.

Setting: May have backdrop of cornfield. May have log or box in the center.

Lighting: No special effects.

Sound: None needed unless pumpkins dance, then appropriate music.

Hint: Costumes were made of paper for second grade play.

Time: The present. A fall day.

Setting: A cornfield, stump or box in the center.

At curtain rise: Two trees and one scarecrow are on stage.

Scarecrow: It's almost that time again. I can tell by the moon and the frosty feel in the air.

1st Tree: What time did you say?

2nd Tree: Not time for my leaves to fall, I hope. I just got real attached to them!

Scarecrow: Well, it is that time, too, but I meant it's almost time for Halloween.

1st Tree: That's when the boys and girls put on costumes and funny faces. It must be fun.

2nd Tree: Better than losing all your leaves!

Scarecrow: I wonder how they think up all those costumes.

1st Tree: Shh! Someone is coming. *(Six children enter. Five are in costume. Johnny walks slowly behind without a costume. See Production Notes for costumes.)*

by Mary Chichester Smith

Anne: I'm so excited! This is my favorite holiday. I love dressing up.

Jane: The costume parade is so much fun. Some of the big boys scare me, though.

Rob: I'm not afraid of anything—at least, I'm not when I'm wearing this!

Joe: Isn't this a great costume my mom made for me? See, she made this Batman suit with a cape and everything. *(He whirls around.)* Look at the bat sign she put on the shirt and this neat hood.

Anne: Bats aren't for me. Mom bought this super costume. It's so pretty. I love being a fairy princess! *(She hugs herself.)*

Jane: This is my sister's costume from last year. She was a cheerleader, and the pom-pom was still hanging in her room. She said I could use it if I'm careful. *(She shakes the pom-pom.)*

Anne: You look good. Maybe I'll be a cheerleader next year.

Rob: Do you like my karate suit? I'm a ninja—Hi-jah! *(He does a karate kick or chop.)*

Tim: Look out! You almost hit me! Snarl! Snarl! You better not mess with the king of the jungle!

Rob: That's great. We all look super. Hey, Johnny, we haven't heard about your costume yet. What are you going to wear?

Johnny: That's what I'd like to know. Mom is too busy to make anything—our new baby has been sick, and Dad is out of town, so he couldn't take me to buy anything.

Anne: Couldn't you use an old sheet? You know, cut out some eyes and be a ghost.

Johnny: We don't have any old sheets. Mom gave them away to the homeless shelter.

Jane: Why not use one of your dad's jackets and a hat and be a detective?

Johnny: Last time I used one of his jackets, I fell in the mud, and he said never again!

Tim: Dress up in your mom's bathrobe, put your hair in a scarf and be a lady. That's what Tony in 6B is going to do.

Johnny: I don't want to copy him. He might not like that.

Joe: Well, buddy, I want to get to school. Sure hope you think of something. Some of the kids aren't dressing up at all, so that's okay, too.

Rob: But it's the only time of the year we really get to dress up. Keep thinking. You'll come up with a good idea yet. Wait for me, Joe, I'm coming with you.

Anne: Good luck. See you at school.

Jane: You can do it. But you had better hurry. *(All children exit. Johnny sits on the stump. He sighs and looks sad. Rabbits enter, hopping.)*

Rabbits: What's wrong? What's wrong, little Johnny Jones?
You look so sad,
clear down to your
bones.

Johnny: I have no costume to wear for the Halloween parade today. I've thought and thought, but no ideas come.

Rabbits: Johnny, that's easy— easy as pie!
Just catch a cotton tail hopping by.
With a bit of fluff and two long ears,
You'd be a bunny. They look so dear!

Johnny: That is a good idea! Now which rabbit shall I catch?

Rabbits: Not me! Not me! Not me! *(They hop away.)*

Johnny: That was a good idea. But I still don't have a costume.

Snails: *(Snails begin creeping across the stage. They speak as they move slowly along.)* Here we come! Please let us through!
We're in a hurry, that is true.
We heard that Johnny needs a plan,
And we have come to lend a hand.
The trouble is our brain is slow,
But we're trying hard, you ought to know.

Johnny: It's nice of you to try, but I need an idea quick. *(Snails creep off stage. Bats fly in.)*

Bats: We're the bats, yes, indeed,
Flying high with amazing speed!
With our sharp ears we heard you say,
You need a costume right away.
We have a plan to make folks shake:
You could go as a roller skate!
(Bats laugh.)

Johnny: Great idea, but how could I do that?

Bats: There's a little problem here, it's true.
But we had the idea, the rest is up to you.
(Bats fly off.)

Johnny: Boy, they weren't a lot of help! I still don't have a costume. All I'm doing is sitting and sitting and sitting.

Three Kittens: *(Enter merrily.)*

If you were knitting as you're sitting,
You'd soon have mittens like little kittens.
Here, you could have a pair to wear—
Little kittens like to share.
(Each kitten offers a mitten.)

Johnny: That is kind, Little Kittens, but what kind of a costume is mittens? It's not a snow parade; it's a Halloween parade.

Kittens: We don't know. It just seems fine.
We use our mittens all the time.
(They look at their mittens.)

Johnny: Well, thank you for your help. I'll keep it in mind. You really are very nice.
(Kittens leave as mice enter.)

Mice: Mice? Mice? Did you say mice?
Well, we are here
With twitching noses, tails, and ears.
Don't listen to kittens—they're known to chase mice.
No costume of mittens would be very nice.
But wearing some ears—now there's a plan!
A reason for cheers! The best in the land!

Johnny: And where would I find ears? Or a tail? Or a nose? The idea might work . . .

(He starts toward the mice. They scamper around.)

Mice: No! No! No! Don't look this way!
We must go! We cannot stay!
(They scurry off stage holding their ears.)

Johnny: So here I am—and still no costume. I need help! *(Owl flaps in.)*

Owl: Folks say I'm wise
'Cause I have big eyes.
I have a way to get it done
With just a part from every one.
The wing of a bat and a pair of mittens,
Shell of a snail on your back could be sittin', Tail of a rabbit all fluffy and white,
With a mouse's big ears—Oh! my, what a sight!
I'll loan you my glasses to make you look wise,
And you'll scare the big moon right out of the sky!

Fox: *(Off stage all creatures are softly saying "No! No! No!" Fox chases owl off stage.)*
Now, fellow, that is much too much.
A costume needs a lighter touch.

Scarecrow: He's right, you know. You're trying too hard. Take a look around to find something to use.

Pumpkins: *(Pumpkins tap onto stage.)*
You should pay attention here.
It's the pumpkin time of year.
Join the pumpkin dancing line—
A pumpkin costume would be fine.
(Pumpkins dance, then tap off stage.)

1st Tree: You could follow their advice . . .

2nd Tree: Or even be a pumpkin pie slice! *(Shakes with laughter.)*

1st Tree: Your leaves are starting to fall! *(2nd Tree stops.)* We would like to help, but all we have are leaves . . .

2nd Tree: And a nest or two. Hey! Wear a nest and be a tree!

Johnny: No thank you. That sounds itchy.

Scarecrow: You are right, there. Straw itches. If I could just take my jacket off, just for a little while, it would help so much.

Johnny: Here, I can help with that. *(He takes jacket off Scarecrow, looks at it, then puts it on himself.)*

Scarecrow: Much better! While you are at it, could you take my hat off, too? I'd have a better view of the moon tonight.

Johnny: Yes, I can do that. *(Takes hat off, looks at it, and puts it on his own head.)*

Fox: I wonder who is wise? Who had the best plan? I think it may be the Scarecrow Man!

Scarecrow: I think you look great . . .

1st Tree: Rush right to school . . .

2nd Tree: But come back tomorrow . . .

Scarecrow: The nights are quite cool.

Johnny: Here I come! The Scarecrow Man. For a costume, this is grand!

Animals: And we get to keep our parts—
That Scarecrow really has a heart!

HALLOWEEN SOUP

How do you make Halloween soup?
You make it by boiling lots of goop (chicken broth).
My spider eggs (barley) and owls' beaks (baby carrots).
Stir in pumpkin vines (celery) and crow's meat (chicken tenderloin).
Add lizards' scales (chopped parsley) and lightning bugs (diced onion),
A dash of pepper, a few rotten slugs (quartered red potatoes).
Boil and bubble until you've cooked the meat,
Your friends will enjoy this Halloween treat.

Spice up the Halloween celebration in your classroom by making and serving Halloween soup. Dress in an orange chef's hat or a Halloween sweatshirt and explain that you are the Halloween host. As the host, you are going to serve Halloween soup. First read the poem aloud and discuss the seasonal contents. Leave out the real soup ingredients when you read the poem. Talk about what you could use to look like lizards' scales, pumpkin vines, and the other "goop" in the soup. Prepare ingredients ahead of time and have them ready in covered bowls so children can't see what you are using. Label the ingredients with their Halloween titles. Describe the ingredients and allow the children to guess what you are using for lightning bugs and owls' beaks. After they guess, remove the lid from that ingredient and show students what is in the bowl. Mix all ingredients together and cook over a hot plate or stove. Allow soup to cook for about two hours or until barley is tender, while enjoying Halloween stories and games. Serve in bowls and let the children slurp it up!

by Jo Jo Cavalline and Jo Anne O'Donnell

Holiday Sing-Alongs
by Mabel Duch

As I Was Walking Down the Street

To the tune of "Here We Go 'Round the Mulberry Bush"

As I was walking down the street,
Down the street, down the street,
A grizzly bear I chanced to meet,
Looking rather wild.
The grizzly said, "Don't be afraid.
Don't be afraid. Don't be afraid."
The grizzly said, "Don't be afraid.
I'm really just a child."

As I was walking down the street,
Down the street, down the street,
A pirate lad I chanced to meet,
Looking rather bold.
The pirate said, "Don't be afraid.
Don't be afraid. Don't be afraid."
The pirate said, "Don't be afraid.
I'm only eight years old."

As I was walking down the street,
Down the street, down the street,
A dragon king I chanced to meet,
Looking rather mean.
The dragon said, "Don't be afraid.
Don't be afraid. Don't be afraid."
The dragon said, "We're dressed this way
Because it's Halloween!"

Discussion

Individual children may be assigned to sing the words of the grizzly bear, the pirate, and the dragon king. Substitute the age of the child singing or the age of most of your children in the last line of the pirate's part.

Let children discuss Halloween costumes. How can they be sure their costumes are safe? They should wear masks that do not obstruct their vision, or use makeup instead. Costumes should be nonrestrictive to allow free walking and short enough to avoid tripping. Children should wear light or bright colors with reflective strips and carry flashlights.

Expand this discussion into general Halloween safety rules.

Activity

Let children draw pictures of themselves in Halloween costumes they will be wearing or would like to wear.

Display the art on a bulletin board under the heading *Our Class Goes Trick-or-Treating.*

Maddie's Yom Kippur Surprise

A Story for the Jewish High Holy Days

"Put those dishes over there, so that we can wash them once more before the Sabbath begins," Madeline's mother gently reminded her. Cleaning, cooking, and keeping a kosher kitchen were important preparations for the autumn celebrations of Rosh Ha-shanah and Yom Kippur, and Maddie was learning a lot of interesting things about her faith and its traditions.

"Why do we have a new year in the middle of the year?" asked Maddie.

"You remember what the rabbi taught at Hebrew school, don't you?" asked her mother. "In Judaism, we have a special calendar and the month of Tishri is the first month of our new year."

"But it is October for the kids at regular school," protested Maddie. "Can it be both?"

"It is both," agreed her mother. "But remember how important faith is for us and for everybody. By celebrating the Rosh Hashanah at synagogue and at home, we remember our history and keep our family strong."

"Is that why the big horn gets blown?" asked Maddie. "In case we forget, it wakes us up."

"You could say that," laughed her mother. "The shofar is a ram's horn that has been hollowed out and straightened."

"Tell me again—how many times it will be blown," urged Maddie.

"Three times," said her mother. "You tell me why."

"Well, one time is after the first prayers, the ones about God ruling the world."

"Yes, and the second time comes after the prayers that remind us that God always listens to our prayers."

"I like that one," smiled Maddie.

"Me too," agreed her mother. "And can you name the last time?"

"I think so," said Maddie. "Isn't it after the prayers that tell us God remembers the things we do . . ."

"The deeds of people," nodded mother. "That's pretty good. Let's get started on that apple and honey cake. It is your dad's favorite, and I want you to make it this year. You are getting to be a big girl, Maddie. It is time to take some responsibilities."

"Like washing dishes and cooking?" asked Maddie.

"And other things," said her mother. "On the tenth day of the new year we have Yom Kippur and that is the most holy day of all."

"Will I have to fast this year?" asked Maddie. She wanted to be a part of the grown-ups' celebration.

"A little bit," nodded her mother, "but there is more. You have to reconcile with those whom you have hurt or whom you need to forgive."

"Not Marc! Not mean, old Marc. He scratched up my new bike on purpose. He's always messing things up. He is new at school, but he is already a big pain in my neck!"

"Well, if Marc is the problem, then you need to do something about those bad feelings if you want to start the new year off right."

"Can't I just make more apple cakes and give them to my friends?" asked Madeline, with a hopeful look.

"That's not exactly atonement," said her mother. "That's more like avoiding the issue."

"But Marc is such a big issue," sighed Maddie.

"Then you need to spend some big time thinking about it. The Holy Days are a time for Jewish families to get in harmony with one another and with others around them. You need to be an example, Maddie, even if Marc doesn't want to get along."

"That's hard," sighed Maddie, again.

"That's why we have the Holy Days," explained her mother. "Hard things are sometimes the most important things in the world."

A few days later, Maddie saw Marc pushing his bike down the street. The tire was flat, and Marc looked angry. Maddie thought, *I ought to say something nice.* So she said, "I'm sorry your tire is flat, Marc."

Marc just glared and kept walking.

Maddie thought, *This isn't working. He's still mean.*

The next day, Maddie saw Marc walking to Hebrew school. He pushed by her and when he did, a notebook dropped out of his backpack.

I ought to throw this notebook in the trash. He's so rude all the time, thought Maddie. But then she remembered the Holy Days coming up. "Hey Marc, you dropped this," she called.

Marc turned around and stuck his tongue out at Maddie, but he grabbed the notebook.

I knew it, thought Maddie.

On the day before Rosh Hashanah, Maddie was eating her lunch and thinking about all the company that would be coming over for the special Sabbath meal. She loved seeing her cousins and aunts and uncles. She was so busy thinking that she almost missed seeing Marc sitting down at the end of the table, with no lunch.

Without thinking, Maddie slid down toward Marc and said. "Did you forget your lunch again?" She handed him half of her sandwich and her whole square of apple cake.

Marc looked around to see if anyone had noticed, and he said, "Thanks, Maddie."

"You're welcome." It felt good, so Maddie asked a question. "What happened to your lunch?"

"My mother is really sick, and I had to get up early this morning to walk my little sister to school, so I forgot my lunch."

"Where's your dad?" asked Maddie.

"He's at the hospital with my mom. We're new here and haven't had time to get to know anybody."

"Well, you know me," said Maddie.

That afternoon, Maddie rushed in the door. "Mother, I need to tell you something."

"Tell me. Tell me," her mother urged.

"Marc isn't mean just to be mean. His mother is sick, and he's worried and sad and lots of other stuff. Can we make them a cake?"

"Let's make a cake and a few phone calls," agreed her mother.

The autumn Holy Days came as usual, in the month of Tishri. There were 13 Holy Days in the month, and Maddie and her family and her new friend Marc participated in all of them! Maddie's family included Marc's family in their celebrations, and Maddie got a very interesting surprise. It wasn't the shofar and it wasn't the honey cakes, it was the good feeling that came when she forgave someone and even tried to be friends.

"L'Shanah Tovah, Maddie."

"L'Shanah Tovah, Marc."

It felt good to greet a friend on Yom Kippur, especially when that friend used to be your worst enemy!

Diwali

Festival of Lights

Diwali is the biggest and grandest festival celebrated by Hindus in India. It takes place sometime in October or November. There is no fixed date because Indians follow the lunar calendar for religious holidays. A lunar month is from full moon to full moon.

The word *Diwali* comes from *Deepavali,* which means "cluster of lights." It was on this day that Lord Rama returned to his kingdom after 14 years of exile in the forest. The Indian people rejoiced at the return of their king, and celebrated by lighting up the town.

And so today, that is the way Diwali is celebrated. Different states in India have different customs and traditions. The celebrations usually start days before Diwali. First, the houses are cleaned thoroughly to invite the Goddess Laxmi into their homes. It is said that the Goddess of Wealth will not enter a dark or dirty home. Candles called *divas* are lit in little earthen bowls and placed all around inside and outside the house. Designs called *rangoli* are made on the front doorstep, using colored powder. Firecrackers abound and for days, long into the night, you will hear their joyful cracks and pops. Friends and relatives visit each other bearing gifts and sweets.

This is a good time to buy gold jewelry and new clothes. Businessmen close their yearly accounts. The account books are laid out in front of the Goddess Laxmi to be blessed.

The day after Diwali is the New Year. The feasting and the celebrations continue. Children go to the elders and touch their feet as a sign of respect. The elders then bless the children by giving them a gift, usually money.

As all good things must come to an end, so do the Diwali festivities.

Activities

Wear a Bindi

Many Indian girls and most Indian women wear a dot in the middle of their forehead called a *bindi,* or a *tika.* In the olden days, it represented the third eye of wisdom; now it is just a fashion statement. In India, the dot is applied with a colored paste or powder. Modern girls in the cities use special stickers. You can make a dot with a non-toxic marker in the middle of your forehead, close to the eyebrows, or you can use small dot stickers.

Draw a Peacock

The peacock is India's national bird. Peacock feathers are greatly prized. They are associated with the Hindu God Krishna.

Say, Namaste!

Namaste means "hello" in Hindi, which is the national language. To say it properly, fold your palms together, bring them up at chest level and bow slightly from the waist.

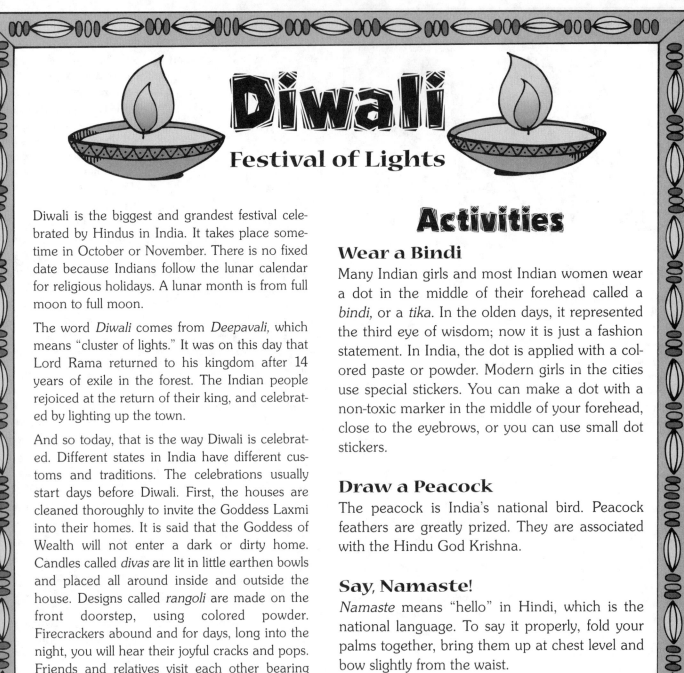

by Bati Patel

Pronunciation Guide

Bindi (Been-dee) or Tika (Tee-kaa): The dot worn by women on their forehead.

Krishna (CRISH-naa): One of the most popular Hindu gods.

Namaste (Naa-MUH-stay): Hello, literally, "I bow to you."

Yoga (YO-gaa): Mental and spiritual exercise.

OM (OHM): Mantra uttered at the beginning and at the end of most Hindu prayers, much like "Amen."

Chutney (CHAT-nee): A thick sauce made out of cilantro, mango, or other fruit, and used as a condiment.

Rakhi (RAA-khee): Ribbon tied on Raksha-Bandhan (RAK-shaa BAND-dhun) or Brother-Sister Day.

Rangoli (RUNG-o-lee): Design made on front doorstep.

Diwali (DEE-vaa-lee): Festival of Lights

Rama (RAA-ma): Indian king exiled to the forest for 14 years.

Laxmi (LAKH-shmee): Goddess of Wealth

Diva (DEE-vaa): Small earthen bowl filled with a candle or oil and a little cotton wick, which is lit.

Do a Rangoli

Rangoli is a design drawn on the front entrance of the house. It is usually done around Diwali, but some people consider it a sign of good fortune and display it year 'round. Draw a design on a piece of paper and put it outside your front door. Or make a design with sidewalk chalk. Choose one of these designs or create your own.

Find India on a Map

Look for the country of India on a world map. Which continent is it on?

Make a Flag

Draw and color a picture of the Indian flag. The orange (top) stands for "courage," the white (middle) for "truth" and the green (bottom) for "faith." The navy blue wheel in the center stands for "duty" and is also the symbol of Indian independence.

Let's Do Yoga!

Yoga is a physical and spiritual exercise done by many Indians. The word *yoga* means "to join" or "to unite"—you try to join your mind, body, and soul in perfect harmony. There are many positions and ways to perform yoga.

Here is one yoga position.

Start by standing totally straight. Bend your right leg slowly and place the sole of your foot against the side of your left knee. Put the palms of your hands together and hold them at chest level. Close your eyes, take a deep breath and chant the word *om*, stretching the sound out, while exhaling.

Make a Rakhi

Just as there is Mother's Day and Father's Day in the United States, in India there is a special day for brothers and sisters. It is called Raksha-Bandhan. This year it falls on August 18th. The sister ties a ribbon called a rakhi on her brother (or if she doesn't have a brother, a cousin or a dear male friend). In return, the brother gives her a gift and promises to protect her forever.

Materials

  thin strip of ribbon about 9" long
  small paper circle, 1 1/2" in diameter
  glue
  pencil
  scissors
  crayons or markers

Procedure

Draw a circle inside the paper circle, about 1" in diameter. In the outer circle, draw lines as in the diagram below. Cut on the lines to make a fringe. Draw a design in the smaller circle. Glue the circle to the center of the ribbon. Let it dry. Your rakhi is ready to be tied!

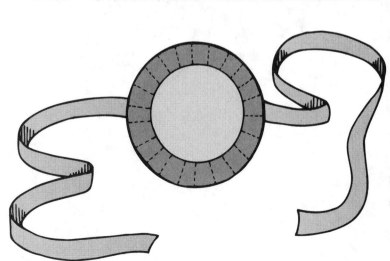

Let's Count in Hindi

Practice writing 1-10 in Hindi. Follow the chart below and sound out the numbers.

९	ek (ayk) one	६	ché (chay) six
२	do (doh) two	७	saat (saat) seven
३	teen (teen) three	८	aht (aath) eight
४	char (chahr) four	९	now (now) nine
५	panch (paanch) five	१०	das (dhas) ten

International DRUM Month

Every year the month of November is dedicated to the percussion instruments, especially the drum. November is International Drum Month, a time to celebrate the worldwide popularity of this instrument. Into their eighth year, the Percussion Marketing Council promotes music education worldwide. "Be a Player" is their slogan—don't just dream and wish, get a percussion instrument and join the fun.

Life is a rhythm. It's a universal mode of expression like a heartbeat, clapping hands, a basketball bouncing, a ticking clock, sounds of a motor, and so on. Children enjoy rhythm and love to use rhythm instruments in the classroom to make sounds and follow a beat. Homemade drums and percussion instruments can be made and explored in music class. Here are a few ideas to try.

FOLLOW THE BEAT

Have the children form a big circle. The teacher will use a drum to give directions. Explain to the children that only the drum speaks. Tell them to move around the circle, listening to the beat. When the beat is slow, the children will walk slowly around the circle. When the beat is faster, they can run around the circle. This is a good listening game.

DRUM GAME

The teacher plays a beat pattern on the drum, changing from loud to soft or soft to loud. The children respond by holding hands close together when they hear soft sounds and then spreading their hands farther apart as the sounds grow louder.

by Tania K. Cowling

DRUMSTICKS

Here are a few ideas for drumsticks to make with your class. You can easily use an unsharpened pencil, but try gluing a thread spool or a cork to one end. Thread a metal nut onto a pencil or dowel end for striking metal on metal. This is great for a snare drum sound. Other materials for drumstick heads could be wooden beads, sponges, padded cloth, or lots of rubber bands wrapped together with thimbles glued on. Listen for the differences in the sounds they make.

COCONUT DRUM

Have an adult cut coconuts in half. Drink the milk and eat the meat for a snack. Sand the edges of the coconut shell. Then get a large balloon, cut off the neck, and stretch the rubber over the rim of the shell. It's a coconut bongo drum just ready for small hands to tap a beat!

KITCHEN KETTLE DRUM

If you strike a metal cookie sheet with a rubber mallet, it will replicate the kettle drum sound. You can outfit your class with all kinds of drums just by bringing in some pots and pans.

SOUP BOWL TAMBOURINES

Decorate two paper soup bowls using crayons, markers and stickers. Discuss what you could put inside to create sounds. You might use rice, dried beans, small pebbles, jingle bells, buttons, and so on. Place a small amount of the noisemakers inside before gluing the bowls together. Shake and tap for fun!

ALUMINUM TAMBOURINE

You can transform an old aluminum pie pan into a music-making tambourine. Just punch holes on the edges and attach old keys, bells, metal washers, and large paper clips with yarn or ribbon. Don't forget to decorate the center of the tin and shake, shake, shake!

COFFEE CAN DRUM SET

A set of drums or bongos can be made from two or three coffee cans with plastic lids. Make sure the coffee cans vary in size. Tape them together with masking tape, making sure the tops are level. Use your hands or homemade drumsticks to beat out a rhythm on the plastic lids of the cans. Notice that the size of each can affects the sound coming from it. A bigger can produces a lower sound, and a smaller can makes a higher sound.

GARBAGE CAN-THE LARGE CLASS DRUM

Use a wastebasket or garbage pail as your class drum. Stretch fabric across the top and affix it with rope or heavy tape. Spread a layer of diluted white school glue on the fabric (several coats are best). This makes the fabric tight when the glue dries and the drumhead will have a better tone.

Celebrate National
SANDWICH DAY

From peanut butter and jelly to a thick juicy club, sandwiches are quick, easy, and popular. Why not celebrate National Sandwich Day on November 3 by making and eating your favorite sandwich at school?

It is said that John Montague, the fourth Earl of Sandwich in the early 1770s, was so involved in a card game that he didn't want to stop to eat. He ordered a servant to bring him two slices of bread with a piece of roast meat between them. Thus the sandwich was born!

Here are some sandwiches you may enjoy putting together and eating, though you're not limited to these. It's fun to create your own, too!

GET THE BREAD

Choose a different bread such as Vienna, Italian, pumpernickel, whole wheat, rye, or oatmeal. And don't overlook pita bread, English muffins, bagels, hard rolls, or specialty crackers.

USING PEANUT BUTTER

Spreading a layer of jelly over a layer of peanut butter is the best-known combination, but try blending the peanut butter and jelly together first and then spreading it. Instead of jelly, try honey or bits of bacon. And topping peanut butter with apples or banana slices is delicious! TIP: Peanut butter is easier to spread on bread that is slightly frozen.

I'M MAKING A SANDWICH

Have the children sit in a circle. The leader begins by saying "I'm making a sandwich, and I need a slice of bread." The next person repeats what has been said and adds something (like mayonnaise, mustard, ketchup, and so on). The next person repeats everything that has been said and adds something else. This continues until everyone has added something to the sandwich. Creativity should be encouraged. Try to avoid duplicating. (Teacher may have to prompt every now and then as the sandwich gets bigger!) When the game is over, have the children draw a picture of this sandwich.

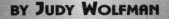

BY JUDY WOLFMAN

SANDWICH COLLAGE

Gather long sheets of mural paper, magazines, scissors, and glue.

Cut out pictures of foods that would be good to put in a sandwich and glue these on the paper. Talk about the various foods—where they come from, what food group they belong to, their importance, other uses, and so on.

CREATIVE WRITING

Have each child write down one food that would be good to put into a sandwich and illustrate that food. Collect the pages and let the children put them in order. Have the class decide on a title for their sandwich story and write it on a cover page. Assemble the book and have it available to read and enjoy.

GIANT SANDWICH

If possible, get a long hoagie roll from a bakery. Have each child bring something to put into the sandwich. Cover a long table with aluminum foil or wax paper and put the roll on the paper. Make sure all hands are washed before making the sandwich. Decide what to put on the roll. Mayonnaise? Mustard? Oil? Allow each child to place his or her food on the roll, spreading it out as evenly as possible. When the sandwich is completed, cut it so each child will have his own sandwich. As the sandwich is made, discuss the various foods, where they come from, how they taste, what food group they belong to, and their nutritional value.

Sandwiches for Everyone!

Mr. Stevens' class had a contest to see who could bring the most soda pop cans to school for recycling. He promised a special prize to the top five students. Today those students get their prize—Mr. Stevens has taken them out for lunch at a favorite restaurant. The waitress just brought six sandwiches to the table. See if you can figure out which sandwich is for which person.

Clues

Lonnie loves to eat. He likes almost everything except cheese and fish.

Maria is allergic to mustard and she can't stand pickles.

Anne is a vegetarian, so she doesn't eat meat or fish.

Scott is a picky eater. He won't eat any kinds of vegetables.

Blake's idea of a good sandwich is "the messier, the better." He doesn't like lettuce, but he loves pickles.

Mr. Stevens says he likes everything on a sandwich, and he likes it big.

Sandwich	Double cheeseburger with mustard, ketchup, pickles, lettuce, and tomato	Bacon, lettuce, and tomato with mayonnaise	Barbecued pork on a bun	Grilled cheese	Tuna salad with lettuce and tomato	Chili dog with cheese and pickles
Lonnie						
Maria						
Anne						
Scott						
Blake						
Mr. Stevens						

by Mary Tucker

VETERANS DAY
MURAL

An activity to facilitate remembering, thanking, and honoring those who fought for our country

MATERIALS
5' long piece of mural paper
markers, crayons, and pencils

SETUP
World War I ended on November 11, the eleventh hour of the eleventh day of the eleventh month of 1918. This day was originally called Armistice Day. It later became known as Veterans Day in the United States and Remembrance Day in Canada.

Prepare for Remembrance Day/Veterans Day by helping children understand the service provided by those who work to preserve peace and those who fought to protect the ideas and beliefs of your nation. Talk about what makes your country special and think about those who gave their lives for their countries.

LET'S MAKE IT
1. Prepare a "thank-you" mural with your group. Begin by taping the mural paper to the floor and providing the drawing and writing tools.

2. Invite children to think about and express their appreciation for the country they live in and the gratitude they feel for those who helped the world. Ask children to express these thoughts and feelings through drawings or words on the mural paper.

BY ROBYNNE EAGAN

NATIONAL CHILDREN'S BOOK WEEK

National Children's Book Week is sponsored by the Children's Book Council and is celebrated in schools, libraries, bookstores, and at home. This tradition is always celebrated during the week before Thanksgiving and is dedicated to the encouragement and enjoyment of reading. Use the following activities as a springboard for your own classroom celebration.

 Design posters and banners announcing Book Week that can be hung throughout the school.

 Students can dress up as their favorite book characters or authors and parade around the school.

 This year's national slogan is "Books Go Everywhere." Come up with your own classroom or school Book Week slogan.

 Have a talent contest where students can read or dramatize a favorite passage, poem, or chapter.

 Plan a book fair during this week.

 Let students design and make their own bookmarks.

Write songs or poems about the joy of reading.

 Make your own books and give them to younger students or write stories and read them to a local preschool.

 Have a school-wide election. Each class nominates their favorite books/authors and the whole school votes.

 Visit amazon.com to find out more about your favorite authors or books.

 For more information write to the National Book Council, 568 Broadway, Suite 404, New York, NY 10012, or visit their web site.

 Tell students they are famous authors and have been asked to write a children's book with one of these titles:

The Day the Rainbow Cried

The Night It Rained Chocolate Chips

Thanksgiving Surprise

My Mom the Astronaut

Two Turkeys and a Duck

 Let students select their favorite title and brainstorm ideas. Each can write a story or collaborate with a friend.

Native American Day

TOTEM POLES

Native American tribes carved and painted totem poles to put in front of their homes. They used animals, plants, and natural objects to represent their family or relatives. Color the totem pole above.

Now think about what objects or animals could represent people in your family. Draw a new totem pole that could represent your family on this page. Color it.

by Ann Richmond Fisher

Thanksgiving

Bytes

by Dr. Linda Karges-Bone

Faith Anderson was in a very bad mood. The Thanksgiving holiday had always been her favorite and she was going to have to spend the week of vacation with her knee propped up on a pillow. Too bad she hadn't listened to her dad when he reminded her about wearing knee pads while roller blading. That last turn had turned out to be a disaster. Faith gently rubbed her swollen knee and bruised leg.

"Not broken, just badly bruised and scraped," the emergency room doctor pronounced. She added, "Too bad you didn't have on the right gear."

"Like a knee pad," added Faith's dad.

"I know," Faith agreed. She had learned a hard lesson, but why did it have to be during Thanksgiving vacation? Her school calendar followed a 12-month schedule, with several breaks during the year. The Thanksgiving break had been wonderful last year. Faith learned to bake pumpkin bread, skated every day with her best friend Margaret, and helped her mom shop for the feast. This year, she was stuck in a chair.

"At least I can work on my Thanksgiving research project," Faith sighed. Her teacher, Mr. Dubois, was big on research. So far this year, he had assigned research projects on: the digestive system, the planet Mercury, and the "origins of your name." That was the best one. Faith talked about how her name came from the Bible, and that girls at the first Thanksgiving had been named Faith. Her parents chose her name because she was born on Thanksgiving Day, and they wanted a name that might have been popular at that time. Their other choices had been "Hope" or "Charity," but Faith was pleased with their final decision. "I'm a person who has a lot of faith in herself," she thought. "I'll get through this."

Carefully sliding her sore leg around, Faith eased up to the desk where her trusty PC (personal computer) beckoned. She signed on the internet and browsed over to her favorite site, "Kids Chat." Using the internet, a system of computers all around the world "talking to one another," kids can do research, find information, or communicate with other people. Faith typed this message:

"Bummer! I hurt my leg roller blading, and have to spend my break writing a research paper. Can anyone tell me about his or her favorite Thanksgiving traditions and where they came from?"

Then she popped in a CD-ROM "encyclopedia" and read about the first Thanksgiving at Plymouth. Usually, it took a while for kids to read and respond to messages. She might as well get started on her research. This is what she wrote.

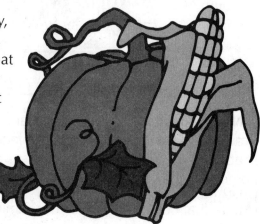

The Pilgrims really did have a feast in 1621, but it wasn't like our Thanksgiving meals today. The governor of Plymouth sent four men out "fowling" and they brought back enough birds for the whole group to eat for a week. That included 90 Native American Indians and their chief, King Massasoit. The Pilgrims were very religious; that is why they left England. They wanted to be free to worship God in their own way. Anyway, the reason for the feast was to give thanks to God for the very good harvest that they had that fall. The Pilgrims probably did have turkey, but it would not have been stuffed, and they probably had pumpkin, but not in a pie. They ate pumpkin stewed, like a vegetable. I think the first Thanksgiving would have been fun, because the researchers at Plimouth Plantation think that the Pilgrims and Native Americans ate outside because there wasn't a building large enough for their group.

Faith finished her opening and noticed that the message light was blinking on her screen. Somebody from Kids Chat had responded!

"My favorite Thanksgiving tradition is eating deer meat that my dad and I cook out doors at our hunting club. I live in a rural part of South Carolina, and on Thanksgiving Day, about 15 families that belong to our hunting club meet to eat an outdoor feast of our own. We eat outside on big trestle tables that we build out of sawhorses and wood. We have turkeys too, but not wild ones. Most of the wild turkeys are extinct, but we do get plenty of deer. Did you know that the Pilgrims probably had more deer at the first feast? Hope your leg gets better. I messed my arm up pretty bad last month, because I forgot to put on pads."

The message was signed by Brad who lived in Ridgeville, South Carolina. Faith sent her e-mail friend a quick reply, because another message was flashing.

This time a girl named La Shaunda from New York had something to share.

"We celebrate Thanksgiving too, but that's not why I'm writing. My family also celebrates the African American holiday Kwanzaa. It is a spiritual holiday, not a national holiday. During the seven days of Kwanzaa, we eat special foods that remind us of our heritage. My grandmother makes a great sweet potato casserole, and I'll send the recipe to you tomorrow. Kwanzaa was started by Dr. Marlene Karenga in 1966, and a lot more people are celebrating it today. Did you know that *Kwanzaa* means "first fruits of the harvest"? Hope your leg doesn't hurt too much. My brother did the same thing. Were you wearing protective gear?"

Faith typed a speedy thanks to La Shaunda, and ended with, "No gear, and I know better now!" She was just about to look at some drawings of what the first settlement at Plymouth might have looked like when her message light flashed a frantic green once more.

This time, Benjamin from California had something to say:

"We do Thanksgiving, sort of. I say sort of, because my parents are vegetarians, so we skip the turkey part. We do have lots of rice and lentil loaf and a pumpkin pie with whipped cream that my mom's grandmother taught her how to make a long time ago. My family does a lot of neat stuff with our church, so we don't just eat the feast at home. We cook a bunch of food and bring it to the mission, so that people who don't have houses can eat, too. Did you know that Thanksgiving is always celebrated on the third Thursday in November? That's kind of weird since the official Thanksgiving Proclamation was signed on June 20, 1676. Hope your leg isn't broken or anything."

Faith wrote Benjamin from California a reply and asked him if he really liked lentil loaf or if his parents just made him eat it. "I'm glad we're carnivores," she thought. She was just about to get back to the drawings of Plymouth when a fourth message beamed in from cyberspace. A girl named Rebekkah from Cleveland had something different to say:

"Shalom. That's a Hebrew word for "greeting." My tradition is Hanukkah. We celebrate the feast of lights during the early winter. Jewish families are remembering a special victory and miracle that happened a long time ago. Maccabees, a Jewish warrior, won a major battle for freedom, and he did it even though we didn't have enough oil to light our lamps. The miracle part is when the oil in the lamps burned for eight days, even though the lamps had been almost empty! So now we have Hanukkah, and eat special foods, go to Temple, and play with special toys. Do you know what a dreidel is? The Hebrew letters on this toy spell out Ness Gadol Hya Sham: A great miracle took place there! Hope you can still have fun even with a hurt leg. My roller blades are too small, maybe I'll get another pair as a Hanukkah surprise."

"Wow," thought Faith. "Winter holidays are a lot more than Thanksgiving, and even the Thanksgiving traditions can be really different. This project is turning out to be pretty cool after all." She saved all of her messages and turned the computer off. It was almost time for her mom to get home. She had a lot to tell her tonight. Maybe she could still help bake, if she sat up on a stool and propped her leg on another stool. Maybe they could try La Shaunda's recipe for sweet potato casserole. She wasn't even going to ask Benjamin about that lentil loaf!

Research Ideas for "Thanksgiving Bytes"

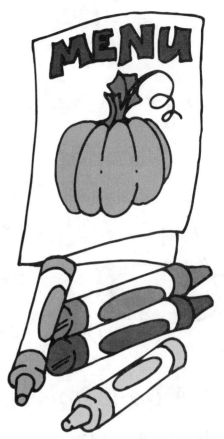

The Name Game

Use baby name books to find out the origin of your name. What culture or country does your name come from? Are you "like" the description of your name? If you could choose a name that really describes you, what would it be and why?

Menu Bytes

Use the internet, CD-ROM encyclopedia, or resource books to find out about the "real" Thanksgiving feast. Use crayons, markers, and fabric to design an authentic menu for the first feast. Hint: Plimouth Plantation is a good source for your search.

Interview Research

Form teams to conduct a study that involves interviews. We call this "ethnographic research." One team of students will interview other students your age. A second team of students will interview people who are ages 25-40. A third team will interview folks ages 40-60. A fourth team can interview older people ages 60 and over. Ask each person the same set of questions, and then compare your results. What did you find out? Does age play a role when one answers the question: What are you most thankful for?

Interview Form

Team _____

Age group _____

Question: "What are you most thankful for?"

Subject 1: _____

Subject 2: _____

Subject 3: _____

Subject 4: _____

Subject 5: _____

Notes

Results

Turkey Carols

Songs to Gobble by . . .

A Do-It-Yourself Thanksgiving Story and Poem

Brad Cunningham was just sitting there doing his homework one chilly November day when the clock radio by his desk started playing, of all things . . . a *Christmas* carol! Now, Brad liked Christmas songs as much as the next kid . . . on Christmas! But that holiday wasn't even close yet. Why, they'd just had Halloween, for Pete's sake! Looking around his room, he could still see the decorations he'd put up for the world's most spooky day.

(All right gang, I KNOW this is a Thanksgiving story, but let's stop right here and take a few good, strong sentences to describe the Halloween decorations in Brad's room. Hanging bats? Crawling rats? Orange and black streamers everywhere? Maybe even a jack-o'-lantern on his dresser? Right now we don't know WHAT Brad's room looks like, so everything you write will be a big help to our story. Remember, write two to three sentences in the space below and really let us know what Brad's room AND his Halloween decorations look like. And remember, have fun!)

Brad probably wouldn't have even minded that *very* early Christmas carol at all, except that at the moment it came on, he was busy writing a report about Thanksgiving for his third grade teacher, Ms. Richards. With a head full of Captain John Smith and Squanto, who wanted to hear about Frosty and Rudolph?

Brad tried to go back to his report, but the jingly, jangly holiday song got stuck in his head and he couldn't get it out. It got him thinking about *all* the different Christmas carols he and his family loved to listen to each year. Then he ripped a piece of paper out of his special note- book and started writing them all down, one after the other, on one side of the piece of paper.

(Here's an easy assignment for you, gang. All you need to do here is LIST every Christmas carol you can think of. Yes, this is STILL a Thanksgiving story, but for this little part of it I want you to "THINK CHRISTMAS!" Use all the space you need and write as many carols as you can think of. The more the better, and don't stop until you've run out!)

by Rusty Fischer

Next, Brad tried a little experiment with himself. On the other side of his piece of paper, right next to *all* those Christmas songs he'd written, he tried to write all the *Thanksgiving* carols he knew. He tried and tried, and couldn't come up with a single *one!* Not . . . one.

He felt bad for poor, little old Thanksgiving. He looked at the stack of thick, dusty history books for the report he was doing, and wondered why such an important holiday didn't have one . . . well . . . turkey carol! Almost every other holiday he thought of had some kind of songs to go along with it.

(We're almost there, gang. List two or three holidays, and then write the name of a song that goes with each one. Remember to use complete sentences, and they should sound something like this: "He thought about all the mushy love songs that went with Valentine's Day." Something like that. You can use Easter, St. Patrick's Day, Halloween, the 4th of July, and yes . . . Valentine's Day. Just remember, for each holiday you use, write the name of a song or the kind of song that you hear around that holiday. Take at least three sentences for this one—if you can't think of that many, two will be all right. Barely!)

It made Brad mad, and when Brad got mad, he did something about it! Without even realizing what he was doing, he ripped another sheet of paper out of his spiral notebook. He forgot all about his Thanksgiving report, and started to write his very own "turkey carol"! It went like this:

(Okay, gang. Here is your very last assignment of this story we wrote together, and you're going to think it's very easy, because all you have to do is . . . fill in the blanks!

On the next page is a short "song" that Brad might have written. It's sort of like a poem, because the lines will rhyme with each other. All I want you to do is fill in the blanks with a word that rhymes with the last word in the line above it. That's IT. Ready, here we go.)

Directions

Read the story and whenever you find italics type, follow the instructions and do some creative writing of your own. Use a separate sheet of paper.

A Turkey Carol

by Brad Cunningham and (You!)

Well, it's that time of year,

Thanksgiving is almost _____.

> (use a word that rhymes with *year*)

November has finally rolled around,

But I don't even hear a _____.

> (rhymes with *around*)

Why can't anybody write

A song to sing on Thanksgiving _____?

> (rhymes with *write*)

When there's four *thousand* songs to play

Every minute of Christmas _____.

> (rhymes with *play*)

Why do I want a turkey song to sing?

Well, it's because of just one _____.

> (rhymes with *sing*)

After every single Thanksgiving dinner,

My Uncle Harvey Phillip _____

> (rhyme a last name with *dinner*)

Likes to take a little nap

With my cat, *Whiskers,* on his _____.

> (rhymes with *nap*)

And from his *nose* come sounds *galore!*

'Cause Uncle Harvey loves to _____.

> (rhymes with *galore*)

But if I had a Thanksgiving song to play,

I wouldn't have to listen to snoring all _____.

> (rhymes with *play*)

TLC10198 Copyright © Teaching & Learning Company, Carthage, IL 62321-0010

Seasonal Science

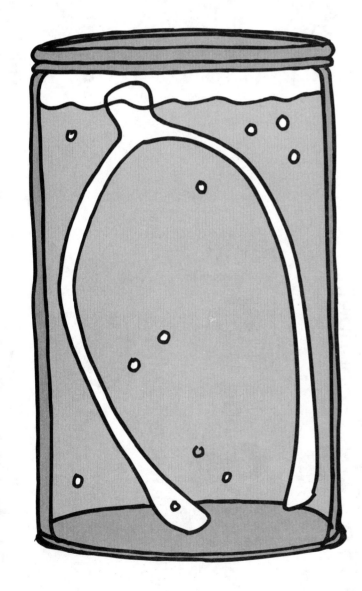

Wishbone Magic

Activity

It's always fun to pretend that our Thanksgiving wishbone wishes will come true, even though it rarely happens. This year, put that wishbone to good use in the classroom to demonstrate the importance of calcium in our diets. First, pass the wishbone to each student and have them describe how it feels—general texture as well as rigidity. Next, place the wishbone in a jar and pour enough vinegar into the jar to cover the bone. For best results, allow the jar to sit overnight. The following day, remove the bone from the jar and again pass the wishbone to each student. Encourage them to comment on how the bone has changed (it should be quite flexible). Explain that the acid in the vinegar has dissolved some of the calcium, causing the bone to bend. Have them contribute their thoughts on why calcium is an important part of our diet. Ask them to name some foods from which we get calcium.

Project

Have students draw pictures or write a few sentences telling what they would wish for if they had a magic wishbone, and why they would choose that wish. Invite them to share their wishes with the class.

Last Thanksgiving

I liked the 🦃

With gravy on top.

I took 🥕 and 🫛

'Til 👦 said to STOP.

There were some good 🧁,

And 🍌 nut bread,

And 🍇 sauce

That was very dark RED.

We went to see 👵

On 🦃 Day.

We gave her big kisses

And a 💐 bouquet.

Our 👶 had 🥛

Of 🍪 juice to sip,

With 🍉 and 🍿

And 🥔 to dip.

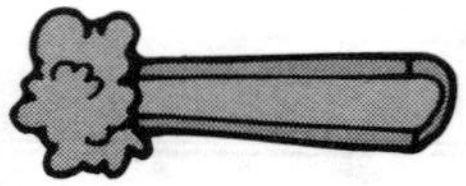

All of us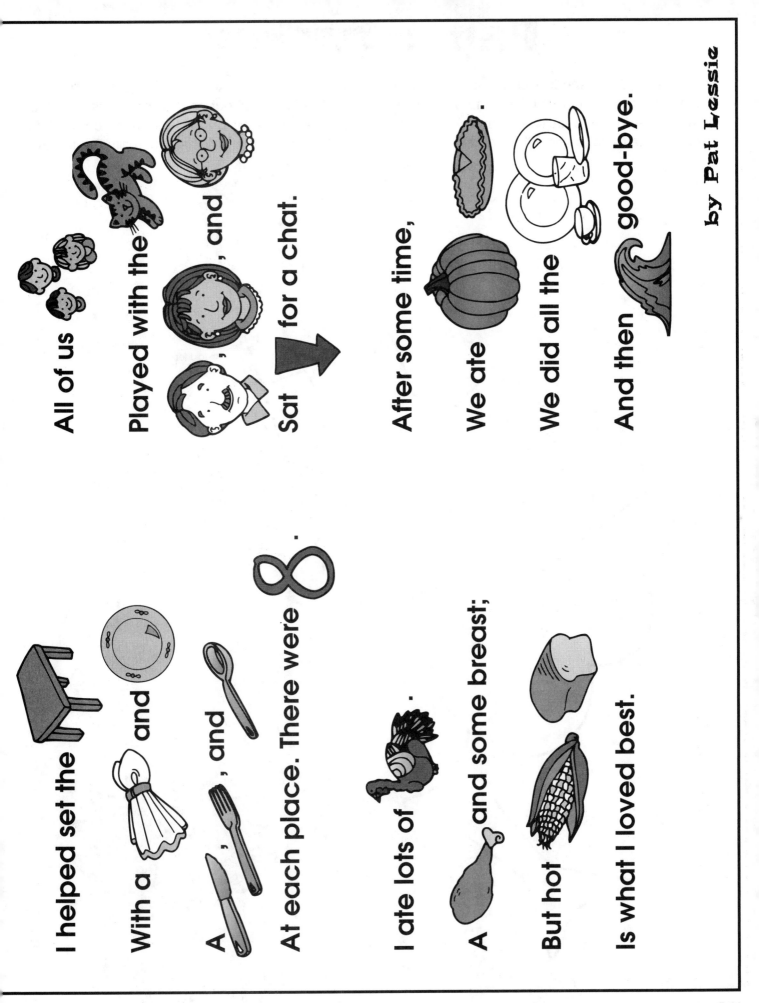

Played with the ⬛🐱 , 👵 , and 👦

Sat ➡ for a chat.

After some time,

We ate 🎃 🥧 .

We did all the 🍽☕

And then 👒 good-bye.

I helped set the 🪑

With a 🧺🍽 and 🥄

A 🔪 , 🍴 , and

At each place. There were 8 🥨 .

I ate lots of 🦃 .

A 🍗 and some breast;

But hot 🌽🥔

Is what I loved best.

by Pat Lessie

Paper Turkey

Fold an 8½" x 11" sheet of construction paper in half the long way (lengthwise). Cut out the pattern. Place the pattern on the fold with the dotted lines against the fold. Cut out on the solid lines. Fold as illustrated. Add any details such as eyes, feathers, and so on. One option is to glue a piece of white paper on the back to show through the middle section. Write what you are thankful for in the turkey.

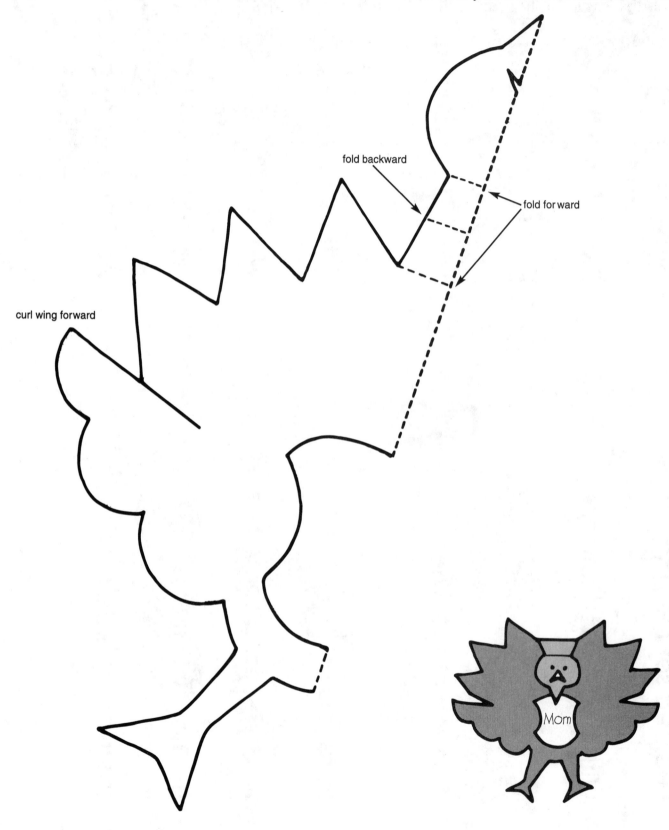

fold backward

fold for ward

curl wing forward

Mom

by Veronica Terrill

Name_____

Turkey Race

These turkeys are all running away from home until Thanksgiving is over. Which one do you think will win the race out of the barnyard? Why?

The turkeys have fun names. Can you guess which name belongs to each turkey?

_____ Speedy Joe   _____ Clumsy Clara   _____ Lazy Louis

_____ Pokey Pete   _____ Mixed-Up Milly

Name_____

Thanksgiving Dinner

There's lots to eat at Thanksgiving dinner. Look at the clues below to
figure out what's on the menu. Color the pictures.

_____

_____

_____

_____

_____

_____

_____

_____

_____

by Jean Powis

Cooking with Kids

Say hello to fall with super snacks and recipe projects your kids will love.

Grandparents are coming to brunch! Send invitations; then set a colorful table. Here is a recipe for pumpkin pancakes that will make enough to serve everyone.

Pancake Brunch

Ingredients

1 c. cooked pumpkin	4 c. pancake mix
2 eggs	1 tsp. cinnamon
3 c. milk	

Place pancake mix in a large bowl. Add eggs, milk, pumpkin, and cinnamon. Mix well with a wire whisk. Cook as you would regular pancakes, on a lightly greased griddle. Serve with maple syrup or honey.

October is Apple Month—the best time for cider.

Warm Fuzzy Punch

Ingredients

1 qt. apple cider	1 cinnamon stick
1 c. orange juice	1/2 tsp. ground cloves
1/2 c. lemon juice	honey (optional)
1/2 c. pineapple juice	

Combine all ingredients in a large crock pot or slow cooker. Heat through and simmer for 10 minutes before serving. Serve warm. Add honey to sweeten, if desired.

Let's celebrate Pizza Month with a delicious "anytime" snack.

Pizza Roll-Ups

Ingredients

pita bread	cheese slices
tomato or pizza sauce	

Slice each pita in half to make two "rounds." Spoon and spread warmed tomato or pizza sauce over the pita half. Tear a cheese slice into pieces and set into the sauce. Begin at one end of the pita pizza and roll it into a cylinder. These can be eaten as is or placed in a hot oven (or toaster oven) for a few minutes, just to warm through. Additional toppings may be added if you choose.

by Marie E. Cecchini

Holiday newsletter

As fall approaches and school bells ring, parents and children alike begin to think about learning again. However, the truth is that we learn something new every day, and every experience is a learning experience in some way. Formal learning experiences in school can be carried over to the home and reinforced in a more informal way. Have fun spending some "together time" with your child and see what you learn.

Simple Science

Popcorn is a favorite food of many children, but how many of them consider the fact that they are actually eating seeds? Examine some popcorn kernels with your child. Note how they look, feel, and smell. Talk about how it is indeed a seed which would grow if planted under proper conditions. Each seed contains moisture which becomes steam when the kernel is heated. The buildup of steam forces the kernels to explode into the kind of popcorn we can eat. Not every kernel pops in every batch of popcorn. Try an interesting experiment and practice estimating by counting out a small number of kernels to pop. Have your child estimate how many will burst. Pop the corn; then count and compare the results.

On the Move

Fall is football season. Set up a backyard practice area that can be used by an individual or a group. Suspend an old tire or a plastic hoop from a sturdy tree branch. Try to toss, "hike," and kick the ball through the hoop. In another area, mark off a space on the ground to form goalposts. Spray paint well. Try to kick the ball through these "goalposts." With a friend, practice passing the ball to one another, catching it on the run, and proceeding through the goalposts. If there are enough players, put up two sets of goalposts and play touch football.

Creative Kitchen

During Popcorn Month in October, invite your child to help you mix up a batch of nacho flavored popcorn.

What You Need:

1/4 c. margarine
1/2 tsp. cumin
1 tsp. paprika
10 c. popped corn
1/2 tsp. red pepper
1/2 c. Parmesan cheese

What You Do:
In a small saucepan, melt the margarine. Stir in the paprika, red pepper, and cumin. Remove from heat. Place the popped corn into a large bowl. Dribble the margarine mixture over the corn. Toss lightly to coat evenly. Sprinkle cheese over the popped corn and toss again. Serve when cool to the touch.

by Marie E. Cecchini

Communication Station

Help your child create a personal journal in which to write and draw about daily events, personal thoughts, opinions, and feelings. Purchase a standard black and white notebook and let your child design a cover with construction or wrapping paper, tape, and craft odds and ends. Glue a small wallet calendar inside the cover to help in dating each entry, and let your child pick out a very special pen or pencil to use only with the journal.

Poetry in Motion

Do you remember "Find a penny, pick it up, all day long you will have good luck" or "Mary Mack all dressed in black"? Share with your child some of the childhood rhymes and chants you remember. Discuss what they mean, and whether they are real or just for fun. Ask your child to share any chants, rhymes, or sayings the youngsters are repeating today. Create your own hand clapping rhythms to do with your child.

From the Art Cart

Invite your child to create an extra-special calendar to give as a gift for Grandparents' Day. Purchase a blank calendar from an office supply store, or photocopy a blank calendar of your own design. Help your child write in the month names and daily numbers on each page. Supply photographs, scissors, glue, and markers, and encourage your child to design a different picture page for each month. Photographs can be cut and glued to each page, and any special details can be added in marker.

Mathworks

This year as you check through the incoming Halloween treats, challenge your child to count and sort each variety. What is there more, less, or the same amount of? How many treats were received in all? Use your discretion and determine the amount that may be eaten in any one day. Use several paper lunch bags and have your child write a date on each, then count the number of treats to place in each bag.

The Reading Room

Share some fun and scary books this fall.

Alice and Greta: A Tale of Two Witches by Steven J. Simmons, Charlesbridge Publishing, 1997.

Bone Poems by Jeff Moss, Workman Publishing, 1997.

Boo! By Colin McNaughton, Harcourt Brace, 1996.

The Dark at the Top of the Stairs by Sam McBratney, Candlewick, 1998.

The Popcorn Book by Tomie de Paola, Holiday House, 1989.

Scary, Scary Halloween by Eve Bunting, Clarion, 1986.

Clip Art for Fall

Fall Is Fantastic

Here's What's
Happening . . .

Clip Art for Back-to-School

Welcome

My school bus is

Welcome Back

welcome!

I got the
point . . .

It's fun
to
READ!

From Your Teacher

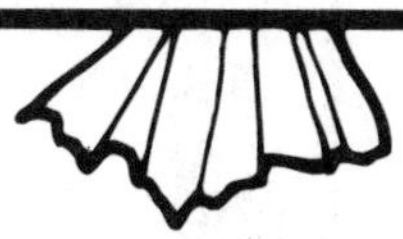

_____
name

was a "sharp" student today!

_____ _____
teacher   date

Cool School Facts

My school's name

My school's address and phone #

Remember . . .

Monday

Tuesday

Wednesday

Thursday

Friday

Weekend

My teacher's name

My room number

My principal's name

Important phone #

Lunch time is

Lunch prices

School's out at

Clip Art for Grandparents' Day

Admit 1 Grandparent

Admit 1 Grandparent

Clip Art for Columbus Day

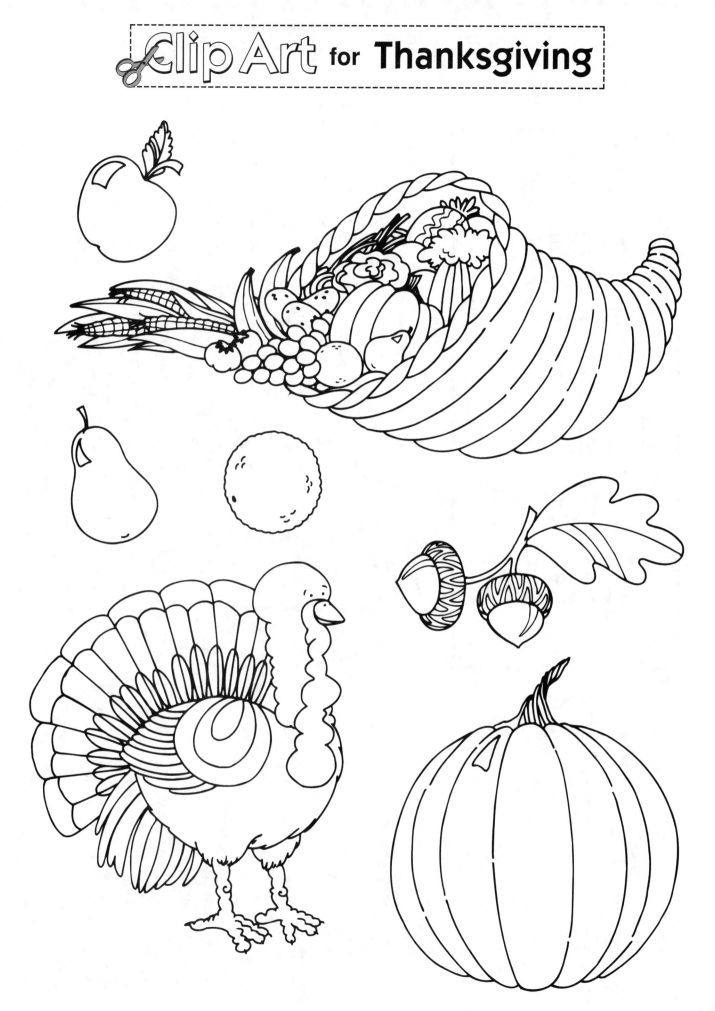

I'm Thankful for Books!

You Should Have Seen It

It snowed and it snowed
And covered the streets.
I climbed in my boots
To unfreeze my cold feet.

I made a snow castle
About fifty feet high
With moats, drawbridges,
And towers to the sky.

You should have seen it.
You were too late!
Last night it melted.
It just couldn't wait.

by Cari Meister

Kid Space
School Yard Learning Adventures
Winter

As autumn turns to winter, your outdoor kid space offers young learners a special place for observation, active learning discoveries, and seasonal outdoor fun.

End of Autumn Observations

Nature Trek
Take a walk into autumn to experience the season up close.
- What do children see, hear, smell, and feel?
- What signs indicate that fall is at its end?

Points to Ponder
Ask children the following questions:
- If you were a poet, what adjectives would you use to describe the scene you see?
- If you were a painter, what colors would you use to paint this landscape?
- If you were a pioneer, what tasks would you be doing now?
- If you lived in the city/country instead of where you are, how might the scenery be different?

Give Thanks at Thanksgiving
Take your group outside to think about Thanksgiving. Have each child choose something he or she is thankful for. The setting is to provide inspiration, but not to dictate what children choose. Encourage children to think about the Earth, nature, family, home, and beyond. In this outdoor setting, have each child think about what he or she is thankful for and report on it to the group.

98

by Robynne Eagan

> Bundle up and make the most of the exciting learning adventures that await your students, just beyond the doorstep.

Weatherproof for Winter

If you are going to make the most of the outdoors in winter, you have to be prepared for anything. No matter how much fun your activity might be, it just won't work if there are cold toes, fingers, ears, or noses.

What can you do to keep kids safe when temperatures dip and the winds pick up? Make your students weather-wise dressers! Talk about how much fun winter is when you dress properly.

- Send a letter informing parents that your group will be participating in outdoor activities. Request that children come to school with proper clothing. Offer to assist parents who are unable to provide warm clothing for their children. Most local charities are willing to help keep kids warm. Organize a clothing swap with another school outside your area—that way it won't be obvious that Johnny is wearing a snowsuit donated by David.
- Teach students to weatherproof themselves for fun and adventure in your Kid Space. Check clothing, boots, mittens, coat fastenings, and face coverings as children venture outside. Encourage children to check on one another and offer reminders if needed.
- Check the thermometer and windchill before venturing out. Plan the length of your outdoor play based on these factors.
- Observe and listen for signs of cold feet, fingers, cheeks, or bodies.
- Apply sunblock to faces on days when you will be outdoors for long periods of time.
- Have children wear lip balm to avoid dry, chapped, or cracked lips. Explain that licking chapped lips only makes the problem worse.
- Fill pockets with tissues and keep runny noses in check!
- Bring along a few pairs of extra mittens to replace the first few soggy pairs. Once many mittens have become wet, you have probably had a good play, and it's time to head inside!

by Robynne Eagan

Games

New Year's Dragon

This is an activity game to ring in the New Year. Don't let snowy weather deter you—this game is even more fun when played in the snow.

How to Play

1. Have players line up single file, holding onto the waist of the person in front so the line becomes a human chain resembling a long dragon.
2. The player at the front of the chain is the head of the dragon; the player at the end is the tail.
3. The object of the game is for the head to catch the tail. All players must stay connected and try to help the head.
4. When the head catches the tail, the head moves in behind the tail and a new "head" takes over.

Snow Maze Tag

Materials
fresh snowfall

Get Ready

1. Divide students into four groups. Select a leader for each group.
2. Have each group follow their leader to create well-stomped paths in the snow.
3. The paths should intersect at various points.

How to Play

1. Choose one child to be "it." This child waits on a marked spot on a path while other players take positions along the paths of the maze. All players must stay on the marked paths.
2. On the signal "go," the player who is "it" attempts to tag other players. Tagged players step outside the maze and observe the final chases of the game.
3. The last player remaining in the maze becomes "it" for the next round of the game.

Blanket of Snow

This game will keep kids warm and teach them about winter survival.

Materials
king-size white sheet
4 tall helpers

Get Ready

1. Have each tall assistant take a corner of the sheet and hold it high up in the air.
2. Have students crouch under the sheet.
3. Have the helpers slowly bring down the sheet until it is almost touching the children's heads. Bring the corners down if possible.
4. While under the sheet, talk about the little mice who survive the winter living under a blanket of snow. Talk about how mice survive in the winter. How important is this blanket of snow? It protects the mice from the cold and from enemies. Does it feel warm under the blanket? Have students step out from under the blanket. Do they notice a change in temperature?

How to Play

1. Tell children that they are now going to be tiny mice living through the winter.
2. Have children stand outside the sheet and hold on.
3. Call out months of the year, one at a time. If a child has a birthday in that month, the child will scurry like a mouse under the "blanket of snow" to the other side of the blanket. When a month is called, other players will raise the sheet and slowly bring it down to the ground. Any mice who are caught under the sheet before it reaches the ground are considered "caught by prey."
4. Players who are "caught" and those who are not join the players holding the sheet and continue to play as before.

Welcome, Winter!

Vasaloppet

Host your own Vasaloppet Festival in your Kid Space, a local park, or visit a cross-country ski trail for the day.

Vasaloppet is a Swedish cross-country skiing festival that is held in late winter in many places throughout Scandinavia and North America. It is held for fun and fitness as well as to commemorate an historical event. In 1521 King Gustav Vass skied a distance of 58 miles (92 km) to gather his people together to defend Sweden.

Vasaloppet events usually occur in January. Teams of skiers participate by traveling on trails covering distances ranging from 1 kilometer (.6 miles) to 160 km (100 miles). In Canada this event has become the most important cross-country ski event of the season.

Host Your Own

Host your own Vasaloppet event in your Kid Space, a local park, farm, or at a cross-country ski facility. If the event is to take place at a facility, you will need to arrange transportation, ski equipment, and fees.

How to Play

1. If you are hosting the event, send out a call for ski equipment, ski instructors, and other volunteers. Some recreation facilities will rent skis to be used off their premises. Parents and friends may be willing to share ski equipment. Your school budget may permit the purchase of a class set of ski equipment from new or used sources. You will need a range of boot sizes to accommodate all. Experienced cross-country skiers in your school or a local high school may be a good source of volunteers for this event. Invite parents and friends to take part or volunteer to assist.
2. Set up the cross-country training course using flags or pylons.
3. Arrange to have other outdoor fun events going on at the same time as the ski activity.
4. Have children proceed through the course, each starting at a different time than other skiers. Allow children to ski with a partner if they choose to do so.
5. Present those who complete the course with a badge of accomplishment.

Provide hot chocolate, warm cider, mint tea, or water to help keep little bodies warm and hydrated.

Snow Baseball

Object of the Game

Not a usual winter tradition—but one that's good for laughter, fun, and skill building.

January 31 is the birthday of Nolan Ryan, born in 1947. Have your students research and report on this baseball great. Ryan struck out more batters than anyone in the history of baseball. Can your students find out how many batters he struck out? Once students have all of the facts, they can take part in a game of baseball with a wintry twist!

Materials

large white rubber ball
baseball bat
base markers

Get Ready

Stamp a small baseball diamond on top of the snow. Include bases and base lines. Divide your group into two teams.

How to Play

Play ball! Play a regular game of baseball or T-ball. Keep the emphasis on fair play and cheers for all.

Frosty Facts

- Frostbite can appear at temperatures of -5° to -10°C and occurs most often at the beginning of winter when you aren't expecting it.

- Hypothermia can occur in above-freezing temperatures when an underdressed person stays in the cold too long.

Spring Detectives

Spring officially arrives on March 21—although you may have to look hard for signs of it at this time.

Turn your students into Spring Detectives for the day. Stay hot on the trail of signs of spring. Take a hike and record signs that indicate spring is on its way. Are there any signs to indicate that spring is not just around the corner? Record your findings back in the classroom.

Dear Parent/Guardian,

Winter is wonderful! Our class is planning to venture outside this term to take advantage of the learning opportunities outdoors in our Kid Space.

Please ensure that your child comes to school with appropriate clothing for cold and wet weather. Please label all items to prevent loss and confusion. An extra pair of socks and mittens can be sent along in a small labeled bag. I will store these in the classroom for the season and use as needed for your child.

Please contact me if you are in need of any outer wear. I can assist you in finding articles needed to keep your child warm this winter.

Thank you for your assistance.

_____

What's Going On?

We know what causes matter to change state—but what's really going on? As the temperature of liquid water cools, the forces between its particles grow stronger and stronger until the liquid becomes a solid—that is, it freezes.

When ice is heated, its particles vibrate (or move) faster and faster and almost overcome the forces that keep them connected. The solid becomes a liquid with loose bonds between its particles.

When water is heated to the boiling point, the particles vibrate so quickly that they break free of the forces that keep them together. The water boils, the liquid becomes a gas, and the particles are free of one another . . . for now.

Is Ice Heavier Than Water?

Experiment and find out. What could you do to investigate? Take a look at a freezing puddle or pond. Where does the ice form first? What does that tell you? Put some ice in a container of water. What happens?

You probably discovered that ice forms at the top of the puddle first and that ice floats in water . . . and you probably concluded that frozen water is lighter than liquid water. You're right!

Skate on Water

Did you know that you never really skate on ice? Your motion and the pressure of your weight on the skate blade cause the ice to melt and you really skate on a thin layer of water.

When can you walk on water? When it is ice!

A Dash of Salt

What happens when you sprinkle a little salt on your ice cube? Put one ice cube in a glass and another in a second glass. Place the glasses side by side in conditions that are exactly the same. Sprinkle a little salt on one ice cube. Observe both ice cubes and discuss your findings.

A Snowflake Is Formed

Water vapor can change directly from a vapor to a solid through the process called *sublimation*. When the temperature in the atmosphere is cold enough, water vapor will turn into ice crystals that often occur around a particle of dust. We call these six-sided (hexagonal) crystals snowflakes.

It is believed that no two snowflakes are the same. The colder and drier the air, the smaller the snowflakes will be. The warmer and more moist the air, the larger and more intricate the snowflakes will be.

Kid Space
School Yard Learning Adventures

Can Matter Change from One State to Another?

Let's Take a Look!

Put some snow or ice in a clear, sealed container and bring it indoors. What happens? The lid was sealed, so we know that snow didn't escape and water didn't break in! It may seem a bit of a mystery, but it's really just a change in the state of matter. When ice (a solid) turns to water (a liquid), it is called melting.

Most substances, including water, can exist in all three states. Early winter provides a wonderful opportunity to investigate this. Watch water change through the three states of matter. Heat ice and it will change from a solid to a liquid. Heat the liquid and it will become gaseous steam. Matter changes state when it melts, freezes, boils, evaporates, sublimates, or condenses.

Freezing: Take a look at a puddle on a cool afternoon. The water (liquid) may turn to ice (solid) by evening when the sun sets and the temperature drops to 32°F (0°C).

Melting: Take a look at a puddle on a cold morning. As the day warms up and the sun shines down, the ice (solid) turns to water (liquid). The melting point of water is the same as its freezing point, 32°F (0°C).

Evaporation: Look at a puddle on a warm morning. By the end of the day, the water (liquid) may vanish into thin air—that is, the heat causes it to evaporate and become a gas without reaching the boiling point.

Boiling: Water (liquid) also vanishes into thin air when heated to 212°F (100°C) at sea level. It boils and becomes a vapor (gas). You see this as steam.

Sublimation: Ice (solid) changes to a gas or from a gas to a solid.

Condensation: Water vapor (gas) turns to water (liquid) when cooled. Look for condensation on windows.

TLC10198 Copyright © Teaching & Learning Company, Carthage, IL 62321-0010

Winter Math Games

for Parties or Practice

What?

Five simple games that can help kids drill the more difficult addition and subtraction facts

Why?

Kids need lots of drill on the ABCs of math. Ideas like these can help avoid boredom.

Where?

Teach the games at school for kids to play at home or for an indoor recess. Some can be used for classroom activities or party games.

Note

For ease in explaining each game, one specific group of facts is used as an example. However, each game can be used for other sets of facts.

Icy Dice

For number pairs that equal 10.

Materials
- 10 regular dice
- 20 small, blank stickers

Two-player game or classroom activity/game

This is a great game to teach children during the winter when it might be too cold to go out for recess. The object of the game is for kids to recognize pairs of numbers that add up to 10. This skill helps make it easier to add long columns of numbers.

One- or two-player game—Use a study sheet listing the groups of numbers that equal 10: $9 + 1, 8 + 2, 7 + 3, 6 + 4, 5 + 5$

Students can make their own study sheets on index cards and decorate them with snowflake stickers or draw their own snowflakes. If you have the *Math Phonics™—Addition* book, use the Travel Folder for Number Pairs for 10 on page 75.

Use five pairs of dice. Cover two sides on each die with small blank stickers and write 7, 8, or 9 on the stickers. Be sure not to cover up the same number on all the dice. The first player rolls the 10 dice. He looks for pairs of dice that equal 10. Player gets 10 points for each pair of dice that equals 10. If all 10 dice can be used in groups to equal 10, player gets a bonus of 10 points and he can call out "ICY DICE."

If you want to have an ICY DICE tournament at an indoor recess or classroom party, use a score sheet with each student's name. Have students pair off and roll the dice five times each, keeping track of scores. If you only have 10 dice, students can take turns with the dice. Announce the winners and give them some kind of reward, like a coupon for a free ice cream cone.

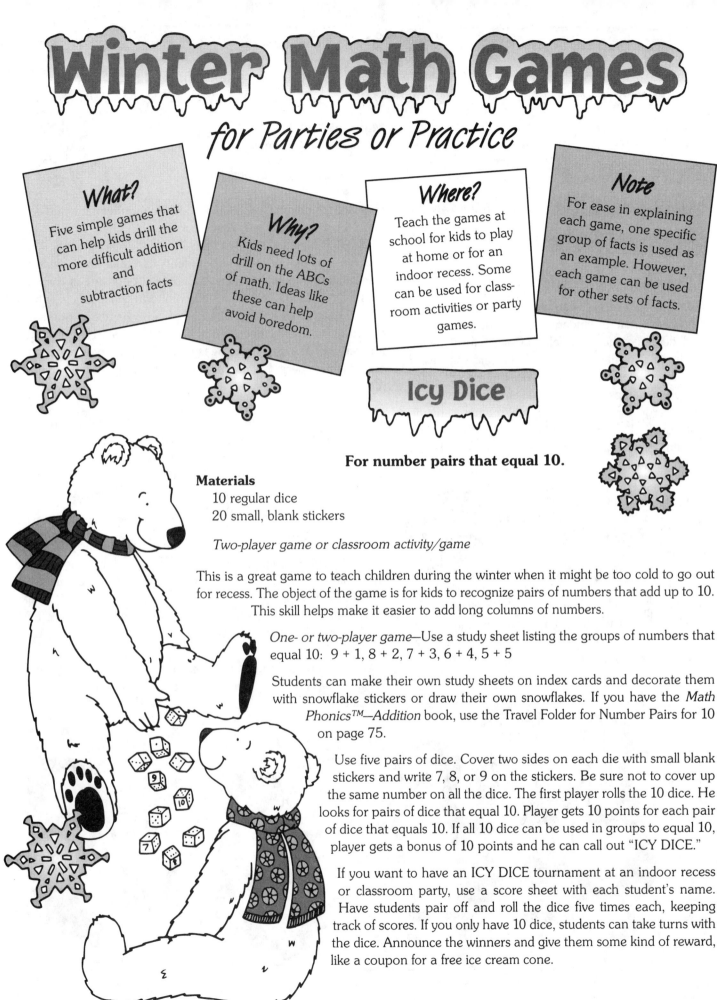

Materials

20 numbered cards or snowflake shapes, or decks of cards with face cards removed
(Ask parents to donate old decks of cards.)

Two-player game or classroom game/activity

Have each student make a study sheet of number pairs that equal 11:

$$10 + 1, 9 + 2, 8 + 3, 7 + 4, 6 + 5$$

Duplicate two sets of numbered snowflakes for each student or pair of students. Have students cut out and decorate the snowflakes. Players turn the 20 cards or snowflakes facedown. Players take turns turning over two cards at a time. If the cards equal 11, player keeps the two cards and turns over two more cards. Players continue until the two cards do not equal 11. Then the other player takes a turn. Continue until all cards have been paired. Player with the most cards wins.

This can also be used as a classroom game or activity. Give each student one numbered snowflake. Divide the class into two teams. One person on team A calls out the names of two students. The students call out their numbers. If the numbers equal 11, team A gets the two snowflake cards and gets to call again. team A continues as long as the two numbers equal 11; then team B takes over. Team with the most cards wins.

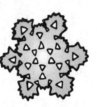

Materials

Poker chips or small party theme pictures

Classroom game or activity

Have each student make a study sheet for number pairs that equal 12: $10 + 2, 9 + 3, 8 + 4, 7 + 5, 6 + 6$

Teacher can be the leader or students can take turns being the leader. Leader points to a student and calls out one of the numbers from 2 to 10—let's say 9. Everyone in the class claps twice and slaps his or her legs. The person who has been pointed to must call out the number that added to 9 equals 12 (the correct answer would be 3) before the leg slap. This can be played at the end of a class period. Students start by standing up, then sit down if they miss.

You can use this as a party game and give prizes. Divide the class into teams. Give each person a poker chip or small snowflake card. Have two boxes at the front of the room. If a member of team A misses, that member must put his or her chip or snowflake in the box for team B. Play for five minutes and then count to see which team has the most snowflakes.

This can also be made into a game for a holiday party by giving each student a small picture to color to use in place of the snowflake. For a Halloween party, use small jack-o'-lanterns. For a Thanksgiving party, use turkeys. For a Hanukkah party, make copies of the star of David. For Christmas, use bells. For Kwanzaa, make copies of an ear of corn.

(If students are just beginning to learn math facts, you might want to have everyone clap four times and then slap their legs to give the student more time to think.)

Fourteens Freeze

Number pairs for 14.

Materials

Playing cards or index cards numbered 4-10

Classroom game or activity

Have students make study sheets for 14.

Tell students that for this activity, they are to move around the room quickly and quietly—without confusion. If there is an odd number of students, the teacher should play.

Give each person a numbered card with any number from 4 through 10. Be sure cards will pair up correctly to equal 14. You can use playing cards, numbered index cards, or the shapes mentioned in the Call the Partner game.

Review the pairs of numbers that equal 14. If necessary, give each student a study sheet for those pairs of numbers.

When the teacher says "go," students silently move around the room holding their numbered cards and look for someone else whose number can be added to theirs to equal 14.

When students find a pair, they immediately sit down in the nearest desk. The last pair to sit down is out of the game. Pick up the remaining cards and pass them out again, facedown. Repeat the process until only one pair of students is left. They get prizes—maybe a ruler with multiplication facts or pictures of Presidents or a free homework pass. (Free homework passes should be given out very rarely. Kids need to do their homework for the practice.)

Flying South for the Winter

Chase away the winter blues and turn your classroom into a tropical beach paradise with these ideas!

BRAIN (SNOW) STORM

Have your class brainstorm a list of words and phrases relating to winter and winter holidays. List the words on a large seasonal cut-out, such as a snowflake. Then have them brainstorm a list of words that suggest differences and opposites, and write these on a palm tree or other tropical cut-out. Divide a bulletin board in half with a strip of border that matches the edges of the board. Cover half of the bulletin board with blue paper and half with yellow. Put the winter cut-out on the blue side and the tropical cut-out on the yellow side. Display students' work from the following activity on the board.

WHAT IF . . . ?

Have students draw and color traditional winter holiday pictures reflecting their cultural heritage and family customs. Then ask them to imagine how the pictures would be different in another climate or locale. Have them draw pictures to illustrate their ideas. Use the resulting drawings as creative writing starters to be displayed on the bulletin board described on the left. Maybe you'll see Santa in a Hawaiian shirt in a sleigh pulled by flamingos!

BY AMY B. BARSANTI

SANDBLAST

Use plain or colored sand for these handy, sandy crafts. Glitter may also be added to the sand for an extra-special effect.

* Create miniature beach scenes in baby food jars using sand, shells, grass, and so on.

* Layer colored sand in baby food jars. Poke around the edges with a toothpick to create a jagged striped effect.

* Draw a picture. Trace the outline with white glue and apply sand, or draw the outline in black marker and fill in sections with glue and colored sand.

* Press sand into air-drying clay sculptures to create sand castles.

* Use a pencil eraser to randomly apply glue dots to snow scenes. Sprinkle sand on the glue and shake the excess onto newspaper to be reused.

SEA"SHORE"NAMENTS

When you have finished all the activities you have planned that require shells, use them to make festive decorations. Have students glue a loop of ribbon to a shell to form a hanger. Then have students paint the shell with white glue thinned slightly with water, and add glitter. Pin backs may be added instead of hangers to make decorative jewelry.

SHE SELLS SEASHELLS

Shells may be collected or purchased from craft supply stores or catalogs for this activity. Divide your class into pairs and provide each pair with an assortment of shells and small, removable, plain stickers. Have students label each shell with a sticker on which they have written a price. Then let them take turns being shell sellers and shell shoppers, using play money and calculators if desired.

SHELL ATTRIBUTES

Use the same shells you used in the activity described above for this sorting and classifying exercise. Divide the class into pairs or small groups. Have students sort the shells into piles according to any attribute they observe. Have students record their method and then try a different strategy. Allow time for each group to share their work with the class.

BEACH BLANKET BINGO

Duplicate the game card on the next page. Have each student color the pictures at the bottom of the page, choose one to glue in each square, then laminate the gameboards for durability if desired. Place a complete set of the pictures in a paper bag for the caller. Play the game like regular bingo, with children taking turns being the caller.

A LIFESAVER!

Inflate several plastic swimming rings. Choose a large indoor or outdoor space to play this game of fun and skill. Have several students stand randomly spaced around the playing area. Assign a point value to each child, with the closest having fewer points. Then have the remaining students take turns trying to toss the rings over the heads of those standing, and have them record their scores. Allow children to switch places until everyone has had a chance to play both lifesaver and victim. Then try having the victims thrash around while the lifeguards are throwing the rings. Your class will have new appreciation for the difficulty of saving a drowning person, and it may help them if they are ever in a similar situation. Provide LifeSavers™ candy for all participants when the game is finished.

POSTCARDS

Divide the class into small groups. Use a large piece of corrugated cardboard, such as a panel from a refrigerator box or similar carton, for each small group. Cut one or two paper-plate sized circles in each piece of cardboard. Have each group design a tropical postcard, drawing the bodies of people under the circles in the cardboard. Encourage students to add details, and to draw their designs in pencil before finalizing them with paints and brushes. When the paint is dry, prop the panels up on chairs and let students take turns standing behind them so only their faces show. Photograph the results and let your class use the photos to write postcard messages and addresses on the back.

FLYING SOUTH

Discuss migration with your class. Ask them to think about what kinds of adventures might occur if children migrated for the winter. Brainstorm pros and cons and record responses on an experience chart. Have children write and illustrate their own migration stories. Compile the stories into a class book.

110

BEACH BLANKET BINGO

		Free		

Extravaganza

Grab your mittens and warm coats—wintertime is here! Get ready for Jack Frost's visit with this array of "ice"citing activities!

Read All About It!

Celebrate the winter season with your class by sharing *Dear Rebecca, Winter Is Here* by Jean Craighead George (HarperCollins Publishers, 1993). It's the shortest day of the year—a perfect time for Grandmother to write to her granddaughter, Rebecca, about the snowy winter season. The loving grandmother talks about the many changes in nature that will occur, as well as the joy of the season. After reading this book to your class, ask children to draw pictures showing outdoor activities that Rebecca might enjoy doing on a snowy day.

Spark up your math lessons by using *The Fattest, Tallest, Biggest Snowman Ever* by Bettina Ling (Hello Math Reader, Grades 1 & 2), Scholastic, 1997. This unique series combines interesting stories with important math concepts. In this winter story, two children try to decide who built the biggest snowman by using a string, paper clip chain, and a stick. Also included in the book are measurement activities.

by Mary Ellen Switzer

Winter Writing Corner

Calling all authors! Write up a winter "storm" with these great creative writing ideas to get you started.

- Snowflake Chit Chat! Write an imaginary conversation between two snowflakes.

- Is it a dream? You look out your window one snowy day and see a penguin in your yard. Tell what happens next.

- Congratulations! You have just survived the worst blizzard in history. Write a "Dear Diary" entry about your unforgettable winter adventure.

- Extra! Extra! Read all about it! You have just won a trophy for "The World's Tallest Snowman." Write a news story telling about your prize creation. Don't forget to include the five Ws: Who? What? Where? When? and Why? Include a news picture with your story.

- Uh oh! Your homework papers got blown away yesterday in a snowstorm, and you ran into a snow monster when you tried to rescue them. You can do better than that! Write a letter telling your teacher what happened to your papers.

- And they lived happily ever after! Write a fairy tale about a prince who rescues a princess from the evil Icicle Palace.

Snowflake Surprises

Here are some surprises that are sure to brighten the winter season!

Hooray for winter! Create a picture of a billboard sign to welcome the arrival of winter to your community.

Write a list of all the words that you can, using the letters in wintertime.

Let it snow! Make a list of some indoor activities that you can enjoy on winter days when the weather is stormy outdoors.

Are you tired of the same old snowmen? Try creating a snow pet instead! Draw a picture of a dog or cat "snow pet," and write directions for building it.

Brr . . . Winter Fun Zone! Meet Sarah and Sammy Snowflake. They will take you on a magical journey thorough our Winter Fun Zone. Our first stop is . . .

Brr! Write a riddle about something cold. Write three clues in complete sentences.

Create a word search or game about your favorite winter sport. Think of a catchy name for your game. Test it on a friend or relative.

Snowflake Amazing Maze

Help the girl find her missing sled in the maze below.

S IS FOR SNOWFLAKE

Color all the items in the picture that begin with the letter S.
Can you find Sarah and Sammy Snowflake hidden in the picture? Color them.

THE ICE IS
SAFE

Bonus: Make a list of all the items you found in the picture.
Now write the words in alphabetical order.

Skills: Beginning and ending sounds

Winter Sounds

There are many wintery words that contain the *S* sound. In *snow*, you hear the *S* at the beginning of the word. In *boots*, you hear it at the end. In *shoes*, you hear it both at the beginning and the end.

Call out the words. Instruct students to take a hop if they hear an *S* sound at the beginning of the word. If they hear it at the end, have them clap their hands. If they hear it both at the beginning and at the end, they should hop and clap at the same time.

1. sleigh
2. holidays
3. sleds
4. singing
5. snowballs
6. storm
7. glass
8. slippery
9. slides
10. dress
11. mittens
12. slacks
13. stove
14. syrup
15. snowflake

Skills: Rhyming words

Have children listen carefully to the word *snow*. Do they hear the *O* sound at the end? Other words that end in the same *O* sound rhyme with the word *snow*. For example, the word *go* rhymes with *snow*. The word *glee* does not, because it ends with an *E* sound instead of the *O* sound. Can the students hear the difference? Call out several words. If the word rhymes with *snow*, have children stand up. If the word does not rhyme with *snow*, children should sit down.

1. blow
2. free
3. no
4. my
5. foe
6. slow
7. toe
8. show
9. pie
10. low
11. play
12. sly
13. crow
14. day
15. glow

"Snow"

by Ann Richmond Fisher

A Watercolor Study of Winter Whites

Let winter wonders inspire your students!

Materials

watercolor paper or heavy white bond paper
variety of good paintbrushes
watercolor paints (blue, gray and white) tube or
    block type

winter scene photographs and pictures for refer-
    ence
cups or paint pots full of water
scrap paper for testing and mixing palettes

Setup

Experiment with the paper you have chosen. How much water works best on this surface? Explain to students that watercolor painting is a very special art that combines the white of the paper, the paint pigments, and water to create subtle effects.

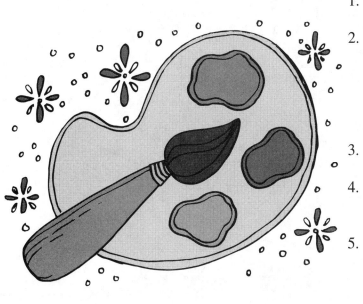

Let's Make It

1. Ask students to observe the snow scene pictures and photographs and to look outside at a real snow scene.

2. Ask students *What color is snow? Does it always look that color? Do you see any other shades? What color is the snow when there is a shadow on it? How could you create those colors using paints?* Children may come to see that "white" snow actually consists of many subtle hues of color.

3. Allow students to explore the colors of snow using whites, blues, gray, or black, and yellows.

4. Have each child fold an 8.5" x 11" (22 x 28 cm) sheet of paper into quarters. Place a splash of water on each block, and then add a tiny drop of the various colors.

5. Have students tilt their papers or use a dry brush to move colors around the water to obtain various effects.

Name _____

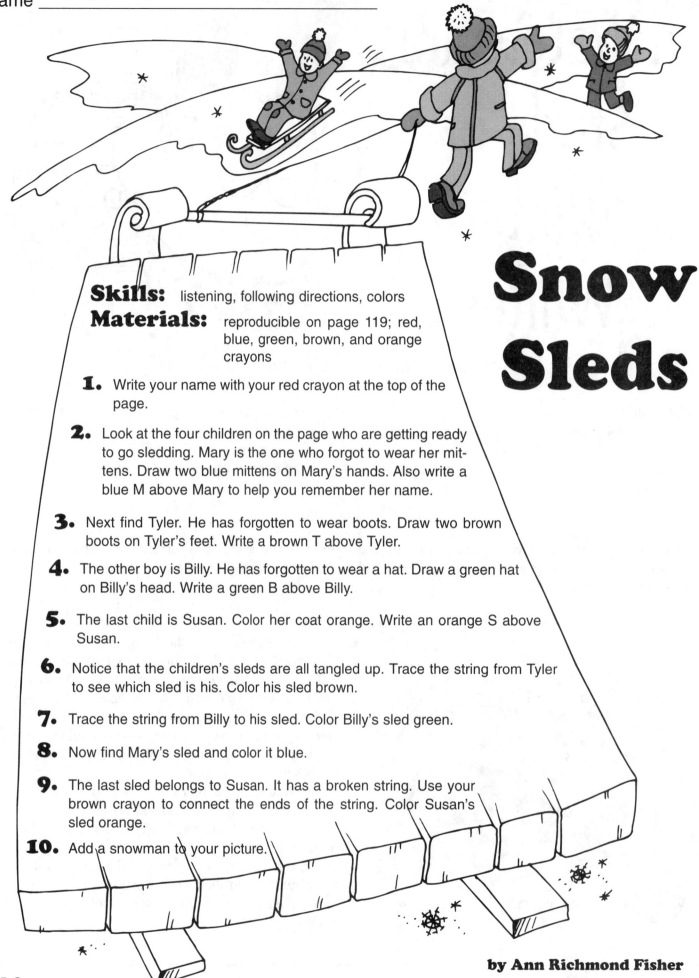

Snow Sleds

Skills: listening, following directions, colors
Materials: reproducible on page 119; red, blue, green, brown, and orange crayons

1. Write your name with your red crayon at the top of the page.

2. Look at the four children on the page who are getting ready to go sledding. Mary is the one who forgot to wear her mittens. Draw two blue mittens on Mary's hands. Also write a blue M above Mary to help you remember her name.

3. Next find Tyler. He has forgotten to wear boots. Draw two brown boots on Tyler's feet. Write a brown T above Tyler.

4. The other boy is Billy. He has forgotten to wear a hat. Draw a green hat on Billy's head. Write a green B above Billy.

5. The last child is Susan. Color her coat orange. Write an orange S above Susan.

6. Notice that the children's sleds are all tangled up. Trace the string from Tyler to see which sled is his. Color his sled brown.

7. Trace the string from Billy to his sled. Color Billy's sled green.

8. Now find Mary's sled and color it blue.

9. The last sled belongs to Susan. It has a broken string. Use your brown crayon to connect the ends of the string. Color Susan's sled orange.

10. Add a snowman to your picture.

by Ann Richmond Fisher

Name _____

Snow Sleds

MEXICAN POSADAS
December 16-24

Everyone can contribute something to this tiny village.

SETUP

1. Discuss the Mexican Posadas celebration with your group. From December 16-24 the traditional Mexican preparation for Christmas includes processions called *Posadas*. These processions represent a pilgrimage leading up to Jesus' birth. "Mary" and "Joseph" go from home to home in search of shelter. These processions eventually come to a pre-arranged home where a celebration takes place.

2. Work together in planning details of your village. How big will it be? What will the platform be made of? Who will work on the platform? The people? The animals? Joseph and Mary? Have children record the details for future reference.

3. Provide reference materials so children can make their Posadas village look like a real Mexican village.

LET'S MAKE IT

Provide the materials listed for children to access as they create the village as planned.

TRY THIS

Children are sure to come up with great ideas of their own, but you could provide samples, or just the supplies, for the following:

- Buildings can be covered with glue and canvas cloth for a stucco look.
- Fine-grained sand can be sprinkled on a glue-covered "road."
- Animal and human figures can be drawn (or cut from magazines),
  pasted to sturdy backings, and propped in pieces of modeling clay.
- The effect of lights, lanterns, and pinatas can be obtained by using crumpled tissue paper.

MATERIALS

small boxes
pieces of cardboard or tagboard
construction paper
masking tape
scissors
craft glue
wooden craft sticks or small twigs
canvas cloth
discarded magazines
    (Christmas theme is best)

BY ROBYNNE EAGAN

Celebrate HANUKKAH!

Cheese Latkes

3 eggs   1/4 cup milk
1 cup cottage cheese   1/4 teaspoon salt
1 cup flour

Use a blender to combine eggs, milk, cottage cheese and salt. Add flour and blend some more. Prepare frying pan with hot grease. Spoon the latkes mixture into the hot grease. Fry on both sides until golden brown in color. Place on paper towels to drain. Makes about 18 3" latkes. Serve warm with applesauce, yogurt or sour cream.

by Ann Curtis

Pretzel Cheese Menorah

Cut celery stalks into long lengths. Spread peanut butter into the celery. Lay this on a plate. Cut small cheese cubes. Provide small pretzel sticks. Children spear a pretzel stick into a cheese cube. Children insert the pretzel stick with the "flame" into the peanut butter/celery holder (menorah). The center candle (shammash) should be placed in first with four more added to each side of the shammash.

by Ann Curtis

- Have a Hanukkah celebration in your classroom using these easy ideas that will spark excitement in all of your students.
- Let students make blue and white paper chains and then go wild decorating the classroom.
- Make Stars of David with craft sticks, glue, blue paint and white sparkling glitter.
- Purchase Hanukkah cookie cutters (menorah, dreidel, and a Star of David) and bake cookies that the students can decorate and enjoy.
- Play spin the dreidel.
- Bring in a menorah and talk about its meaning. Encourage children that have their own menorah to bring them in.

by Marianne Cerra

Hanukkah Books for Kids

Backman, Aidel. *One Night, One Hanukkah Night*, Jewish Publication Society, 1990.
Kimmel, Eric A. *The Chanukkah Guest*, Holiday House, 1992.
Kimmelman, Leslie. *Hanukkah Lights, Hanukkah Nights*, HarperTrophy, 1994.
Nerlove, Miriam. *Hanukkah*, Albert, Whitman & Co., 1992.
Rosenberg, Amye. *Melly's Menorah*. Little Simon, 1991.
Rothernberg, Joan. *Inside Out Grandma, A Hanukkah Story*, Hyperion Press, 1995.
Rouss, Sylvia A. *Sammy Spider's First Hanukkah*, Kar-Ben Copies, 1993.
Topek, Susan Remick. *A Turn for Noah, A Hanukkah Story*, Kar-Ben Copies, 1992.
Zalben, Jane Breskin. *Beni's First Chanukah*, Henry Holt & Company, 1994.
Ziefert, Harriet. *What Is Hanukkah?* Harper Festival, 1994.

by Adrienne Cohen

Playdough Menorah

Provide children with playdough and purchased birthday candles. They can make a base with the playdough rolled into a long menorah. Children place a larger candle in the center for a shammash and then four small candles on each side to complete the menorah. Make sure that there is no way the children can light the candles.

by Ann Curtis

STAR OF DAVID

Place a sheet of waxed paper over the top of the pattern. Fill the outlined area with white glue and sprinkle with glitter as illustrated. Let dry completely (about 5-7 days) and carefully peel from waxed paper. Attach string to hang.

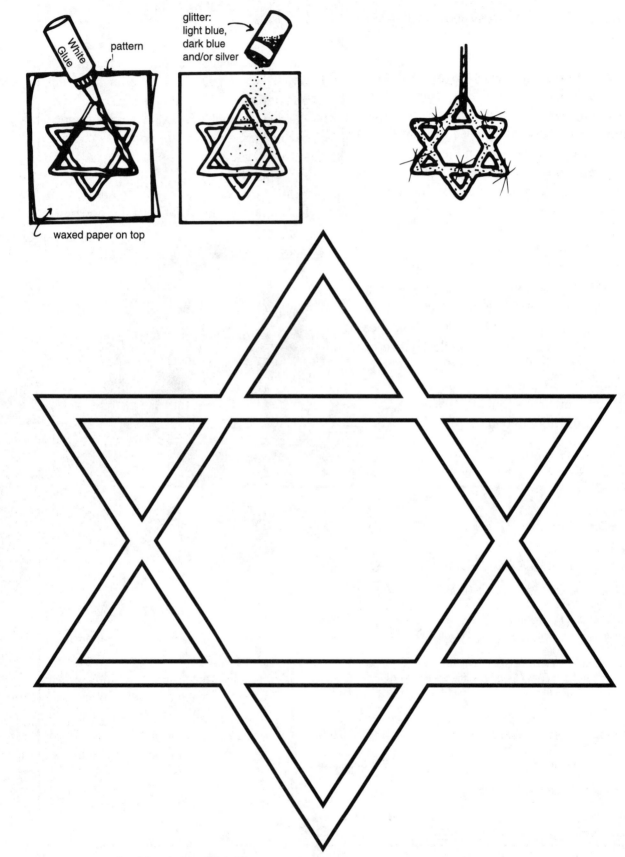

    by Veronica Terrill

Durwood Dragon
Makes a Christmas Friend

Christmas Eve! And Durwood Dragon's
Friends were all away,
Visiting their relatives
Till after Christmas Day.

Flakes of snow were softly falling;
All the world was white.
And Durwood walked, a wee bit sadly,
Out into the night.

The moon came out. He made a snowball,
Rolled it right along,
And underneath the purple sky,
He hummed a Christmas song.

Suddenly a bright idea!
"I know what to do.
I'll make myself a Christmas snowman!
Then I won't be blue!"

At last it stood, all white and silent.
Durwood frowned and said,
"He must be cold. I think I'll get him
Something for his head!"

At home, he found a hat and scarf
Of green and brightest red.
A perfect fit! "I think I'll call you
Happy Jack!" he said.

All at once, the snowman spoke
And then began to stir.
"I'm very glad to get to know you.
Merry Christmas, Dur!"

Who'd have guessed, on Christmas Eve,
That such a friend he'd find?
It's true, the coolest things can happen
When your heart is kind!

by Irene Livingston

The ABCs of Giving

The Alphabets were sitting in their classroom, anticipating the Professor's arrival. They were very excited. Except for Christmas itself, this was their favorite day of the year. This was the day they would take a trip to the mall.

The Professor walked in holding a huge candle shaped like a Christmas tree. "This is the Christmas candle," he said, heading for Cs desk. "Since both *Christmas* and *candle* start with the letter C, I will put it on C's desk."

"'Let's light it," said C impatiently.

"No," said the Professor, "we cannot."

"Why not?" asked G.

"This is a magic candle," explained Professor Thesaurus. "It will light up only when the spirit of Christmas is realized."

The Professor demonstrated by lighting a match and trying to light the candle with it. It did not light. Then T tried to light it, but could not.

"It really is a magic candle," said T.

"Well," said the Professor, "it's time to go on our shopping trip for Christmas."

Each of the Alphabets had picked another Alphabet for their Kris Kringle so that each had to buy only one present.

The Alphabets eagerly jumped on the alphabet bus which was decorated for the Christmas season. There was silver and gold sprayed all around the edges of the bus which gave it a festive, glittery look. There were jingle bells hanging from the ceiling. As the bus rolled along, the bells jingled, which kept the cheerful Christmas mood in full swing.

The Alphabets loved Christmas so much. On their way to the mall, they talked about why Christmas was so special.

"I love the snow," said S, looking out the window.

"I love the presents," said P.

"I love the wonderful food," said F, licking his lips.

"I love everything about Christmas," said E, "especially the excitement."

"I love the story about Jesus and the Wise Men," said J.

"I hope Rudolph and the other reindeer can get to everyone's house before sunup," said D.

"Of course he can," said P. "He always does."

"Suppose the elves don't get all the toys finished on time?" asked T. "Then what?"

"The toys are always ready on time," said B. "The elves have been working a whole year."

"Do you suppose Santa and Mrs. Claus will remember everybody?" asked C. "I do hope the sleigh is big enough to hold all those toys."

"I'm sorry for Santa Claus," said S. "He works so hard. He must be very cold, very tired, and very hungry when he gets back to the North Pole."

124

by Constance LaCapra

"Don't worry," said H. "As soon as Santa Claus gets home, Mrs. Claus feeds him some good hot soup and sets up his bed in front of the fire. Then he can sleep and rest for two days if he wants to."

The bus finally arrived at the Christmas store. The Alphabets filed out and lined up behind the Professor. It was one o'clock. The Professor told the Alphabets to shop for three hours and to meet back at the same spot at four o'clock.

The Alphabets entered the store and were struck by the beauty of it. There were huge chandeliers hanging from the ceiling, all decorated with big red bows. Christmas trees were all around, each a different color. There were red, gold, silver, green, and even pink and blue trees. The largest tree stood in the middle of the store and had all the colors of the rainbow on it. A beautiful angel swirled on top, its wings and hair gleaming and shimmering in the lights.

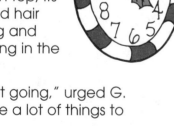

"Let's get going," urged G. "We have a lot of things to get."

The Alphabets scattered to do their shopping. K bought L leggings because L's legs were so long and she liked to keep them covered. F bought E earmuffs because he always complained about his cold ears. J chose a large pad and some pencils for W because W was always writing. C bought a new book for B because he knew how much B liked to read. U bought Q earrings because she loved jewelry so much. D bought a ski sweater for I.

The Alphabets were having such a good time shopping they almost forgot it was getting close to four o'clock.
The Professor and some of the Alphabets were assembled at the designated spot. As they waited, they noticed another group of youngsters accompanied by an elderly woman. All of the children were shabbily dressed. They had no packages in their hands.

Professor Thesaurus approached the woman. "Excuse me," he asked, "do these children all belong to you?"

"Good heavens, no," answered the woman. "These children are orphans. We had no money to buy presents, but we thought we might enjoy looking at all the pretty things in the store."

Some of the Alphabets heard what the woman said. They started to whisper among themselves. Then they called the Professor and whispered something in his ear. A big smile brightened the Professor's face. He called the woman and her orphans over and said, "My Alphabets would like to give your children their gifts for Christmas."

The woman and the children were astounded. They could not believe their good fortune. As the children clutched their new presents in their arms and thanked the Alphabets, the woman said to the Professor, "You have shown these children the true meaning of Christmas. This has been a wonderful day for us."

The Alphabets and the orphan children hugged each other and wished each other a Merry Christmas. Then the Alphabets got on the bus. The Professor was beaming. "I'm so very, very proud of you," he told his Alphabets. "You have learned what many people do not know. The spirit of Christmas is giving. You have all shown that spirit today."

The Alphabets were jubilant as they rode home. They felt so good. They sang Christmas carols all the way home.

When the bus pulled up to the school, the Alphabets were surprised to see the school completely lit up.

"I must have left the lights on," said the Professor. "But how can that be? I remember turning them off."

He took out his keys and unlocked the door. The alphabets followed closely behind him. There, on C's desk, was the Christmas candle, glowing so brightly that it lit up the whole school. It was truly a magic candle!

"This," said the Professor, "proves that we really and truly realize the true spirit of Christmas.

Santa's

Santa's book bag is overflowing with lots of seasonal favorites just for you!

Ho! Ho! Ho! Tickle everyone's funny bone this winter with *Jingle Jokes, Christmas Riddles of Deck the Ha Ha Halls* by Katy Hall and Lisa Eisenberg, illustrated by Stephen Carpenter (HarperFestival, 1997). Lift the flaps and find out *What subject do elves like best in school? Why does Santa Claus plant a garden?* and *Why did Jack Frost call the doctor?*

For more fun with riddles, don't miss *I Spy Christmas, A Book of Picture Riddles,* photographs by Walter Wick, riddles by Jean Marzollo (Scholastic, Inc., 1992). Challenge your students to find the hidden objects in the beautifully photographed holiday pictures. Young readers of this book are also encouraged to write their own rhyming riddles to accompany any of the pictures.

Enjoy a cornucopia of stories and poems in *The Family Read-Aloud Christmas Treasury,* selected by Alice Low, illustrated by Marc Brown (Little, Brown and Company, 1989). Some of the seasonal selections include *The Elves and the Shoemaker, Uncle Wiggily's Christmas, The Christmas Whale,* and *Emmett Otter's Jug-Band Christmas.*

Take your class on a magical trip around the world to learn all about Christmas festivities and customs in other countries. *Merry Christmas, Children at Christmastime Around the World* by Robina Beckles Willson, illustrated by Satomi Ichikawa (Philomel Books, 1983) will give everyone a first-hand look at Christmas celebrations in countries such as France, Italy, Germany, Mexico, India, Japan, and Australia. Craft ideas and holiday recipes are also included. Create your own Mexican piñata, or design a Swedish straw star decoration. Treat your class to a Norwegian holiday treat called gingerbread house cookies, or letter cakes called letter-blankets from the Netherlands. Merry Munching!

Elf Help

http.//www.falala.com
by Margie Palatini
illustrated by Mike Reed
Hyperion Books for Children, 1997

When Alfred E. Elf types up Santa's gift list on the computer, he causes the wildest mix-up in history! Will a little boy in Alaska like his brand-new surfboard? Or will a girl in sunny California enjoy a pair of winter skis? How about the ranch girl in Arizona with her new ice skates? Luckily for our poor computer whiz, Alfred, the surprised children seem to adore their mismatched holiday gifts!

• Draw a picture of the best gift you ever received. Tell why you liked this special present.

• Invent a new toy that children everywhere will rave about. What would you name your new toy? Write a few sentences to describe the toy.

• Design a billboard sign to advertise your new toy.

by Mary Ellen Switzer

Book Nook

Albert's Christmas

by Leslie Tryon
Atheneum Books for Young Readers
1997

Shh, it's a secret! Santa is planning a Christmas Eve "pit stop" in Pleasant Valley and a duck named Albert, along with his friends, will be his official crew. Will Albert and his animal team be able to keep Santa running on time for his busy schedule?

• Write an interview with Albert the duck. How did he help Santa during the pit stop? What friends helped him?

• Design a thank-you card for Santa to send Albert, thanking him for his help on Christmas Eve.

• Be an author! Write a story about the Christmas Eve that you helped Santa.

Emily and the Snowflake

by Jan Wahl
illustrated by Carolyn Ewing
Troll, 1995

Join Emily as she and her family prepare for the Christmas holiday. After much waiting, Emily manages to finally catch the first snowflake of the season. On Christmas morning, the delighted girl gets another special "Snowflake"—a new puppy!

• Give Emily three tips on how to take good care of her new puppy.

• Design a new doghouse for Emily's new puppy.

• What a dream! Emily had a dream about meeting a snowman named Mr. Woggle. Draw a picture of her snowman friend.

Nate the Great and the Crunchy Christmas

by Marjorie Weinman Sharmat & Craig Sharmat
illustrated by Marc Simont
Delacorte Press, 1996

Our favorite detective—Nate the Great—is back just in time to solve a perplexing holiday whodunit. Seems that Annie's dog, Fang, is unhappy because his annual Christmas card and treat are missing. Will our dedicated detective be able to follow the trail in such a heavy snowstorm? We'll never tell!

• Design a detective's badge for Nate the Great.

• Write a "help wanted" advertisement for a new detective. Be sure to include the qualifications needed for the job.

• Be an author! Write your own mystery story called "The Case of the Missing Holiday Cookies."

The Legend of the Poinsettia

Retold and illustrated by
Tomie dePaola
G.P. Putnam's Sons, 1994

Tomie dePaola re-creates the timeless Mexican legend of how the lovely poinsettia came to be. When Lucinda can't finish weaving a blanket for the village nativity scene, she brings a simple gift of tall green weeds instead. Her humble gift is suddenly transformed into beautiful red Christmas "stars." These lovely red flowers, now known as poinsettias, appear every Christmas as a holiday symbol.

- Find Mexico on a map or globe. Pretend you are taking a trip to Mexico. What places would you like to visit there?

- Make a list of all the words you can think of using the letters in *poinsettia*.

There's Music in the Air!

Sing a merry song or two this holiday season with the help of these marvelous songbooks. Lyrics and musical arrangements are included in these beautifully illustrated books.

The Raffi Christmas Treasury by Raffi. Crown Publishers, Inc., 1988.

Joy to the World! Carols selected by Maureen Forrester. Dutton Children's Books, 1993.

Hark! A Christmas Sampler by Jane Yolen and Tomie dePaola. G.P. Putnam's Sons, 1991.

Tomie dePaola's Book of Christmas Carols by Tomie dePaola. G.P. Putnam's Sons, 1987.

Computer Corner

Software

All aboard for a magical trip to the North Pole in this interactive CD-ROM version of *The Polar Express* by Chris Van Allsburg. In this classic holiday tale, a boy takes an unforgettable train ride to the North Pole to visit Santa Claus. When Santa offers the boy a holiday gift, he chooses a silver bell from the reindeer harness—a gift he will cherish forever.

CD-ROM, Houghton Mifflin, 120 Beacon Street, Somerville, MA 02143.

Add sparkle to the season by creating your own personalized holiday cards, invitations, and stationery—thanks to Broderbund's *ClickArt Celebrations & Holidays*. There are over 40 holidays and events featured in this clip art software program such as Christmas, Chanukah, Kwanzaa, and New Year's Day.

CD-ROM, Broderbund, P.O. Box 6125, Novato, CA 94948.

128   **by Mary Ellen Switzer**

TLC10198 Copyright © Teaching & Learning Company, Carthage, IL 62321-0010

Hi, Gramps!

The Gift of Time

Christmas bells toll throughout the land;
It's time to lend a helping hand.
Giving a smile and a warm hello;
Watching a tree all aglow.

Visit an old person all alone;
Bring him some cookies, contact by phone.
There is more to Christmas than toys and gifts;
Go out and give someone's spirit a lift.

The greatest gift is your precious time;
The best part is it doesn't cost a dime.
Share a special moment, show someone you care;
Love and friendship—what a pair!

by Carlene Americk

Paper Christmas Trees

Fast, easy and fun!

Materials

various shades of green construction
   paper
brightly colored tissue paper
craft glue and glue sticks or brushes
red, white, or blue construction paper

Setup

Provide a sample to illustrate the craft—no
instructions will be needed.

Let's Make It

1. Children will choose a colored background, other than green, for their project.

2. Children will tear off pieces of green construction paper and paste them in the
   shape of a Christmas tree to their chosen
   background.

3. Tissue paper will be crumpled into tiny
   balls to resemble Christmas lights.

4. The tiny tissue lights will be carefully
   pasted to the torn paper tree.

by Robynne Eagan

Gingerbread Bar Graph

Instructional Goal

To illustrate the concept of measuring statistics using a bar graph.

Materials Needed

gingerbread cookies*   crayons
reproducible cookie pattern   scissors
tape

*Plain sugar cookies made from a gingerbread cut-out can be substituted for gingerbread.

Directions

1. Hand out a gingerbread pattern to each student. (See page 195.)

2. Instruct students to color their "cookies" and cut them out, writing their names on the back.

3. Pass out a real cookie to each student, but tell them NOT to eat the cookies until they receive further instructions.

4. After all students have received their cookies, ask them to take ONE bite, and one bite only, from the cookie!

5. Instruct students to put their cookies down.

6. How many chose to eat an arm first? How many chose to eat a leg? How many chose to eat the head?

7. Have students use their scissors to cut their paper cookies to match their real cookies. (Cut off head, right leg, left leg, and so on.)

8. Ask each student to come to the board individually. Have students use masking tape to "stack" their paper cookies in one of five columns: head, right arm, leg arm, right leg, left leg.

Questions

What does this graph tell us?
Which body part was chosen the most?
The least?
Why are pictures a good way to explain "how many"?

If you want to go further . . .

Reorganize the cookies in each column by boy and girl to create a stacked bar graph.

Sweet Themes

Holiday Ornament

Here is a holiday ornament project that comes out looking wonderful, no matter what the age of the child!

Materials

white, red, or green round ornament balls
1/2" wide satin ribbon, cut in 8" strips
glue
flat-bottomed ice cream cones
colored baking sprinkles

Directions

Glue each end of the ribbon to the inside of the ice cream cone so it forms a loop that can be hung on a branch of a Christmas tree. Place the loop about two inches from the edge of the cone.

Have each child dip the tip of the ornament into glue, then dip it in colored sprinkles, just to cover the top. Then have children glue the ornament on top of the ice cream cone, making sure the ribbon is outside of the cone.

To personalize the ornament, write the child's name on the cone. If the surface is too bumpy, write under the sprinkled part of the ornament using a permanent marker.

These ornaments fit perfectly into a square tissue box. Cut off the top of the box and place the ornament inside. Cover the top with a piece of construction paper or aluminum foil. Then have students paint the entire box with either red or green poster paint. They can dab Christmas-shaped sponges over it in a contrasting color.

by Angela Marie Calabrese

Nutcracker Suite Ballet

To use "sweets" as your Christmas theme, introduce your students to Tchaikovsky's *Nutcracker Suite*. It is a delightful and fun way to acquaint them with a traditional ballet. Rent a condensed version to avoid boredom and disinterest. Try to see a live performance at a local theater. Discuss which performance was more enjoyable to your students. Why?

Then, while they are doing seatwork, play the tape to familiarize them with the music. Discuss the "Land of Sweets" segment, where desserts from different lands dance in various ways. Let them write about their favorite ones and explain why they like them.

132

Candy Cottages

Materials

- small milk carton
- various candy (M&Ms®, gumdrops, licorice, Skittles®)
- Styrofoam™ or cardboard tray
- 1 can vanilla frosting
- 1 box graham crackers
- masking tape
- plastic knife

Directions

To culminate this Christmas theme, make a candy cottage. Use a school-sized milk carton, wash it out thoroughly with soap and water, and tape the carton onto the tray.

Cover each section of the milk carton with frosting, using a plastic knife. Place part of the graham cracker on top of the frosting, which acts as a glue. Continue this until the carton is completely covered with graham crackers. For the roof, use a sharp knife to score a cracker in the shape of a triangle or whatever shape you need, then break it. Now your students are ready to decorate their houses by placing a small dab of icing wherever they want to put candy pieces. They can use an inverted ice cream cone (the cylinder shape) as a tree and tint the icing green. Marshmallows can be snowpeople, gumdrops can form a path from the house, and two miniature candy canes situated just right can create a heart-shaped door. Licorice can be cut to form square windows and doors. Allow the students to use their own creativity and ideas.

Set up a special table and invite other classes to view your candy cottages. Play holiday music to create a festive atmosphere while the visitors are looking. Give awards to all of your students, for the most unique, most delicious looking, neatest, gooiest, most colorful, most outrageous, and so on (don't leave anyone out).

Creative Writing Ideas to Culminate This Theme

Have your students write stories to tie in with these projects. Here are some topics to get your class started.

If you lived in a candy village, what would be some of the occupations of the people?

If you could be one candy, which one would it be and why?

Assign a "how to" essay. Let students create their very own made-up desserts. Give them an example to set their brains in motion, perhaps marshmallow lemon pie sprinkled with peanut M&Ms® or lollipop pudding. They must explain, step by step, how their unique desserts are prepared. What beverage compliments each treat?

Make up 15 characters who would live in the candy village your class has built. Their first and last names must begin with the same letter.

    Michael Marshmallow
    Linda Licorice
    Gary Gumdrop

Ask each student to draw one of these characters. Use glitter or colored sand for texture and color.

A Multicultural Christmas

Around the World at Christmas is a 30-day celebration. From December 6 to January 6, countries of Europe, North and South America commemorate Christmas in many ways. It's a holiday season with wonderful sights, sounds, smells, and tastes. Expose the children to a multicultural Christmas by making and enjoying these holiday activities.

GERMANY

Froliche Weihnacten says, "Merry Christmas" in German. The people of Germany love Christmas and have brought us many traditions. The Christmas tree comes from Germany, as well as the famous carol "O Tannenbaum;" the English version is "O Christmas Tree." Gingerbread also originated in Germany, so we have them to thank for gingerbread men cookies and gingerbread houses.

On the night of December 5, German children wait for a visit from St. Nicholas. They set out their shoes before bed and awake to find them filled with cookies, candy, nuts, and small toys. For a class project, cut out a large shoe shape from construction paper. Search through magazines and catalogs to find pictures of food treats and special toys. Cut these out and glue them onto the paper shoes.

For a cooking activity, gather the children and prepare a gingerbread cake from a recipe or packaged mix. Serve this with whipped cream for a holiday snack. Then use a brown grocery bag to create a "gingerbread man." Cut out two doll figures from the brown bag. Using a hole punch, make holes around the edges of the figure. Lace the two shapes together with yarn, leaving a space open for stuffing. Give the gingerbread man facial features, and decorate him by gluing on buttons and trims. Stuff him with fiberfill or tissue. Finish lacing the open space, then enjoy your own stuffed gingerbread man.

by Tania K. Cowling

POLAND

Christmas is celebrated on the eve with a traditional Wilea supper (no meat is served). It begins as soon as the first star is seen in the night sky. Stars are important Christmas symbols in Poland. This celebration symbolizes love and peace. For an activity, teachers can cut out paper stars and hide them around the classroom. Prior to snack time, have the children hunt for the stars. After the first star is found (or after all are found), serve the meal. It is customary to serve 12 different foods at the Wilea supper to represent the 12 apostles. Today, a fruit compote including 12 different fruits is common. In a large bowl, try combining these fruits: cherries, apples, pears, figs, apricots, peaches, oranges, raisins, grapes, plums, blueberries, and prunes. Serve this snack in paper cups.

MEXICO

Beginning on the night of December 16, Mexicans start celebrating Las Posadas. On each of the nine nights before Christmas, families reenact the story of Mary and Joseph's search for lodging in Bethlehem. People go from house to house caroling and finally reach a destination for the evening's festival.

The highlight of the party for the children is breaking the piñata filled with fruit, candy, nuts, and small toys. The piñata is hung from the ceiling. The children take turns, blindfolded, trying to break the piñata with a stick. When the goodies fall, all the children scurry to gather up their share. Use a brown grocery bag and fill it with goodies and crumpled newspaper. Gather up the top securely and tie it with twine (enough to hang it from the ceiling or doorway). Decorate your piñata with colorful markers, crayons, paint, and crepe paper steamers. Play the piñata game in class.

Mexico is noted for Christmas ornaments made of brightly colored foil and tin. To make a homemade replica, outline and cut out an ornament shape from the bottom of an aluminum pie pan. Affix tape all around the edges to protect tender fingers. Sketch designs and punch holes with a large nail. Make a larger hole at the top to thread a ribbon. You can leave these silver or color over the tin with crayons and markers. When using the nail to punch holes, pad the table with a stack of newspapers. You could also use aluminum foil to make this craft. Cut a square of foil and sketch a design. Use a hole punch to make holes along the design lines. Glue or tape the foil onto a piece of bright construction paper. The colors will show through the holes. Cut this into an ornament shape and hang it with ribbon.

GREAT BRITAIN

The traditional English Christmas greeting is "Happy Christmas." Many of today's customs have come from Great Britain. The Christmas card, for example, originated in England. It is said that school children made beautiful cards to send home to parents, informing them of the child's progress and a "wish" list of gifts. The first Christmas card was printed in England in 1843.

Look in your recycle box for collage materials and you're on your way to making lovely cards. To make one such card, fold a piece of construction paper in half. Glue on a picture cut from an old Christmas card and add trims, or cut many pictures from old cards and glue these onto the front cover in collage style.

Holly, ivy, and mistletoe are important parts of an English holiday. Children search the woods for branches of holly to decorate the home. The carol "Deck the Halls" is a reflection of this tradition. Make an English holly napkin ring to decorate your snack table. Cut a cardboard toilet paper tube in half. You can paint these if you wish. With green construction paper, cut out three holly leaves for each napkin ring. Glue these on the tube and add three red paper berries in the middle. Print the child's name on one of the leaves.

Another great activity that came from England is making pomander balls. Take an orange, lemon, or lime and using a toothpick, gently poke holes in the fruit. Press a whole clove into each hole until the fruit is entirely covered. It's best to wrap the fruit in a square piece of nylon netting. Make a ribbon hanger for the ball. As the fruit dries, it will shrink, become lighter, and the sweet smell will grow stronger. A spicy holiday scent will permeate the classroom.

136

BRAZIL

At Christmastime, Brazilians greet you with "Feliz Natal" meaning "Happy Christmas." Since Brazil has a warm climate, Papa Noel (the gift giver) goes in through an open window. Most homes have no fireplaces. He places gifts in the children's shoes, which have been left under the Christmas tree. The people gather together for dances, picnics, and fireworks. Large, colorful flowers decorate the Brazilian festivals. In class, make these flowers from colorful tissue paper. Cut five circles from tissue paper. You can zigzag or fringe the edges if you wish. Poke one end of a pipe cleaner through the middle of the circles. Grasp the stem and base of the flower and twist them into a point. Tape the stem to hold the flower base together. Separate and fluff out the petals.

NIGERIA

Christmas is a joyous holiday in Nigeria. Music is important to these people, so on Christmas the children go from house to house singing carols. They are rewarded with cookies and candy treats. Drums are considered the most important musical instrument. Make homemade drums and march to a rhythmic cadence.

Find empty oatmeal containers or coffee cans with lids. First decorate some paper with a holiday theme to use on the drum. Use cookie cutters and dip them into tempera poster paints. Press them down onto heavy paper to make holiday prints. Cover the paper with these designs and let it dry. Then wrap the container with this paper; trim it to fit. Place glue underneath for an adhesive. You can use the container's original lid for the drum top or for a softer sound, use a balloon. Cut off the neck and stretch the rubber over the opening of the container. Secure this tightly with several rubber bands. Use an unsharpened pencil for a drumstick.

Holiday Sing-Alongs

by Mabel Duch

Early Christmas Morning

To the tune of "Here We Go 'Round the Mulberry Bush"

Children may be divided into groups to sing
the song.
Group 1 can sing verses 2, 3, 6, and 7.
Group 2 can sing verses 4, 5, 8, and 9.
All sing verses 1 and 10.

Here we go 'round the Christmas tree,
The Christmas tree,
The Christmas tree.
Here we go 'round the Christmas tree
Early Christmas morning.

A little panda I can see,
I can see,
I can see.
A little panda I can see
Early Christmas morning.

I hope that bear is meant for me,
Meant for me,
Meant for me.
I hope that bear is meant for me
Early Christmas morning.

And I can see a building set,
A building set,
A building set.
And I can see a building set
Early Christmas morning.

Is that the present I will get,
I will get,
I will get?
Is that the present I will get
Early Christmas morning?

I see the gift I'm giving you,
Giving you,
Giving you.
I see the gift I'm giving you
Early Christmas morning.

I hope that you will like it too,
Like it too,
Like it too.
I hope that you will like it too,
Early Christmas morning.

And there's my gift for Mom and
Dad,
Mom and Dad,
Mom and Dad.
And there's my gift for Mom and
Dad
Early Christmas morning.

I hope that it will make them glad,
Make them glad,
Make them glad.
I hope that it will make them glad
Early Christmas morning.

Let's all go 'round the
Christmas tree,
The Christmas tree,
The Christmas tree.
Let's all go 'round the
Christmas tree
Early Christmas morning.

Discussion

1. Which is more fun for you: opening the gifts you receive or watching others open the presents you give them?

2. What do you like about opening the presents you receive?

3. What do you like about watching others opening the gifts you give?

Snowball Ornaments

A quick, easy Christmas idea that sparkles with the lights of Christmas!

Directions

Cut a pipe cleaner into fourths and push one piece into a Styrofoam™ ball about 1½". Pull it out and put a drop of glue in the hole, then push the pipe cleaner back into the hole.

Cut out two to three designs from the napkins that will fit on the ball. The designs don't have to be cut perfectly because the white part of the napkin will blend in with the ball. Carefully separate the layers of the napkin so there is only one layer with the design.

Mix equal amounts of water and glue in a cup. Use the paintbrush to spread the glue mixture onto the Styrofoam™ ball.

Gently place the design from the napkin onto the ball, tapping it down into the glue. Start from the middle and work out to the edges to avoid wrinkles. More glue mixture can be added if needed. Be sure the first design is stuck to the ball, then add the other design(s) in the same manner.

Liberally add more of the glue mixture with the paintbrush, then sprinkle glitter all over the ornament. Hang the ball to let the glue harden.

When the glue is dry, ribbon can be added at the base of the pipe cleaner. These ornaments sparkle and glitter as they reflect the lights of the tree. The ornament is ready to be hung on the Christmas tree or to be wrapped as a gift for someone special.

Materials

Styrofoam™ ball
Christmas napkins
white glue
one-sided glitter (it looks clear to white)
ribbon
pipe cleaner
paintbrush

Happy Holly Days

Santa's Super-Duper Story Starters

Calling all authors! Here are some story starters to brighten your holiday season.

Extra! Extra! Read all about it! "Kid Saves Christmas." Write a news story for the Holiday Herald about how you helped Santa one year.

You look out your window on Christmas Day and see a strange elf in your yard. Tell what happens next.

You're an Inventor! Write a story about how you invented the most popular toy of the year. Draw a picture of your new creation.

Write a story about the tallest Christmas tree in the world.

Write a story about Santa's newest reindeer. His name is Randy Reindeer, and he's the fastest reindeer at the North Pole.

by Mary Ellen Switzer

Holiday Activity Cards

Reproduce and laminate these holiday activity cards for your class to enjoy.

Pretend you are a Christmas card. Write about your journey after landing in a dark mailbox.

Round up some facts about reindeer. Use an encyclopedia or reference book to find out more about this fascinating animal. Create an All About Reindeer trivia or board game.

Write directions on how to wrap a holiday present.

Santa's Word Challenge! How many words can you make using the letters in CHRISTMAS TREE?

Congratulations! While baking your holiday cookies, you make the biggest gingerbread man in the world. Draw a picture of your giant cookie. Tell what happens next.

You have just been hired by Sherlock Elf's Detective Agency. The Acme Candy Store needs your help. All of their candy canes are missing. Write a story about how you solved the mystery.

Make a word search or crossword puzzle using "red" and "green" words.

Happy New Year! Write three New Year's resolutions that will help your school.

Design a holiday card for your favorite sports star.

Happy New Year! Write three New Year's resolutions that will help our planet Earth.

Name_____

Where Are the Gingerbread Boys?

Help these children at a holiday party locate their missing cookies.
Find and color all the hidden gingerbread boys in the picture.

142   by Mary Ellen Switzer

Let's Trim the Christmas Tree!

These children are busy trimming their Christmas tree.
Color all the items in the picture that begin with the letter T.

Help the children trim their tree.
Add a yellow star to the top of the tree.
Draw two bell ornaments on the tree.
Add five candy canes on the tree.
Finish coloring the tree.

by Mary Ellen Switzer

143

Seasonal Science

Science projects invite children to observe changes taking place around them and encourage them to ask questions about the changes. Here are a few simple activities that demonstrate changes. These activities will prompt questioning and lead into projects that incorporate these discoveries into your holiday learning experiences.

Project Recycle

Activity

A product in wide use during the holiday season is paper, as used in wrapping, cards, and gift tags. This year, invite your class to join in the process of making recycled paper. Have the children each create a cardboard frame, then help them staple a piece of burlap over their frames. To prepare paper mash for this burlap screen, have them tear paper towels and construction paper scraps into bits over a bowl. Soak the paper pieces in warm water for 10 to 15 minutes, then pour the mixture into a blender. Blend until the mixture is mushy. Pour the mush into a bowl. Have the children remove pulp from the bowl, squeeze out the excess water, then pat it flat onto their burlap screens. Work over several thicknesses of newspaper to absorb the water. Prop the screens up in a warm, dry place and allow the paper to dry thoroughly. When dry, it should peel right off the burlap. Help the children understand that they have created a new, usable product from "trash."

Project

Have the children draw and cut holiday shapes from their papers, then decorate these shapes with glitter, sequins, buttons, ribbon, and so on to make unique holiday ornaments. Paper punch a hole at the top of each and thread ribbon through for hanging.

Variation: Cut each homemade paper sheet in half, creating two paper strips. Decorate these paper strips in the same manner as above, and use them as bookmarks to give parents.

Merry Christmas

by Marie E. Cecchini

Going Up

Activity

During the holiday season, many families incorporate the use of live trees or seasonal floral arrangements into their home decor. If possible, provide one for your classroom, or make use of a pine tree branch. Help the children note that these trees and arrangements need water to remain "fresh" longer, then help them discover how the rootless plants receive water through capillary action. Demonstrate the upward movement of water molecules using two containers, water tinted with food color, a clean white rag or several paper towels, and a box. Set one container on a tabletop. Set the box next to it, and the second container on top of the box. Pour tinted water into the container on the table, then set one end of the rag into the water and the opposite end into the container on the box. Observe as the tinted water crawls up the rag and into the second container. Help the children conclude that the trees and plants nourish themselves with water in the same manner.

Project

Provide the children with white coffee filters, eyedroppers, and containers of tinted water in various colors. Have them work over several thicknesses of newspaper and drip tinted water onto their coffee filters. Note the capillary action and color mixing. When the filter pictures are dry, have the children create black paper frames, cut the coffee filters to fit the frames, and glue them in place. Add a hole and yarn hanger to the top of each frame and hang these in a window to simulate stained glass.

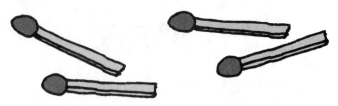

Candle Power

Activity

Candles are widely used in many holiday celebrations. Have the children use dictionaries and encyclopedias to determine the origin of wax, from which candles are made. They may be surprised to discover that it is another animal by-product we find useful. Bring in beeswax, available at craft stores, for the children to observe. Note the color and texture. Demonstrate the art of candle making by placing the wax into a coffee can, setting the coffee can into an old pot, filling the pot one quarter full of water, and heating the water. What happens to the wax? What caused the change? Dip a length of wick into the wax and allow the wax to harden over the wick. What caused the wax to harden? Wrap one end of the wick around a metal washer and set the washer into a half pint milk container. Pour a small amount of wax into the container to solidify the washer in place, then fill the container with wax. Wrap the top of the wick around a pencil and set the pencil across the top of the container to keep the wick centered. Allow the wax to harden overnight, then light the candle the following day to complete the demonstration. Please remember at all times that this is a science demonstration. Hot wax is not safe for children's use.

Project

Purchase a set of beeswax candle making sheets from a local craft store. The wick is included and the price is under five dollars. Provide each student with a 2" x 8" strip of beeswax and a length of wick. Show them how to roll the wax strip around the wick to form a votive candle. Use these candles as holiday gifts for parents.

Christmas Money Adds Up

Read the money problem on each present. Add up the coins to find the total.

Add
one quarter
one dime
one nickel

Add
one quarter
one nickel
two pennies

Add
two dimes
two nickels
five pennies

Add
two quarters
one nickel
three pennies

Add
one quarter
three dimes
four pennies

Add
five dimes
three nickels
ten pennies

Add
two quarters
two dimes
two nickels

Add
five dimes
three nickels
nine pennies

Add
six dimes
five nickels
four pennies

by Jeanne Grieser

A Logical Christmas

Lisa and her friends went Christmas caroling at the senior citizen home where her grand-mother lives. Almost everyone wanted to give them a little present or treat. When the boys and girls left, they each had a Christmas bag of goodies! Read about them and fill in the chart below. Then answer the questions.

Denton was given 2 apples, 4 candy bars, 2 boxes of raisins, a bag of cookies, and a ball.

Katie's bag contained 3 apples, 2 boxes of raisins, a yo-yo, and a coloring book.

Ryan had 4 candy bars, 3 bags of cookies, and a ball.

Mia received 4 bags of cookies, a yo-yo, 2 coloring books, and a ball.

Chip's bag contained 2 apples, 4 candy bars, 2 boxes of raisins, 3 bags of cookies, 2 yo-yos, a coloring book, and 3 balls.

1. Who got the least?

2. Who got the most?

3. Who didn't get any healthy treats?

4. Who got the most healthy treats?

5. Who got some of everything?

6. Whose Christmas bag would you like to have?

GOODIES	apple	candy bar	raisins	cookies	yo-yo	coloring book	ball
Denton							
Katie							
Ryan							
Mia							
Chip							

148   **by Mary Tucker**

Name_____

A Holiday Message

Using page 150, follow the directions to find out the holiday message. The first one has been done for you.

Put an *A* in the snowflake/bell square.
Put an *H* in the candy cane/snowman square.
Put an *E* in the holly/party whistle square.
Put an *A* in the angel/stocking square.
Put an *M* in the candy cane/Christmas tree square.
Put an *R* in the star/stocking square.
Put an *I* in the candy cane/bell square.
Put a *Y* in the angel/bow square.
Put an *A* in the angel/snowman square.
Put an *E* in the holly/Christmas tree square.
Put an *S* in the candy cane/candle square.
Put a *W* in the holly/bell square.
Put an *R* in the holly/candle square.
Put a *Y* in the star/Christmas tree square.
Put an *N* in the snowflake/stocking square.
Put an *M* in the star/party whistle square.
Put a *P* in the angel/present square.
Put a *Y* in the holly/present square.
Put an *R* in the candy cane/party whistle square.
Put an *R* in the star/present square.
Put an *S* in the candy cane/stocking square.
Put an *N* in the holly/snowman square.
Put a *C* in the candy cane/Christmas ornament square.
Put a *D* in the snowflake/present square.
Put a *P* in the angel/Christmas tree square.
Put an *A* in the holly/bow square.
Put an *E* in the star/bell square.
Put an *A* in the candy cane/bow square.
Put a *T* in the candy cane/present square.
Put an *H* in the angel/bell square.

by Jeanne Grieser   **149**

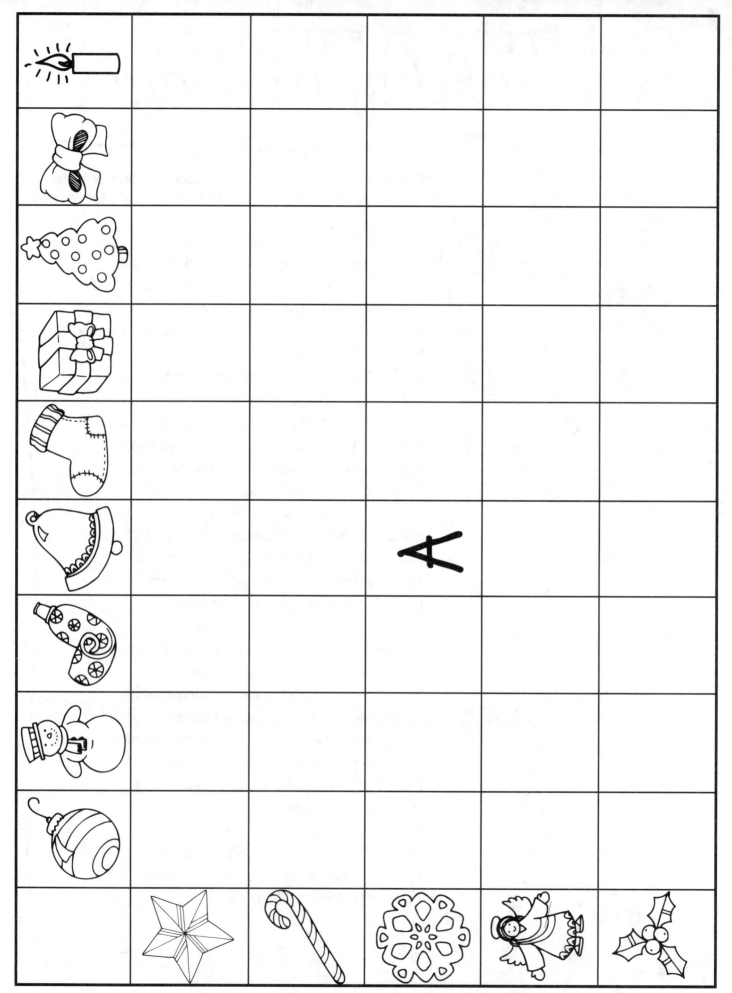

First Fruits of Kwanzaa Bowl

Reproduce the patterns below. Color and cut out. Glue the bowl, as illustrated, to red, green or black construction paper to form a pocket. Place the fruit in the pocket as you learn the seven principles of Kwanzaa.

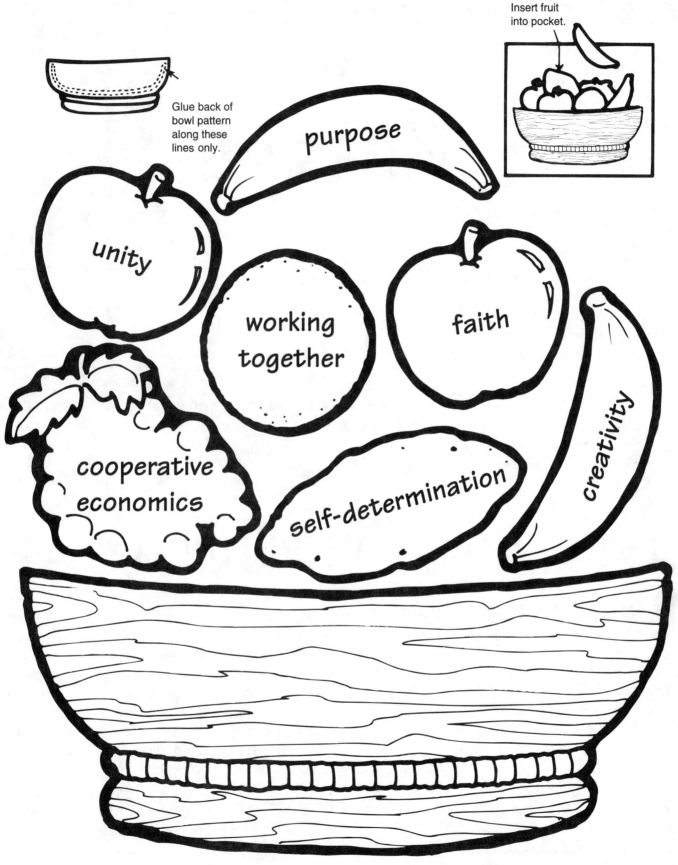

Insert fruit into pocket.

Glue back of bowl pattern along these lines only.

purpose

unity

working together

faith

cooperative economics

self-determination

creativity

by Veronica Terrill

KWANZAA AND KARAMU

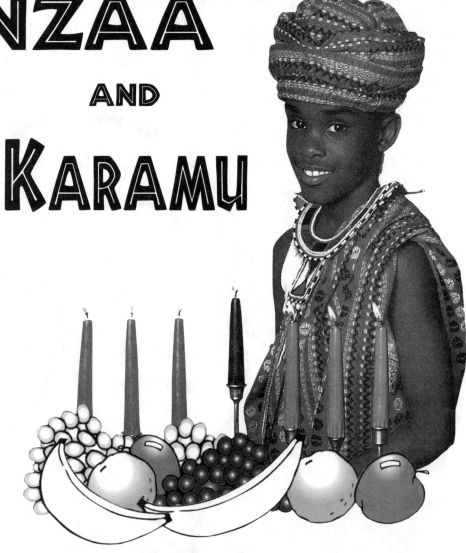

To the tune of
"Row, Row, Row Your Boat."
It has a drum-like rhythm.

Come, come, come, my friends,
Come and celebrate.
Happily, happily, happily, happily,
Karamu is great.

Come, come, come, my friends,
Come and share some food.
Happily, happily, happily, happily,
Ethnic meals are good.

Red, black, green, my friends,
The colors that we show,
Happily, happily, happily, happily,
Display what we should know.

Praise, praise, praise, my friends,
Praise leaders old and new.
Happily, happily, happily, happily,
We'll be leaders, too.

Come, come, come, my friends,
We will dance and sing.
Happily, happily, happily, happily,
Fun's a Kwanzaa thing.

BACKGROUND

Verse 1: A Karamu is a special feast celebrated with family and friends on the sixth day of Kwanzaa (December 31). Often it is a community celebration—a cultural festival. *Karamu* is a Swahili word meaning "a feast."

Verse 2: Ethnic food is served throughout Kwanzaa, but at the Karamu there is a lavish feast. Everyone brings his or her favorite food. There are dishes of African, Caribbean, and South American origin, as well as local family favorites.

Verse 3: Participants wear African garb, often in the colors of Kwanzaa: red, black, and green. These are the colors of the African American flag (Benara), and the colors of the seven candles lit during Kwanzaa. The three red candles stand for past suffering and struggle, the center black one represents the people, and the three green candles stand for hope for the future.

Verse 4: As on other days of Kwanzaa, past and present leaders are honored and praised. One of the purposes of Kwanzaa is developing leadership qualities in children and young people.

Verse 5: Singing and dancing, important parts of the Karamu, bring a special joy to Kwanzaa.

152   **BY MABEL DUCH**

Learning More About Kwanzaa

Team children in your class who have experienced Kwanzaa with those who have not. Set aside a time for the pairs or groups to hold question-and-answer sessions. Provide paper and crayons or markers, so the teaching children can illustrate their information if they like.

Contact an African American group in your community to see if someone would talk to your class about Kwanzaa. Your local library may be able to help you locate the right person.

Make Kwanzaa Drums

Cover large coffee cans or oatmeal boxes with off-white or beige paper. Using red, green, and black paper, decorate the drums with geometric or stylized designs. Cut some of the paper into strips 3/4" and 1 1/2" wide, or use colored adhesive-backed plastic tape to create designs.

Singing the Song

Have some children sing while others drum. Then switch roles. Or all can drum and sing at the same time. The verses can be sung as rounds.

Kwanzaa Candles

Materials

white paper
yellow paint in small containers with eyedroppers
drinking straws
thin black marker and crayons

Directions

1. Children draw seven candles with crayons.

2. Children place a drop of yellow paint on their paper above each candle and blow it around with a straw to form a flame. Leave flat to dry.

3. When the paint is dry, children print one principle in each flame.

Seven Principles of Kwanzaa

Unity
Self-determination
Working together
Sharing
Purpose
Creativity
Faith

Over the holidays, seven candles are lit to represent these guiding principles.

Read About Kwanzaa

Kwanzaa: An African-American Celebration of Cooking and Culture by Eric V. Copage. Design and illustration by Cheryl Carrington (New York: William Morrow and Company, 1991.)

You may find this book in the cookbook section of your library or bookstore, but it is much more than that. In addition to the recipes, it tells how various families observe Kwanzaa and provides stories of heroes and leaders for Kwanzaa sharing and discussion.

New Year's Day Waxy Resolutions

January

Materials

- white wax crayons or candle stubs
- wax crayons of all colors
- white bond paper of any shape or size

Setup

Discuss reasons that students think people make resolutions at this time of the year. For many people it marks a new beginning, new hope, and new possibilities. Some people think that resolutions should be kept simple and easy to achieve; others think you should reach for the stars and set goals that are a challenge to achieve. What do your students think? Everyone agrees that we shouldn't get discouraged if we don't live up to our resolutions . . . there is always next year!

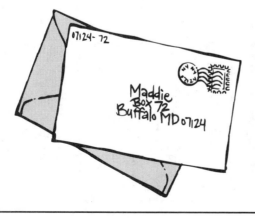

Let's Make It

1. Students will write their resolutions on white paper using clear wax. These resolutions will be "invisible" and "secret" at this time.

2. The only person who can make a resolution come true is the person who makes it. As a symbol of this, children can color over the invisible resolutions with a color or various colors of crayons and make it appear.

Try This

Have the children put their resolutions in envelopes, seal them, and address them to themselves. At the end of the year you can mail the envelopes to the students as a reminder of the aspirations and goals they have for themselves.

by Robynne Eagan

155

Ring in the New Year with good news. Rhyme a little, write stories, and review math skills with New Year's News.

New Year's News

50 cents

2 pages   2 sections   Jan./Feb./Mar. 1999   Carthage, IL 62321   by Terry Healy

Welcome Back to Our New Year's News

| School | Home | Friends |

Classroom Helpers

On your classroom helper board, follow the theme of New Year's News by covering the board with newsprint. Make labels for the following: Manager (classroom helper), Editors in Chief (peer reviewers), Food Editor (lunch count), Production Staff (hand out papers), Sports Editor (playground equipment), and Director of Special Projects (pets, and so on).

Recycling Newspaper

Make a New Year's resolution for your class to begin recycling. Ask students to collect newspapers from home and bring them to school before winter break. Collect the newspapers for the exercises in New Year's News. Use the remaining pile for skills practice. For example, use page numbers from the newspaper to practice ordinal numbers and counting. As a class, weigh the newspapers on a bathroom scale. Estimate how many pages are in all of the newspapers. Decide which day's edition of the newspaper is the heaviest. Cut out pictures from the newspaper for comparison and sorting. For older students, cut out the articles attached to the pictures.

Bulletin Board

Set up your New Year's bulletin board by first covering it with newspaper. With large letters, title the bulletin board, Welcome Back to Our New Year's News. Label one section as School, one section as Home, and one section as Friends. As a writing exercise, ask a student to write or dictate something that is new this new year about school, home, or a friend. Instruct the student to illustrate his news. Mount these news flashes on your bulletin board.

Where in the News

With a large map, ask older students to identify the location given for one of the newspaper articles and pictures you clipped. Pin the article next to the map and connect the article with a piece of string to its location on the map.

Instruct students to sort articles and pictures according to whether the location is local or at a distance. Continue map practice by attaching each article next to the map and connecting it to its location.

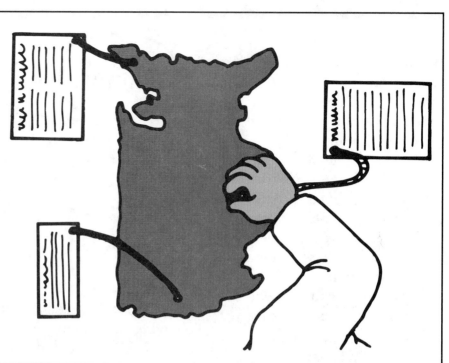

Newspapers

Newspapers and advertisements provide an excellent way to practice letter and word identification. For younger students, give each a small section of an advertisement or newspaper. Present an over-sized letter to the class and instruct students to locate and circle that letter as many times as possible. Count the number found. For older students or readers, present the same skill using sight vocabulary.

Sorting News

Living and Nonliving. For younger students, attach a picture of an animal to one shoe box and a picture of a rock to another. Review the definitions for living and nonliving objects. Provide a large selection of pictures cut from newspapers. Ask students to sort the pictures into the Living or Nonliving boxes.

Living   Nonliving

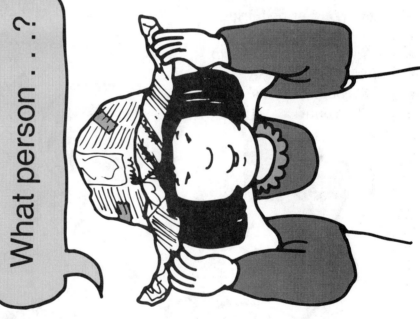

What person . . . ?

New Year's Hat

Provide each student with several sheets of newspaper and three or four feet of masking tape. Instruct each student to create a hat that a community helper might wear. Use additional scraps of construction paper to decorate the hats. When the students are done, gather them for a discussion. Ask, *What person in our community might wear this hat? What job does that person do in our community?* Ask older students to write a story about the hat and community member who wears it.

Rhyming New Year

Print each of the following words on separate cards. Ask students to agree whether the word rhymes with *new*, *year*, or is not a rhyming word.

bear	tear	knew
blue	zoo	true
cheer	dear	sue
clue	boo	brew
fear	gear	flew
grew	drew	pew
hear	near	shoe
two	you	who
sheer	pear	care

Daily News

At calendar time, tell about upcoming events such as class plays, programs, or field trips. Record the upcoming New Year's News on a paper next to the calendar. Highlight the days of upcoming events. Ask a student to count how many days are left before the event.

New Year's Noodles/Snack

Following the theme of New Year's News, prepare alphabet-shaped pasta according to the instructions. Flavor by sprinkling with cinnamon and sugar.

What Time Is It?

Enlarge a picture of the New Year's Baby carrying a clock. Put moveable hands on the clock. Review time-telling skills. Ask students what they might do at each of the times listed below.

New Year's Eve midnight
New Year's Day noon
New Year's Eve 6:00 p.m.
New Year's Day 3:00 p.m.
New Year's Day 8:00 a.m.
New Year's Day 10:00 a.m.

Give each child a copy of a blank clock face. Instruct them to draw in the hands showing the time which was their favorite time of New Year's. Ask them to draw or write a sentence about what they did at that time.

New Year's Resolutions

New Year's is a time for thinking about the past and what changes would be good for the future. Ask students what New Year's resolutions they have made. Discuss possible goals for the rest of the school term. Give students 3" x 5" cards. Instruct them to each write one personal goal on the card. Tape the goal to the upper corner of the student's desk. Possible goals might include keeping a neat desk, mastering math facts, or improving handwriting.

My New Year's Resolutions
1. Do my chores without a reminder.
2. Improve my handwriting.
3. Don't talk in class.

Stone Soup

January Is National Soup Month

To celebrate this special month, read the book Stone Soup by Marcia Brown to your class and follow up with these fun classroom activities.

Talk About Soup

- Think of all the kinds of soup you have eaten.
- Which is your favorite? Does it have noodles in it? Or vegetables? Or bits of fish or meat?
- Does eating it warm you up?
- Do you ever slurp it? (poor manners, but fun!)
- Do you eat it from a cup or bowl?
- Have you ever helped make soup at home? If so, tell how you did it.

Talk About Stone Soup

- Did the soldiers really plan to have just stones in their soup?
- In what way were the stones in the soup magic?
- The villagers had hidden their food. Why did they go and get some for the soup?
- Did the villagers realize they were being tricked? Was it a good trick or a mean one?
- Do you think the soldiers had ever made Stone Soup before?
- Why did the soldiers share the soup with the villagers?
- Why do you think the soldiers laughed as they went on their way?

by Elaine Hansen Cleary

Some Other Soupy Things to Do in School

Cooperative Group Activity

Get in groups of three. Invent a soup of your own. Give it a name. Write a recipe for making it. Design a label for the can it could be sold in. Cut out that label and paste it on an empty soup can. Display your can with cans from other groups. Tell your classmates about your soup.

Language Arts Activity

Make several batches of alphabet noodle soup. Give each child a bowl.

1. See how many letters of the alphabet each child can spoon out of his soup.

2. How many spelling words can each child make from his soup (or combined with a partner's soup)?

An At-Home Soup Activity

Try making your own stone soup—without the stones. First, boil water in a pot. Then add one vegetable, then another and another. How does the taste change? Include seasonings such as salt, pepper, parsley, and catsup. Maybe add a bit of meat or fish. Don't use foods you are allergic to, and make sure an adult is present to supervise you!

Math Activity

Collect labels from as many soup cans as possible. Count the labels. How many do you have of each kind? Which flavor of soup has the most labels? Which soup flavor has the least labels? Help children graph the results.

Just for Fun

Ask parents to help by coming to school to assist children in making a variety of soups. (Either canned soups or those made from packets of dry soup.)

Put soup samples in three-ounce paper cups (filled half full). Let each child try as many soups as he or she prefers. Have crackers available to eat with the soup and water to drink. Note: Be sure to make allowance for any allergies! And check with cafeteria staff to make sure health laws are observed!

Art Activity

Once the label collection has been used in math, use those labels to make a collage.

J. Armbrust

160

Name _____

Soup Scramble

After the soldiers left, the villagers made a list of the ingredients in the stone soup so they would never forget them. But they wrote so hurriedly that they mixed up the letters in every word. Can you unscramble them?

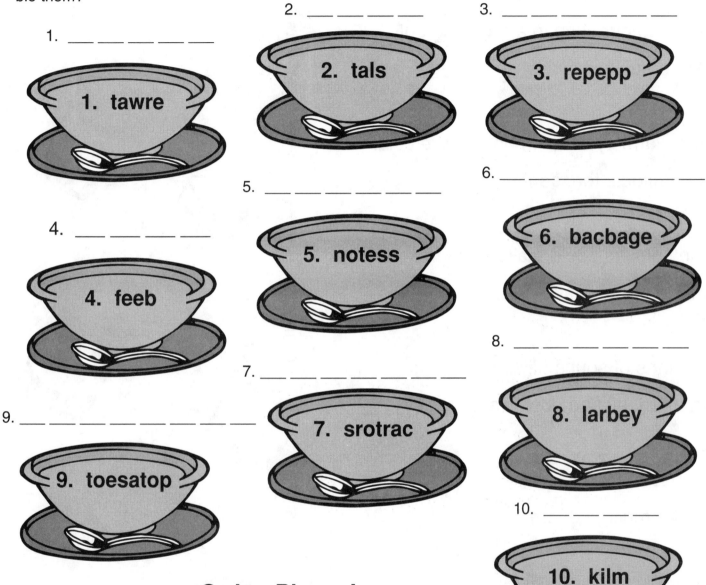

1. __ __ __ __ __

1. tawre

2. __ __ __ __

2. tals

3. __ __ __ __ __ __

3. repepp

4. __ __ __ __

4. feeb

5. __ __ __ __ __ __

5. notess

6. __ __ __ __ __ __ __

6. bacbage

7. __ __ __ __ __ __ __

7. srotrac

8. __ __ __ __ __ __

8. larbey

9. __ __ __ __ __ __ __ __

9. toesatop

10. __ __ __ __

10. kilm

Order, Please!

When the words were finally spelled correctly, they still were not listed in the correct order in which they were put into the soup. Can you rearrange them correctly?

1. _____
2. _____
3. _____
4. _____
5. _____

6. _____
7. _____
8. _____
9. _____
10. _____

Poetry Soup

When words rhyme, they sound alike. For example *bee* and *see;* or *day* and *may.* Use the words on the cans below to complete the rhyming poems about soup.

We made our soup in a great big pot.

I like to eat it while it's ___ ___ ___.

Soup warms you up when you are cold.

It's nutritious, too, so I am ___ ___ ___ ___.

If the soldiers could make soup from stones,

How come we make it using ___ ___ ___ ___ ___?

The kinds of soups I like are many;

I eat them all and don't waste ___ ___ ___.

Whenever soup is on the table,

I eat as much as I am ___ ___ ___ ___.

If soup is good for me and you,

Is it good for animals in a ___ ___ ___?

Alphabet soup is my favorite kind;

It warms my tummy and tickles my ___ ___ ___ ___.

Name _____

Martin Luther King, Jr.

Dr. King had a dream.

I have a dream, too.

To live in a world

where his dream

comes true.

Draw your dream for the world.

BY ELIZABETH GILES   163

Martin Luther King, Jr. Day

January 15

Materials

magazines, catalogs, photographs, and newspapers
scissors
paste and glue sticks or brushes
colorful markers, crayons, and colored pencils
mural paper

Setup

Talk to your class about this civil rights activist and what it means to them to be free and equal. Set up a center with magazines, pencils, markers, scissors, paste, and mural paper.

Let's Make It

Have your group make a Martin Luther King, Jr. collage tribute by filling the mural with words, symbols, pictures, and magazine cut-outs that represent the dream of Dr. Martin Luther King, Jr.

by Robynne Eagan

Literature

Incorporate books about music and instruments into the classroom. Add them to the classroom library or reading space. Read them aloud for story time. Don't forget other areas of the classroom when introducing books. Place a book about music or instruments in the music area, near the record player or cassette player, or in a movement and exercise area. Try these books about music and instruments.

Music, Music for Everyone by Vera B. Williams, William Morrow & Co., 1988.
The Alphabet Symphony by Bruce McMillan, Apple Island Books, 1989.
I See a Song by Eric Carle, Scholastic Trade, 1996.
Dance, Tanya by Patricia Lee Gauch, Philomel Books, 1989.
Clap Your Hands by Lorinda Bryan Cauley, Paper Star, 1987.

February Is National Music Month

Cooking: Musical Instrument Snacks

Cracker Drums

Lay a square or rectangular cracker on a paper plate. Use soft, spreadable (or squeeze) cheese to place a zigzag line on the cracker so that it looks like a drum. Lay two thin pretzel sticks across the top as drumsticks.

Banana Cymbals

Cut banana in slices. Gently push thin pretzel sticks into one edge of a banana slice. Position the pretzels as the cymbal stand.

Pear Guitar

Cut pears in half and scoop out the seeds and part of the center with a melon baller or the tip of a spoon. Cut a thin slice from the rounded side of the pear so that it will lay flat with the scooped out center up. Cut red string licorice or very thin carrot strips the length of the pear, three or four per pear half. Lay the licorice or carrot strips lengthwise on the pear like the strings of a guitar.

by Carol Ann Bloom

The Sound of Music Game

Assemble a variety of classroom instruments: sand blocks, rhythm sticks, tambourines, drums, cymbals, triangles, maracas, bells, and xylophones. Add to the variety using homemade instruments.

Familiarize the group with the name and the sound of each instrument. Choose one child to hide his or her eyes. Choose another child to pick an instrument and play it. Give the child with eyes closed three chances to guess the musical instrument being played. Give each child a turn to be either an instrument player or a guesser.

Why Is Music Important to Us?

Talk about different kinds of music and music preferences. Invite children to talk about music in their homes. What kinds of music do they hear? What kinds of music do they like? When do they listen to music at home? Do any family members play musical instruments?

Brainstorm a list of "Good Things About Music." How does music make us feel? What would the world be like without music?

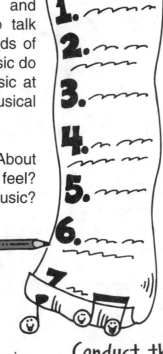

Music, Music for Everyone

Read *Music, Music for Everyone* by Vera B. Williams.

Play a variety of different kinds of music: marches, country, opera, rock and roll, Broadway show tunes, classical, rap and folk. Include music that reflects the families and cultures of the classroom and the community.

Talk about each selection. Invite children to indicate by raising their hands whether they like each type of music. Make a graph of music types and classroom preferences. Help children to understand that music, like so many other things (food, books, movies, games) is a matter of personal taste. Encourage children to bring music from home to share.

Count the Beats Math

Use a variety of drums—real drums, toy drums, and homemade drums such as coffee cans, peanut cans, oatmeal containers, and margarine containers, and pots and pans. Knees can even be used as "body drums." Give each child a drum. Beat a number of taps on a drum. Children count along and beat the same number on their drums. Beat and count individually or as a group. Give each child a turn to lead the group in drum beating a number for others to count and follow.

Number cards can also be used in the activity. Display a number for children to identify. Children then tap the appropriate number on their drums.

Conduct the Orchestra

Use classroom instruments and homemade instruments for this activity. Wrap a chopstick or a pencil with aluminum foil (shiny side out) to use as a conductor's baton.

Talk about the conductor as the leader of the band or orchestra. Though the conductor does not play an instrument, he or she determines how and when all of the other instruments will be played. Musicians must watch the conductor and his or her baton carefully. Give children turns conducting the classroom orchestra with the silver baton. Encourage children to point the baton at different sections (drums, bells, and so on) for solo playing, as well as leading the entire orchestra.

Art: Music Makers

Make several traditional musical instruments and try two new ones.

Paper Plate Tambourine

Put a handful of dried beans, buttons, or pebbles between two paper plates or aluminum pie pans. Staple the edges. The plates can be decorated with markers. Lace or ribbons can be laced through holes placed around the edges of the tambourine.

Shoe Box Guitar

Place a number of large rubber bands around an open shoe box or shoe box lid. Try different thicknesses of rubber bands for different sounds. The shoe box and lid can be painted or covered with paper before rubber bands are added. Use plastic tab fasteners (from bread bags) as guitar picks.

Ankle/Wrist Bells

Thread jingle bells on yarn to tie on wrists and ankles. Make music when you move and walk.

Cardboard Tube Flute

Place a row of holes in the top of a paper towel tube. Cover one end with waxed paper and secure the paper with a rubber band. The child hums in the open end and uses the fingers on the flute holes. The tube can be colored with markers or decorated with stickers.

Can Drum

Tape the plastic lids on coffee cans and peanut cans for safety purposes. Use pencils, chopsticks, or wooden craft sticks as drumsticks. Wrap a rubber band several times around one end of a pencil to make a drumstick with a different sound. Cut wallpaper or gift wrap to tape around can drums. Attach a zigzag of yarn with glue to complete the drum.

Buzzing Button

Thread a 36" piece of string through both holes of a large two-hole button. Tie the ends of the string together. Hold a loop of the string in each hand with the button in the middle. Keep one hand still and rotate the other hand to wind the string tightly. Pull both loops to tighten the string and spin the button. Rewind the button by moving both hands closer together. Slowly move hands closer together and apart to keep the button spinning. Listen to the buzzing music.

Air Whistler

Cut a 4" x 6" piece of cardboard. Remove the center of the cardboard leaving a 1" border on the long side and a 3/4" border on the short side. Place a hole in the center of one of the 6" sides and tie a 2" string through the hole. Slide four rubber bands loosely around the 6" sides of the cardboard. Hold the end of the string and whirl the cardboard over the head in a circle. Listen as the air whistler makes its music.

National Children's
Dental Health Month

Sink your teeth into these fun activities during the month of February. Good dental health habits now will promote years of bright smiles.

Taking Care of Teeth Business

Most young children have 20 teeth. These are called milk or baby teeth. When you grow up you should have a total of 32 teeth. How many teeth do you have now?

The surface of your teeth is hard, covered with strong white enamel. You must keep your teeth healthy or they will decay.

1. Brush your teeth at least twice a day.

2. Limit sugary foods and drinks.

3. Eat crunchy foods like raw carrots, apples, and celery. These foods help scale the tartar from teeth.

4. Eat calcium-rich foods such as cheese, milk, and yogurt. Calcium builds strong bones and teeth.

Together Time Teethbrushing

Have each child bring a toothbrush to school, or better yet, ask if a local dentist will donate new brushes to the class. Label each toothbrush with a child's name. Then designate time during your class day where everyone brushes their teeth together. Demonstrate the correct way to brush. Remember, practice makes perfect!

Show Us Your Pearly Whites

This photo opportunity will have your students excited about keeping their teeth white and shiny. Obtain a Polaroid™ camera and snapshot of each child showing their pearly white teeth. Attach photos on a bulletin board.

by Tania K. Cowling

Brush an Egg

Pretend that the surface of a hard-boiled egg is your tooth. Notice how the egg color is close to the color of tooth enamel. Discuss how certain foods and drink can stain the teeth. Soak eggs in a few soft drinks overnight such as grape soda, red fruit punch, and even cola. The next day, remove the eggs and examine any staining. Let children take turns gently brushing an egg with a toothbrush and toothpaste. Work on getting the eggs back to a "happy tooth" color.

Tooth Fairy Envelopes

Give each child a white envelope to decorate with crayons and markers. Suggest drawing the "Tooth Fairy." Make copies of the following poem and have students glue them to the center of their envelopes. Instruct students to take their envelopes home to use when they lose their next tooth. The child can place the tooth inside and tuck the envelope under his or her pillow at night.

> Dear Tooth Fairy,
>
> My mouth no longer needs it.
> I really want to keep it.
> But I know it belongs to you.
> So slip it away while I sleep
> And leave a surprise
> For me to keep.
>   Love,

Teeth Learning Center

Use the tooth shape to help teach skills during the month of February. Cut out several tooth shapes. Make several matching games to help teach specific skills.

- place squares of color on one tooth—color words on the other tooth
- place capital letters on one tooth—lowercase letters on the other tooth
- place numbers on one tooth—dots to match the numbers on the other tooth
- place simple addition problems on one tooth—answers on the other tooth

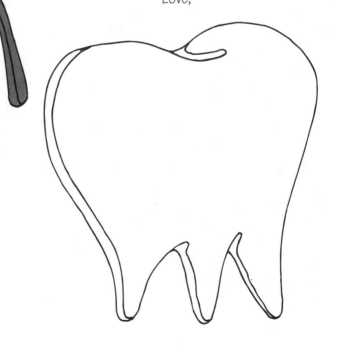

Did You Brush Your Teeth Today?

Duplicate the outline of a mouth on red construction paper for each student. Ask the class, "Did you brush your teeth today?" For every day the student brushed, have him or her glue one white navy bean representing a tooth in the mouth. Keep each child's mouth on display in the class and use them like a calendar, adding a new bean every day until the mouth is full.

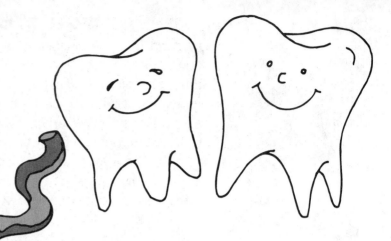

Happy Tooth Wand

Cut tooth shapes from white poster board. Have students glue or staple them to craft sticks. Instruct each student to create a "happy face tooth" by gluing on facial features such as wiggly eyes, a small pom-pom for the nose, and yarn for a smiling, happy mouth. Have the children wave their wands and sing this song.

To the tune of "Row, Row, Row Your Boat"
Brush, brush, brush your teeth,
Shine them every day.
Healthy habits are a must
To keep decay away.

Healthy Snack Faces

Place bowls of healthy snacks in the center of your table. Give each child a small paper plate. Ask children to make cute faces by arranging these foods on the plate. Use foods such as broccoli florets, cauliflower florets, apple slices, orange slices, nuts, raisins, popcorn, and carrot rounds. After they have finished creating their edible art—snap a picture for the memory, then let them eat and enjoy it.

Literature List

The Story of the Tooth Fairy by Tom Paxton, William Morrow & Co., 1996.
A Quarter from the Tooth Fairy by Caren Holtzman, Scholastic Trade, 1995.
My Tooth Is About to Fall Out by Grace MacCarone, Cartwheel Books, 1995.

170

Gung Hay Fat Choy

The biggest and most festive holiday for the Chinese people is the Chinese New Year. Its date, which falls between January 21 and February 19, is fixed according to the Chinese lunar calendar as the second new moon after the winter solstice. Traditionally the Chinese New Year is also considered everyone's birthday.

It is especially exciting for children because they receive presents of money in red envelopes. Red, the symbol of happiness, is used in decorations and presents for the New Year festivities.

This holiday marks the beginning of a new cycle of life and symbolizes the end of winter and the beginning of spring. Families scrub their houses clean, purchase new clothes, and prepare special foods. The homes are decorated in "lucky red." The festivities last for 15 days with gifts, music, dancing, fireworks, and a visit from a fierce-looking dragon who dances through the streets to chase away "evil spirits."

The Chinese New Year

1999 was the "Year of the Rabbit." Every year is named for one of the 12 animals in the Chinese zodiac cycle. It takes 12 years for the same animal to appear again. Take your birth year and find the animal on charts that corresponds with that year. Chinese horoscopes claim that people born in the Year of the Rabbit (1951, 1963, 1975, 1987, 1999, 2011) are nice to be around. They like to talk and many people trust them.

Following are activities to help celebrate this interesting holiday in the classroom.

Dragon Banner

Symbol of goodness and strength.

1. Reproduce the picture of the Chinese dragon.
2. Have children color it with crayons and markers.
3. Have each child place his or her dragon picture in the middle of a 6" x 6" square of clear adhesive plastic and seal it with the same-sized top sheet.
4. Have children make red construction paper frames and tape the laminated dragons in the center.
5. Use a black marker to write the words *Gung Hay Fat Choy* (Happy New Year) on the frame.
6. Punch two holes at the top of each frame and thread them with red ribbon or yarn.
7. Hang these banners in the classroom, then send them home with students to bring "good luck" to their homes.

Fortune Balloons

1. Write "good fortunes" on slips of paper. Create clever wishes such as *"you will have a fun day at school," "you will taste a sweet treat," "you will play many games today,"* and so on.
2. Slip strips into the necks of several balloons.
3. Blow up each balloon and tie off the ends. Have a balloon for each child in class.
4. Scatter the balloons throughout the classroom and have each child pick one.
5. Let children play with the balloons, tapping them up into the air and catching them.
6. Call "time" to break the balloons. Have children sit on the balloons or use pushpins to pop them. Read the fortunes together.

Lucky Red Punch

Pour strawberry soda into a plastic glass. Add one scoop of strawberry ice cream. Squirt on a row of whipped cream and top with a maraschino cherry. Sip this punch through a straw. (Serves one.)

Lanterns

The New Year's celebration ends with the famous Lantern Festival. Children and their families fill the streets holding lighted lanterns. This is when the giant dragon (made of silk fabric and bamboo) is carried through the streets to ward off evil spirits. Make paper lanterns.

1. Have children fold a 9" x 11" sheet of construction paper in half lengthwise.
2. Instruct children to draw a line across the paper about 2" down from the top of the open edge.
3. Have children cut slits 1" apart from the fold up to the marked line.
4. Open and curve the paper into a cylinder and staple the sides together.
5. Punch holes around the bottom edge, and have children tie colorful yarn or ribbon in each hole.
6. Punch two holes at the top (opposite sides). Attach a 12" piece of yarn to the top of the lantern for hanging.

Almond Cookies

Ingredients
1 cup margarine
1 cup sugar
2 eggs
1 teaspoon almond extract
2$\frac{1}{2}$ cups flour (sifted)
$\frac{1}{4}$ teaspoon baking soda
roasted almonds

Beat margarine and sugar together until light and fluffy. Add one egg and the almond extract. Mix. Slowly add flour and baking soda. Chill this dough before shaping. Shape walnut-sized balls of dough with your hands. Press the ball flat on an ungreased cookie sheet. Brush the cookies with the other egg (beaten), pressing an almond into the center of each cookie.

Bake the cookies for about 20 minutes in a 350^{0}F oven, checking the last few minutes for doneness. All ovens vary; you may need more or less time. Cool and enjoy!

Red Envelopes

Children receive Lai Se (lucky money) for Chinese New Year. Make these lucky red envelopes in class.

1. Take a square of red construction paper.
2. Tape a shiny penny in the center.
3. Fold each corner into the center and seal it with a large adhesive gold star. Note: this can be an activity done by the children or made by the teacher and given as a gift.

Holiday Sing-Alongs

by Mabel Duch

Groundhog's Song

To the tune of
"The Bear Went over the Mountain"

The days were growing warmer,
The days were growing warmer,
The days were growing warmer.
It felt so good to me.

So, I went out of my burrow,
I went out of my burrow,
I went out of my burrow
To see what I could see.

A great big scary shadow,
A great big scary shadow,
A great big scary shadow
Was all that I could see.

I ran back to my burrow,
I ran back to my burrow,
I ran back to my burrow
Where I could safely be.

For six more weeks, I'll stay here,
For six more weeks, I'll stay here,
For six more weeks, I'll stay here.
I'll come out when it's spring.

Ground-
hog
Day

Activity

Acting "Groundhog's Song"

Choose one child to be a groundhog. The other children stand in a circle holding hands. "Groundhog" is within the circle. All sing the song.

After the first verse, "ground-hog" approaches two children who lift their arms to let him out of his "burrow."

If possible, have a light positioned so "groundhog" can actually see his shadow.

He should act frightened at this point.

While the fourth verse is being sung, the two children who let him out should raise arms to let him back into his "burrow."

If your class is large, have several "groundhogs" and "burrows." Or let some children be the singers while "groundhog" and "burrows" do not sing.

If time permits, let children take turns being "groundhogs."

Discussion

1. Why was the groundhog frightened? (He was scared by his shadow.)

2. Why would he be afraid of his own shadow? (He hasn't seen it all winter and has forgotten what it looks like. He probably went out early in the morning, and early morning shadows are tall.)

Activity: Shadows

On a sunny day, take children out as early in the morning as you can. Let them trace each other's shadows on large sheets of white paper. Repeat at noon and as late in the afternoon as possible. Cut out white "shadows" and use them as patterns for making black paper "shadows." Display "shadows" and label with the times they were traced.

Activity: Groundhog Day Follow-Up

What would a groundhog predict for your area? Place an outdoor thermometer outside your window. Have students take turns writing the temperature on a calendar each day. They should do this at the same time every day. (suggestion—1 P.M.) Have them note what the weather is like, using symbols. You can buy weather stickers or let the children draw pictures.

sun   rain   snow

clouds   sleet   wind

At the end of six weeks, let the class judge whether or not the groundhog predicted correctly.

Groundhog Day Shadow Rubbing

Reproduce the pattern. Color and cut out. Lay pattern under a sheet of thin paper. Gently rub with a pencil or crayon. Cut out the "shadow" around the outline created by the rubbing. Glue groundhog and shadow to a piece of paper, as shown. Add background or details as desired.

by Veronica Terrill

This page may be used as a coloring page, book cover or story starter sheet. To use as a story starter, have children color and cut out the picture. After writing a story about the picture on one or more pages of writing paper, have children glue the picture to the first page of the story. Additional pages of the story can be attached vertically.

Glue here.

Valentine's Day

On [Valentine] 's Day,

Where I go to  ,

Each  in  ,

Get's a  . That's a rule.

I made my own

Out of  and

And  I  out

And  d in place.

"  are  ;

are  .

If I had a  ,

I would ride as your ".

"If I were a  ,

I'd sit next to U ,

And then I would  ,

'Cock-a-doo-doodle-doo.' "

TLC10198 Copyright © Teaching & Learning Company, Carthage, IL 62321-0010

"When I see your 🙂,
My ❤ starts to 🎵,
And I feel like a 🪁
In the sky with no 🧶."

"My very best 💌
Was a 🐱.
It said, 'Will U be mine?'
And it was from Matt."

It took a long 🕐.
But for me it was fun
To make all **23**.
A 💌 for each **1**.

Our 📦, 💗, and
Was 🍬, 🍪, and 🍫
This is what some of
The 💌 said.

by Patricia Lessie

Make all the little valentines in your class giggle with glee by sharing *Hearty Har Har, Valentine Riddles You'll Love* by Katy Hall and Lisa Eisenberg (HarperFestival, 1997). Find out: *What did the valentine envelope say to the stamp? How did the cat call her sweetheart on Valentine's Day?*

For a magical journey through February and other months of the year, don't miss *A Year Full of Stories, 366 Days of Story and Rhyme* by Georgie Adams (Doubleday Books for Young Readers, 1997). Your primary students will enjoy such seasonal selections as *Mrs. Bear's Valentine, The Snowman,* and *Winter Trees.*

Word Bird is busy again! This time he's building a special "word house" filled with words pertaining to Valentine's Day. *Word Bird's Valentine Words* by Jane Belk Moncure (The Child's World, 1987) is the perfect book to introduce young primary children to the vocabulary of the valentine season. Have your children create holiday poems and stories using the vocabulary words in this handy book.

Clifford's First Valentine's Day
by Norman Bridwell
Scholastic, 1997

Uh oh! That mischievous puppy, Clifford, is trying to help his owner, Emily Elizabeth, make valentines. First, he manages to make a sticky mess and later falls down the mail chute at the post office. Will Emily Elizabeth ever find her lost puppy?

• Be an author! Write a funny story titled "I Took My Dog to the Post Office." Use these words in your story: *letters, chase, mail chute,* and *postman.*

• Clifford the puppy grew up to become America's best-loved giant red dog. Plan a holiday to honor this special dog. Decide on a name for the holiday and make a list of ways everyone will celebrate this special day. Don't forget big red balloons and doggy decorations!

• Hip, Hip, Hooray for Clifford! Draw a picture of Clifford's holiday celebration.

Arthur's Valentine
by Marc Brown
Little, Brown and Co., 1980

Valentine's Day is coming and Arthur has a big problem already! Seems that all of his friends are teasing him because he keeps getting valentine messages from a secret admirer. Will Arthur be able to find out his admirer's identity in time for Valentine's Day?

• The students in Arthur's class were making special valentine boxes to hold their cards. Design a special valentine box for Arthur.

• Calling all detectives! Write your own valentine mystery about a secret valentine. Use these words in your story: *valentine, purple, ink, handwriting,* and *stamp.*

• Marc Brown has written a series of books about Arthur. Which is your favorite book? Tell why you enjoyed this book. Design a bookmark to advertise the book.

by Mary Ellen Switzer

Book Nook

One Very Best Valentine's Day

by Joan W. Blos
Illustrated by Emily Arnold McCully
Aladdin, 1990

When Barbara's special bracelet of colorful hearts breaks, she searches until she finds them all. She decides to "share" the hearts with her family on Valentine' Day as a wonderful holiday present.

- Candy conversation hearts have delighted people since the early 1900s. Everyone enjoys their cute sayings and sweet taste. Cut out some small valentines from colorful construction paper. Create your own sayings for your family and friends.

- Make up a word problem using candy conversation hearts.

- Put on your creative thinking caps! Write a list of other uses (besides eating!) for those tiny conversation hearts. For example, they make perfect bingo or other game markers!

Puppy Love

by Dick King-Smith
Illustrated by Anita Jeram
Candlewick Press, 1997

Calling all dog lovers! You will enjoy reading about the many dogs that the author's family has owned over the years. He also gives some helpful tips on being a good pet owner.

- What dog did you like best in the story? Tell why. Design a valentine for your favorite pet dog.

- Just imagine! Pretend you traded places with a pet dog for a day. Tell about your exciting day.

- Being a dog owner is a big responsibility. Dogs depend on their owners to be fed, groomed, and exercised. Design a poster, showing tips on how to take good care of a dog.

I Love You So Much

by Carl Norac
Illustrated by Claude K. Dubois
Doubleday Books for Young Readers
1996

Poor Lola the hamster! One morning she wants to tell her parents she loves them, but they are too busy. She decides to say her special words to someone at school, but everyone seems too busy. Later she finally gets to say those magical words to her parents, "I love you so much!"

- Design a special valentine that Lola could give to her parents on Valentine's Day.

- Make a list of ways that Lola could show her parents how much she loves them such as making a homemade gift or surprising them with a bouquet of wildflowers.

It's Video Time!

Valentine's Day is the special holiday that everyone loves—a time for friendship and sharing. This is the perfect season to share these excellent videos reflecting the true meaning of friendship.

Winnie the Pooh New Found Friends

Walt Disney
Running Time: Approximately 44 minutes

Come along for a merry visit to Hundred Acre Wood with Winnie the Pooh and his faithful friends. In "Find Her, Keep Her," Rabbit becomes a new "parent" when he finds a tiny baby bird. He soon discovers that raising a baby bird can be extremely difficult at times. Winnie the Pooh and his animal friends come to the rescue and help Rabbit in his new role. This appealing video also features "Donkey for a Day," and "Friend, in Deed."

The Berenstain Bears and the Trouble with Friends

Story by Stan and Jan Berenstain
First Time Video, Approximate Time: 30 minutes

The bear family is delighted when a new girl cub moves in the neighborhood—Sister will have a new playmate. Sister isn't so sure about her new friend, because the new cub is too bossy. The two soon discover the secret "ingredients" of being a good friend—sharing and taking turns. Also included in the delightful double feature is "The Berenstain Bears and the Coughing Catfish." The two bear cubs meet a talking catfish at Grizzly Lake who gives them a lesson in ecology.

Poetry Corner

Poems can provide the perfect springboard for other creative writing activities with your students. The charming collection of poems in *It's Valentine's Day* by Jack Prelutsky (Greenwillow Books, 1983) can set the stage for any writing activity. Here are a few ideas.

I Made a Giant Valentine

Pretend you made the biggest valentine in the world. Describe your valentine. How big was your valentine? Draw a picture of what your giant card looked like.

Our Classroom Has a Mailbox

Write a "Dear Diary" entry about the day that your classroom valentine box overflowed with a thousand cards.

Be a Poet!

Write your own Valentine's Day poem.

Computer Corner

Web Sites

Everyone has been charmed with *The Mitten* and other marvelous books by author Jan Brett. Enter the wonderful world of this popular author by visiting her web site. www.janbrett.com/index.html. Educators will love the "Piggybacks for Teachers" section brimming with motivating ideas they can use with her books. Animal masks, coloring pages, art and writing activities will captivate your children. Information on Jan Brett and her writing is also included on this web site.

A top-notch literature site on the web is Mary Cavaraugh's www.children story.com.

This appealing reading site features selections from four groups: Holiday Stories, Interactive Stories, Fairy Tales, and Nursery Rhymes. Have fun reading the tales yourself or hear them by downloading the audio player from this site.

Need a quick, creative art lesson? Crayola has a variety of appealing classroom art lessons that will surely inspire your young artists. Just visit the popular web site at www.crayola.com/art education. Other kid-pleasing activities are also included, such as coloring pages, greeting cards, stories, games and science lab activities. Put this handy site at the top of your list!

by Mary Ellen Switzer

A Valentine for You

The stores are full of valentines
With ribbons, hearts, and lace.
Even valentines with jokes
I'm finding everyplace.
Instead, here's one I made myself.
It may not look as fine.
But my heart's tucked right inside,
'Cause you're my valentine!

by Bonnie Compton Hanson

To: _____

From: _____

Message: _____

_____

A Valentine for You

Be Mine!

Colored Treats

Here is a box of candy conversation hearts.
Follow the directions below to color each heart.

If the heart has no words, color it light green.

If the heart has 3 letters or less, color it orange.

If the candy has 4 or 5 letters in one word, color it pink.

If it has 5 or 6 letters in two words, color it yellow.

If the heart has 7 or more letters, color it white.

Design another candy for each color. Draw the new hearts on the back.

184   **by Ann Richmond Fisher**

Meet the PRESIDENTS Matchup

Help your students learn interesting facts about Presidents Washington and Lincoln as they play this game. Make two copies of the cards below and on page 186. Cut out the cards. (You may want to cover them with clear adhesive plastic first to make them more durable.) Mix up the cards and place them on a table facedown. Let children take turns turning over a card, then trying to turn over the matching card. When a match is made, the child keeps the two cards. The winner is the child with the most cards when the game is over.

After the game, ask questions about Washington and Lincoln to review what the children have learned.

first President

called "Father of His Country"

a general in the Revolutionary War

grew up in a wealthy home

refused to become "king" of America

called "Honest Abe"

sixteenth President

President during the Civil War

grew up in a poor home

was shot and killed while President

Holiday newsletter

"Mom, Dad, I'm home!" Are you searching for projects to occupy your child's time during the holiday break? Try some of these ideas for learning fun, activities you and your child can enjoy together. Use them as a springboard for creating some of your own.

Simple Science

Turn your Christmas tree into a science exploration by trimming a sample from the tree trunk. If you do not celebrate Christmas or you use an artificial tree, ask a friend or neighbor to save a sample for you. Examine the trunk stub with your child. Count the rings and determine the age of the tree. Note the texture of the bark and how it looks under a magnifying glass. Take the trunk outside and compare the bark with other trees you may have in your yard or in a nearby park. For special fun when you come back, use a paintbrush to paint a section of the bark, then press the painted section onto a piece of paper to make bark prints. Bark-print paper can be turned into holiday cards and wrapping paper.

On the Move

Looking for a quiet way to entertain the children at the next holiday gathering? How about some simple, silent games? For the first game, divide the players into two teams. Choose a sport or outdoor game, such as catch, tug-of-war, or weight lifting, then let the players perform the sport/game with imaginary equipment. It's a wonderful way of encouraging everyone to work together and to think about how they are moving. A second imaginary game can be played on a more individual basis. Like charades, the players take turns acting out an activity, such as jumping rope, swimming, riding a bicycle, or golfing. The remaining players try to name the activity. Invite the adults to join in the games and make it a time of real family fun.

by Marie E. Cecchini

Poetry in Motion

Although we tend to think more about performing good deeds for others during the holidays, it could become a healthy habit throughout the year. Help your child develop this healthy habit now. Begin a collective paper chain that can be added to day by day, link by link, detailing good deeds performed. Place the following rhyme at the beginning of the chain, then have your child write the good deed for the day on a strip of paper. Slide each strip through the previous loop, shape it into a ring, and use tape to secure.

Chain of Good Deeds

My chain of good deeds
Grows longer each day,
As I help others
Along the way.

Mathworks

Whether your child needs to purchase gifts or supplies to make them, now is a great time to begin to learn the value of a dollar. Let your child make a list of gifts/supplies needed, then together estimate the cost per person. Have your child determine the total amount needed for the purchases. As an alternative, you might match the dollar amount your child has saved from allowance for gifts, then help your child to determine the amount available to spend on each person.

The Reading Room

Teach your child to be a careful listener. Ask questions as you read and reread stories. Here are a few reading suggestions.

Country Angel Christmas by Tomie dePaola, G.P. Putnam's Sons, 1995.

The Little Drummer Boy by Ezra Jack Keats, Aladdin Paperbacks, 1987.

The Magic Dreidels: A Hanukkah Story by Eric A. Kimmel, Holiday House, 1997.

Over the River and Through the Wood by Lydia Marie Child, Henry Holt & Co., 1996.

The Story of Kwanzaa by Safisha Madhubuti, Third World Press, 1989.

Communication Station

Meaningful communication among family members has become increasingly more difficult as additional activities and obligations rob us of together time. Overcoming this hurdle requires a bit of creativity. One idea would be to have each family member design a personal mailbox. A simple one can be made by removing the top portion from a cereal box, covering the box with paper, and decorating it with markers, stickers, and so on. Next, poke a hole at the top of each side panel, thread yarn through the holes, then knot the yarn ends together. Each person can hang the mailbox on his or her bedroom doorknob. Then, whenever someone has something to tell, an invitation to extend, a question to ask, or an apology to offer, it can be written and placed in the correct mailbox. This is a great way to interest children in using their language skills, as well as improving overall family communication.

Holiday newsletter

When winter weather is too cold, icy, or rainy for outdoor play,
keep your child busy indoors with activities that put creativity to work.

Simple Science

Ring in the New Year with a mobile project you can use to prove a scientific principle. First, have your child draw or trace then cut out the numerals in the year from colorful paper. Cut four lengths of yarn and tape one end of each length to the top of a numeral. Set these aside. Next, cut a strip of cardboard, bend it into a ring, then staple it together. Cut three lengths of yarn and tape one end of each to the ring, spacing evenly. Gather the opposite ends of the yarn together and knot them into a loop for hanging. Now tape the yarn lengths of the numerals around the ring, spacing evenly. Cut and decorate a paper strip to fit around the ring. Tape or glue this in place. Suspend the New Year mobile above your hot air heating unit (no flames, please) and observe what takes place. When the heat is on, the mobile moves. What does this demonstrate? Warm air rises because it is lighter than cold air. Happy New Year.

On the Move

Games and activities reinforce a child's physical skills and coordination. Although these types of activities generally require adequate play space, many can still work indoors. Bowling is one such activity. Empty plastic soda bottles, cans, or milk cartons can serve as "pins" and any ball will work. Why not set up a Valentine Bowl-a-Thon for the family or a group of friends? Have your child draw and cut several paper hearts; then write a different numeral on each. Tape one heart at the top of each bottle, then set up the pins. Each player takes one roll at a time, then adds up the numbers on the fallen bottles. The person with the highest total after 10 rolls is the top bowler.

Creative Kitchen

Warm up your kitchen this February with a quick and delicious cobbler in observance of National Cherry Month.

Quick Cherry Cobbler

Combine one 21 oz. can cherry pie filling with 2 tsp. lemon juice in a small bowl. Pour into an 8" square baking dish and spread evenly. Mix 1 c. biscuit mix with 1/4 c. butter or margarine in a separate bowl, then add 3 T. boiling water and stir until a dough forms. Spoon dough over cherries. Combine 1/4 c. granulated sugar with 1 tsp. each of cinnamon and nutmeg. Sprinkle this over the dough. Bake 25 to 30 minutes at 400°F until golden brown. Top dessert with softened vanilla ice cream for a special treat.

by Marie E. Cecchini

Communication Station

The start of a new calendar year is the perfect time to encourage your child to develop organizational skills which are essential for success in school and life. Begin by providing a calendar with blocks large enough to write in. Have or help your child add all family and friends' birthdays, as well as any upcoming special events. You can also help your child fill out a personal address book listing names, addresses, and phone numbers of relatives and close friends. This is a great way to practice making use of alphabetical order, and your child will learn how to use the telephone book as you search for information. Finally, your child can set up a personal filing system in a box or drawer. Provide folders for your child to label such items as schoolwork, correspondence, photos, or creative writing endeavors. As your child uses the filing system, calendar, and address book, the value of organization will become self-evident.

Poetry in Motion

A New Year's resolution is a promise we make to ourselves in the hopes of improving some aspect of our life or behavior in the upcoming year. Talk with your child about why living up to our resolutions is sometimes a difficult task; then try the following song with the whole family.

Promises to Keep

To the tune of
"Did You Ever See a Lassie?"
I will make a resolution,
Resolution, resolution.
I will make a resolution
To do something new.

Let each family member have the opportunity to promise one resolution. Afterward, have everyone write their resolutions. Encourage family members to help each other keep these resolutions through the year.

Mathworks

Another way to celebrate Presidents' Day is to help your child begin a savings program. Create easy coin banks by cutting paper to fit around two empty plastic frosting containers. Have your child place one sheet of paper over a quarter, then rub over the quarter with the side of a crayon, creating a coin imprint. Do this several times to decorate the paper. Make a similar paper using a penny, then tape each paper around a plastic container. Cut a slot in each container lid for depositing coins. Can your child name the person depicted on each coin? Does your child know the value of each coin? Have your child fill the containers with excess change; then help to count and roll the coins. Open a savings account with this money.

The Reading Room

Set aside a special time and place each day to share a book or two with your child. Here are a few for both of you to enjoy.

Dumpling Soup by Jama Kim Rattigan, Little Brown, 1998.

The Hat by Jan Brett, Putman Publishing Group, 1997.

One-Hour Nature Crafts by Janelle Hayes and Kim Solga, Publications International, Ltd.

The Paper Dragon by Marguerite W. Davol, Atheneum, 1997.

Riddle-icious by J. Patrick Lewis, Knopf, 1996.

When I Was Five by Arthur Howard, Harcourt Brace, 1996.

Cooking with Kids

Create a few of these holiday snacks and help your children begin to understand the meaning behind the celebration.

Pancake Roll-Ups

February—National Pancake Week

Ingredients
"complete" pancake mix
cream cheese, softened
variety of fresh fruits—berries, bananas, melons, etc.

Prepare pancakes as directed on package. Have children slice and dice the fresh fruits as desired, and place them in separate serving bowls with individual serving spoons. Let children spread cream cheese over their pancakes, add fresh fruit pieces, then roll them up and eat.

Kwanzaa Fruit Shapes

Ingredients
4 4oz. pkgs. fruit-flavored gelatin
2$\frac{1}{2}$ c. boiling water
fruit chunks and slices

Combine gelatin and boiling water in a mixing bowl. Stir to completely dissolve gelatin, then pour into a 9" x 13" oblong baking dish. Allow gelatin to stand for about 30 minutes, until it begins to thicken. Then place fruit chunks and slices throughout pan. Refrigerate until firm, then cut into shapes with cookie cutters.

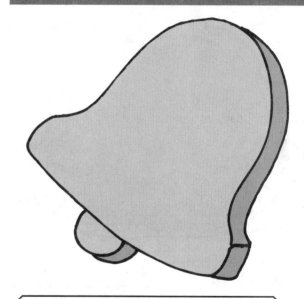

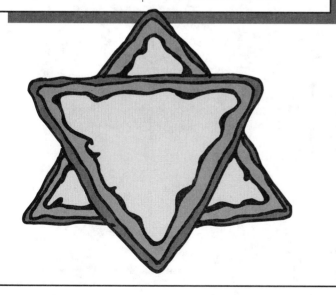

Star of David Sandwich

Ingredients
bread slices   mayonnaise
hard-boiled eggs   grated cheddar cheese

Peel and chop the eggs. Combine the eggs with a small amount of mayonnaise and set aside. Toast the bread slices and cut them into triangles. Spread egg mixture over two triangles. Set one egg triangle over the other, egg sides up, to form a six-pointed star. Sprinkle cheddar cheese over the star.

by Marie E. Cecchini   **191**

Edible Angel

Ingredients

bread slices   pretzel rings
cheese slices   golden raisins
cream cheese   cucumber slices

Toast the bread slices and cut into triangles. Top one triangle with a cheese triangle and set on a plate for the body. Spread cream cheese over two additional triangles and set at the top point of the body for wings. Place a cucumber slice above the wings for a head. Add a pretzel ring above the head as a halo. Set raisin feet below the cheese body.

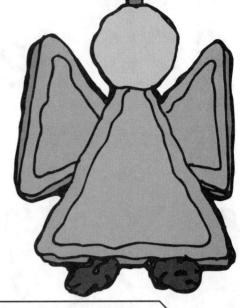

Candle Sundae

Ingredients

ice cream   maraschino cherries
bananas   flaked coconut
whipped cream   green food coloring

Tint coconut with green food coloring. Sprinkle green coconut over a plate. Top with a scoop of ice cream. Use a craft stick to form a hole in the center of the ice cream. Insert half a banana, flat side down, into the hole. Spoon a small amount of whipped cream on the top of the banana and top with a cherry.

Spicy Rice

Ingredients

6 c. uncooked rice   4 tsp. onion powder
1/2 c. parsley flakes   1 tsp. garlic powder
3/4 c. chicken bouillon   1/2 tsp. thyme powder

Combine all of the ingredients in a mixing bowl and mix well. Divide mixture by 1 cup measures and place into plastic bags. Twist-tie each bag and add directions for use. To use, put this rice mix into a saucepan. Add 2 c. water and 2 T. margarine, then bring to a boil. Reduce heat, cover, and simmer for about 15 minutes or until liquid is absorbed.

Clip Art for Winter Holidays

Happy New Year

Let It Snow!

Just a little reminder:

Presidents' Day

Clip Art for Winter Holidays

I Love This **Book!**

Please be a sweetheart! Look over these papers and sign below.

_____

Remember to bring your **valentines!**

_____
_____
_____
_____
_____

U R Nice

"Bee" Mine!

To My Valentine

Happy Valentine's Day!

This is a
cool book!

Please look
over these
cool papers.

Return by _____ Signed _____

_____
**is a
cool student!**

_____
teacher

_____
date

Winter Holiday Take-Home Notes

Reproduce the notes below on plain or colored paper. Cut out and send them home with your students to share your holiday lessons with parents and other family members.

Today we learned about Presidents' Day! Let me share with you what we learned.

We learned about Hanukkah today. Let me tell you about it!

I know how to celebrate Kwanzaa. Ask me to tell you about it!

Let me share with you what we learned about Christmas today!

by Veronica Terrill

It's a Spring Thing

"**Did** you see the first crocus push up through the snow?"
I asked my friend Sarah. But she didn't know.
"It's a Spring Thing," I said. "The flowers come out,
Yellow and purple. I just want to shout!
Spring has come back, without a doubt."
"It's a what?" asked Sarah, trying to figure it out.
"It's a Spring Thing," I told her and went on my way,
And ran into Miguel, who wanted to play.

"Did you see the snow melting and the icicles dripping?"
I questioned Miguel, who was too busy slipping.
"Melting and dripping. Yuck! Who would care?"
"It's a Spring Thing," I told him. "And we're almost there!"
"Where are we going?" Miguel called to me,
But I was off running and shouting in glee.
"It's a Spring Thing! A Spring Thing!" I called to the twins,
Marcus and Mary, who answered with grins.

"Are you singing?" they asked when I got close enough.
The twins stopped to chat, their arms full of stuff.
"It's a Spring Thing," I answered, not singing at all.
"And why are you carrying that old basketball?
It's time for softball, for tennis, or walking."
"Are you crazy?" Mary laughed. "It's too cold just for talking."
"But spring's on the way. I can hear the wind changing.
The sunshine is warmer. The Earth's rearranging."

I tried to convince them, but the twins kept on going.
They were all missing spring, though the season was showing.
Showing birds building nests, and trees getting green.
Grass peeking out from where snow once had been seen.
Kids wearing jackets instead of their coats.
And ice skates replaced with small sailing boats.

"It's a Spring Thing," I told my best friend, Marie.
Though she only smiled and said, "I can see."
How could they miss it? The coming of spring.
The Earth's most exciting, refreshing new thing.
New every year, fresh every day,
More lovely and interesting than anyone could say.
And then I saw them, in a pet store display.
Creatures who knew just what to say.

A chick and a bunny, soft and still.
But welcoming springtime in that windowsill.
"It's a Spring Thing," I whispered, and I know that they heard,
Though the bunny nor chick uttered a word.
"Let them all miss it," the pets seemed to say.
"But we'll all celebrate this marvelous day."

So if you get too busy to welcome the spring,
Just remember this wonderful thing.
Spring will keep coming, warmed by the sun.
And it's better to be here, to join in the fun.
It's a Spring Thing, I tell you. Don't let it go by.
Plant a flower or bush or let a kite fly.
Take off your mittens and play in the sand.
For spring is a blessing, a joy in your hand.

by Dr. Linda Karges-Bone

201

Enrichment Activities

Language Arts

 Practice phonics skills by creating a "Garden of Word Families." Using the flower pattern provided, help the children write or dictate "rhyming words" on each petal of the flower. Use patterns started in the story—for example *fun, sun.*

Continue to work on phonetic blends by using the flower pattern to identify initial blends: *fl, pl, bl, cr.* Write the blends that you find in the story on cut-out flower petals.

 Reinforce auditory memory and auditory discrimination by "listening" for specific words in the story-poem. Give each child a bell or tambourine and ask them to respond musically when they hear a specific word, such as *spring.*

Use a story chart to continue the discussion about "Signs of Spring." Ask children to describe springtime in their own words and write their responses on the chart. This activity strengthens expressive language.

Write and illustrate "Welcome Spring" postcards to be sent to shut-ins or nursing home residents. This is a good opportunity to practice penmanship.

Flower Pattern

Counting and Problem Solving

Use the flower pattern to practice counting ordinal numbers. This can be done in a center by laminating the flowers so that they can be written on with a marker. In the center of each flower, write a number between 0 and 9. Then instruct the children to write the numbers that come next, in order, on the petals. If a "4" was in the center, the next numbers would be 5, 6, 7, 8, and 9.

Collect empty or new packets of flower and vegetable seeds for sorting and patterning. Place the packets in an old watering can for fun and help the children distinguish the packets by color, shape, and other attributes. For example: "Sort out the packets that show flowers that look tall and thin when they bloom."

Practice using the calendar to mark time. Count the days in March. Mark the days that the children are in school with a flower or a sticker. Count those days separately. Look ahead to April. Is it a longer month or a shorter month? How can you tell? Continue with questions that require the children to use the calendar to find the answers.

Make a flower graph. Use the seed packets again, but this time, select three "favorite" flowers. Place these packets at the top of a large sheet of paper or use an old plastic shower curtain. Have the children "vote" for their favorite spring flower and record their choice. You can use washable markers on the shower curtain or stickers on the paper to let children mark their selections. Count and graph the results.

TLC10198 Copyright © Teaching & Learning Company, Carthage, IL 62321-0010

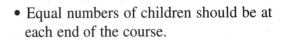

Creative Arts and Music

 Sing the song "A Tisket, a Tasket" and play the game in a new way by dropping a silk flower instead of a handkerchief. Make sure that every child has the opportunity to be chosen. Pair wheelchair-bound youngsters with a partner so that they can participate.

Pair a gross motor activity with music for a sure hit. Use a large plastic beach ball and several deep plastic laundry baskets to play a springtime game called Musical Baskets.

- Place three baskets in an obstacle course setting, a few feet apart.

- When the music starts, a child skips, runs, or walks to each basket and drops the ball in, then takes it out and proceeds to the next basket. (A nice choice for music is a CD or tape of piano favorites by Vivaldi or Schubert. Very "springy.")

- At the end of the course, a partner waits. He or she retrieves the ball and starts back through the course.

- Equal numbers of children should be at each end of the course.

- When the music stops, the child holding the ball must sit in the basket and hold the ball until the music starts again.

This a great "first day outdoors" activity for spring, because the children are moving all the time.

Combine fine motor skills with the creative arts by making mosaic flowers. Use the same flower pattern on page 11, but this time let the children tear, cut, or roll colored tissue paper and glue it onto the pattern to make a three-dimensional flower. Use potpourri-scented spray to "scent" your creations.

Create a "Welcome Spring" banner or flag for your classroom by using an old bedsheet and fabric pens. After reading the story-poem, encourage children to draw their impressions of "It's a Spring Thing" on the cloth and then display it as a welcome to your classroom.

Spring and Summer

Let the great outdoors bring you and your students to their senses in your outdoor Kid Space. Develop a patience to observe and a willingness to learn by tapping into a child's sense of wonder in the outdoors. Look, ask questions, get your boots and hands dirty, and have fun!

Chart the Flowers

April showers bring May flowers—but in what order?

Directions

1. Have children observe and record the flowers they see in bloom. Have each child make a drawing of the flower spotted, along with the date of the sighting and the child's own name. If the flower can be identified by the child, include the name of the flower as well.

2. Provide a spot on a bulletin board, wall, or chalkboard to display the record of flower sightings. Provide some flower identification keys and books for those who care to search for their flowers. Keep the emphasis on spotting and describing the flowers, rather than the actual naming of the plants.

3. Create a chart to illustrate the flower sightings in the order that they occur. Record the sightings in order throughout the spring and summer.

- Use this chart to talk about ordinance.
- Encourage children to compare the various flowers. What differences are noted between the springtime and summer flowers?

May Day Flower Festival

Don't let this wonderful spring holiday pass without a celebration!

- Invite students to bring in flowers to decorate your classroom.
- Scatter wildflower seeds in an outdoor space that will blossom into color.
- Take a flower hike—search for flowers, identify flowers, smell flowers.
- Sketch a flower.

by Robynne Eagan

What Does a Flower Do?

Watch some flowers for a while. Do your students have any ideas about the job of the flower? Do they notice any activity on and around the flower? Flowers are important in helping a plant reproduce. The flowers attract birds, animals, and insects to a plant to help with pollination. Colors and scents of a flower are signals to pollinators that the flower has nectar to offer. In return for nectar, the visiting insect pollinates the flower.

Landing Pads

Flowers and leaves are the landing pads for the insects and birds. Just watch! Flat-topped flowers and leaves attract large flying insects while upside-down hanging flowers attract tiny hummingbirds. The shape of a flower will usually tell you what kind of pollinator is likely to visit.

Open, Sesame

Some flowers are very choosy and want only particular pollens. These flowers have a special way of ensuring that only insects carrying the pollen they want can pollinate their plants. These flowers will only open when an insect is heavy enough to trigger the flower to open. Take a look at a snapdragon, a lupine, or the flower of a pea plant. Can you get the flower to open for you?

Bright and Beautiful

Flowers are not colorful just for us to enjoy—those beautiful colors help to attract pollinators to the plant. The color is caused by pigments that are part of a flower's cells. The colors let a pollinator know that the flower has nectar to offer. Flowers with bright colors attract insects with good eyesight—like bees. Different insects are attracted to different colors. Butterflies and hummingbirds can see red and are attracted to red colors. Can you find out what colors attract various kinds of pollinators?

"Scent"sational

Most flowers attract pollinators with their colorful flowers, but not all pollinators have good eyesight. Flowers need another way to attract visitors. Can you guess what that might be? Flowers attract some pollinators with their sweet or foul-smelling scent. Investigate the flowers that you have found.

Turn Toward the Sun

Is it true that flowers turn their faces toward the sun? Investigate and find out! If you are lucky enough to have a field of sunflowers nearby, be sure to visit and watch the flowers' motion throughout the day.

Thoughts to gROW On

Many of us include seed planting in our springtime lesson plans. There are so many lessons to be learned from seeds, why stop there? This year also include music, math, and art activities, and watch the interest grow!

Where Do Seeds Come From?

Seeds come from little paper envelopes in the store, right? Many children do not realize that plants are "mothers," producing seeds for many baby plants.

A springtime field walk can yield a variety of weed, flower, fruit, and tree seeds. Look for dandelions, winter pansies, and strawberries. Supplement these with fruits, nuts, vegetables, and seeds from your store. Examine each item, discovering how many seeds are in each one. Make a graph of your results. Why does each plant produce so many seeds?

Grow with Love

What do seeds need to grow? Ask for ideas, then set up several experiments. Place seeds between paper towels in clear plastic cups. Grow seeds . . .

> in sun with no water.
> with water and no sun.
> with water and sun.
> under water with sun.

After seeds sprout, ask students to notice which experiments had seeds that sprouted. What conditions do they think are necessary to keep the seeds growing? Continue growing the plants under the original conditions. What happens? (Remember that seeds may sprout in the dark, but how long can they live without light?) Help children draw a conclusion: What do plants need to grow?

Give each child a copy of a chart that lists each type of experiment your class is doing. Under each experiment, show a picture of a sprouting and a non-sprouting seed. Have students record their original hypotheses by circling either the sprouting or the non-sprouting seed in each category. Have students record the final outcomes by drawing a picture of each plant that grew in the appropriate category.

Extension: Discuss what children need to grow. Do children need the same things that plants need? Draw pictures to illustrate what children need to grow. Your students may be interested to learn that babies grow better with hugs, and plants grow better with kind words and classical music!

by Gloria Trabacca

Seed Sorting

How many ways can you sort seeds? By size? Shape? Color? Provide empty egg cartons and an assortment of seeds. Remember that dry beans, peas, lentils, popcorn, and birdseed are all inexpensive sources for seeds. For extra fun, include some colored popcorn kernels!

Planting Song
To the tune of "Twinkle, Twinkle, Little Star"

Planting seeds into the ground,
Here they grow, see what we've found:
Some grow flowers tall and round;
Some grow veggies underground.
Thanks to just a little seed,
We grow many things we need.

This can easily be sung with actions: 1) act out planting seeds; 2) fingers around eyes, binocular style; 3) act out flowers growing up; 4) act out veggies growing down, underground; 5) bow, or do thank you gesture; 6) arms moving away from body, outward, palms facing up, indicating many things around us.

Growing Needs Collages

Discuss what kinds of things come from seeds and the plants that grow from them. Remember to include foods, wood, paper, furniture, clothing (cotton, flax, rayon, linen), dyes, beauty (from flowers and trees), and more trees (which attract rain and clean air).

Have children use old magazines to make individual or group collages, showing useful things that come from plants. Learn the "Planting Song."

Above and Below

Some plants bear foods that grow above the ground, others bear food underground. Discuss which foods grow up or down. Sing "Someone Has a Little Seed." Insert each child's name and allow them to choose what grew. How will they use it? Finish each verse with either "underground" or "above the ground," depending on the chosen plant. Students can act out planting the seed, above or underground; reaching for the sky to indicate above ground, and crouching, ducking head under arms, to indicate below ground.

Someone Has a Little Seed
To the tune of "Mary Had a Little Lamb"

_____ (child's name) had a little
   seed,
   little seed,
   little seed,
_____ had a little seed, (s)he
   planted in the ground.

It grew something that (s)he needs,
   that (s)he needs,
   that (s)he needs,
It grew something that (s)he needs,
a _____ under/above ground.

"Scent"sational SPRINGTIME
Curriculum

Medical researchers now report that the scent of vanilla wafted through the air or the smell of freshly crushed cucumber applied to the body can help patients undergoing an MRI scan (magnetic resonance imaging) to relax, even when they suffer from panic or anxiety. As teachers who have spent the fall and winter seasons largely cooped up indoors with restless youngsters, there is an application here. We, too, are challenged with directing energy and focusing attention in our closed classrooms and with children who may not always want to cooperate. The season of spring is our last "hurrah" in the curriculum. Standardized testing looms close ahead. Teachers need a lift themselves. Scent can help us to accomplish our goals. We can use scent in many, varied, creative ways to stimulate thinking, creativity, and reflection in our springtime curriculum.

by Dr. Linda Karges-Bone

What Scents Can Do

The brain processes scent and other stimuli *first* thought the limbic center. Interestingly, this center is also home to emotions and feelings. If teachers can pair a scent with a feeling, there is the opportunity to make learning easier and more intense. In my book, *Beyond Hands-On,* available from the Teaching & Learning Company, the science and application of scent and the brain is more fully discussed. However, in the springtime curriculum, there are many natural ways to use scent to enhance learning.

With Testing

Does testing carry a big stick in your school? Few can deny it. Tests and the issue of accountability are critical issues for the public and for teachers. Although the year of instruction preceding the test is most important, there are some simple techniques that teachers can use to help students be more alert and attentive during these lengthy, tiresome examinations.

Peppermint on the Brain

The scent and taste of peppermint, spearmint, or wintergreen can help learners to be more attentive. It is best if one offers the mints both during the review sessions and during the test. One teacher took my advice last spring. She offers this anecdotal report:

My principal called me into her office in late May. She wanted to know what I had done with my class, since the group scored an average of 12 points higher than the other fourth grade classes in our school (10 classes). I told her about the peppermints. This year, everybody will be using the mints!

Flower Power

The scent of rose and lavender help children to relax and reflect. This is a wonderful opportunity to do some springtime poetry. Children need lots of modeling to feel comfortable with poetry, so start by offering a bar of rose-scented or lavender soap for the children to wash their hands with, then go outside for a poetry reading. Create original verses about spring. Start by simply having the children write the word *SPRING* and then offering adjectives that describe the season. Here's an example.

S *Spring*
P *Pretty*
R *Rose-scented*
I *Interesting*
N *New*
G *Green*

Observation Opportunities

One of the six science process skills is observation, and it is critical. However, observation is a skill that must be practiced and developed over time. Use the scents of springtime to help shape observational skills. Try having a scent scavenger hunt. Pair children and offer them brown lunch bags (for collecting) and a checklist of "scents." Create a class chart to list the data (another process skill) and discuss your findings.

Scavenger Hunt Checklist

_____ Something fresh and green-smelling   _____ Something sweet and floral-smelling

_____ Something warm and sunny-smelling   _____ Something dark and earthy-smelling

---

Create Your Own Lesson

Use the "Scent"sational Learning Chart below to help you create a unique springtime lesson. Are you reviewing material for a test? Use a scent for alertness. Are you writing or drawing? Go for a creative scent. Do you want the children to relax and listen quietly? Select a reflective scent. Scents deliver messages right along with the content and curriculum. Don't overlook an important opportunity to make your springtime classroom absolutely "scent"sational.

Outcomes		
Alertness or Attention	**Relaxation or Reflection**	**Creativity**
peppermint	chamomile	sage
wintergreen	jasmine	apple
pine	lavender	rosemary
lemon	sandalwood	rose
eucalyptus	marjoram	basil
spearmint	honeysuckle	cinnamon

Spring 'n' Flowers

Classroom life just got easier with this exciting bulletin board idea that is set up to last the next two months with student-generated work.

Materials
construction paper
pipe cleaners
large and small buttons
scissors
flower pattern

On the first day of school, leave one bulletin board empty for students. Use a long piece of white paper to write the slogan, *Spring 'n' Flowers*. Ask students to use the pattern to trace and cut out flowers from pink, blue, yellow, red, and brown construction paper. On the flower petals, ask students to write their favorite colors, favorite subjects, favorite sports or hobbies, favorite books, favorite foods, and favorite television shows. Have students bring in small photographs of themselves for the centers of the flowers.

For the next month, have students take their flowers home. Re-create flowers again, using elements of a book report as a theme. Ask students to choose books to read. Enlarge and cut out the reproducible and make flowers again. Have each student draw an important scene from the book in the flower's center. On each petal, write the title, the author, the setting, main characters, theme or main idea, and book recommendation.

For additional flower decorations, use the reproducible and cut-out flowers in the same way. Choose a button for the center of each flower. Poke the pipe cleaner through the flower, through one button-hole, and down into the next hole. Twist the end of the pipe cleaner. Decorate the bottom border of the bulletin board with these flowers.

by Donna Clovis

WATERMELON
Teaching Tool
You will "seed" the results!

Paper Plate Watermelon

Materials
- one paper plate per child
- pink, green, and black tempera paint
- scissors

Paint the outside edge of the paper plate green for the rind. Paint the inside of the plate pink. When dry, make the seeds using black paint. For small children, you may have to make a cardboard stencil to paint on the seeds. Cut the watermelon in halves or fourths to teach simple fractions.

Watermelon Seed Art

Materials
- paper
- glue
- lots of watermelon seeds

Let the students' imaginations go wild on this project. Have the children design their own seed people, animals, flowers, and strange creatures. Work in small groups to add cooperation to this lesson.

Watermelon Rind Printing

Materials
- 5" square of watermelon rind
- semi-sharp knife to carve rind
- ink pad
- paper

Carve a design in the watermelon rind using a knife. You may also use the handle end of a spoon as a carving tool. Teach older students to use reverse printing for letters and numbers. Press the carved rind on the ink pad. Stamp the design on paper. Try making wrapping paper, stationery, or greeting cards.

Curly and the Wild Boar
by Fred Gibson, Harper & Row Publishers, 1979

Read the story *Curly and the Wild Boar* to the class. Then have students develop their own adventure story about a watermelon. An adaptation would be to tell the story into a tape recorder and illustrate. The new talking books would make a great addition to your class library.

Watermelon Flags

Materials
- lots of watermelon seeds
- white paper 8$\frac{1}{2}$" x 11"
- blue tempera paint
- red tempera paint

Cut the white paper into the shape of a watermelon. Make a flag design on the paper with a pencil. Draw stars in the upper left corner and stripes going horizontally across the watermelon shape. Paint some of the seeds red and the others blue. Glue the blue seeds on the watermelon flag for stars and the red ones across the flag to make the stripes. Leave the white stripes blank. Hang these on a bulletin board display with the caption *The USA is really "ripe" for me.*

Just for Fun

After the students have worked hard all day graphing, measuring, counting, and writing about watermelons, take them outdoors to enjoy a good old-fashioned seed-spitting contest. Measure the distance that the seeds travel. Award a certificate to the winner. This is an activity that won't be forgotten!

If you are fortunate enough to have access to a swimming pool, you can dazzle your students with a greased watermelon in the pool. What fun it is to try and hold on to a slippery watermelon. Enjoy eating the watermelon when the fun is over.

Watermelon soup can be enjoyed anytime by you and your students. Cut up chunks of watermelon in a big bowl. Smash with a cooking utensil until it becomes a liquid. Pour into cups and enjoy.

Watermelon People

Materials
- whole watermelon
- yarn, lace, old hats, shirts, and so on
- paper or paint for facial features

Dress the watermelon to look like a person. If you are fortunate enough to have more than one watermelon, turn the activity into a contest. Name each watermelon person, and write creative stories about the lives of the watermelon people. Stress the importance of who, what, where, when, and why.

Hard-Boiled Watermelon

Materials
- one hard-boiled egg per student
- green tempera paint
- black tempera paint
- paintbrushes

Ask each student to bring in a hard-boiled egg from home. Cover a table with newspaper. Place green paint, black paint, and paintbrushes on the table. Allow them to work at the table in groups, painting their eggs to look like watermelons. Put them all together to make a watermelon patch.

214

Watermelon Math Worksheet

Lesson 1 Instructions:

Fill out the estimation part of your worksheet. Look at the classroom watermelon and think carefully about your answers. After the estimations are complete, work through each question to determine the facts. Some of the facts will have to wait until the watermelon is cut.

	Estimations	**Facts**
1. How much does the watermelon weigh?	_____	_____
2. How long is the watermelon?	_____	_____
3. How many seeds are in the watermelon?	_____	_____
4. How many melons do you weigh?	_____	_____
5. How do you measure a round object?	_____	_____
6. What is the average number of seeds in a slice?	_____	_____
(Base your estimation as if each student had a slice of the watermelon.)		
7. What percentage of the melon do you actually eat?	_____	_____
8. How much will all the seeds weigh?	_____	_____

Lesson 2 Instructions:

1. Draw on the watermelon to show $1/2$, $1/4$, and so on.

2. Weigh each slice of the real melon your teacher has given you. (Don't eat it!) Add the totals. Do they weigh the same as the whole uncut melon? _____ Why? _____

3. What is the average weight of each slice? _____

4. Use the seeds as counters. Make up your own math problems. Your classmates will answer with the seeds on their desks. (20 - 7 = ___)

CORNER

CRAFT

How to Plant a Garden

A step-by-step visual guide to planting a garden

Materials

    sample "How to Plant a Garden" diagram
    11" x 14" (28 x 35 cm) legal-sized paper for each child
    garden magazines
    scissors
    glue
    brushes
    sand
    seeds
    glitter
    yellow and orange fabric paints
    markers, pencils, and crayons

Let's Make It

1. Set up a station that includes paper, scissors, magazines, glue, glitter and sand, paints, markers, pencils and crayons.

2. Talk with children about the steps involved in creating a garden. Show children the diagram that you created to show these steps. Your diagram should look something like this:

    soil + seeds + shovel/hoe/gardener + rain + sunshine = growing plants

3. Guide children through the center, allowing them the freedom to think and create their own diagrams to describe the gardening process.

Try This

Children can work with words or pictures to enhance their diagrams. Introduce words such as *labor, endurance, patience, seedlings, weeding,* and *harvest.*

Designer Seed Packages

Bring art and gardening together

Materials

    sample seed packages
    gardening catalogs
    4" x 5" (10 x 13 cm) paper (2 per student)
    drawing instruments

Let's Make It

1. Encourage children to look at various seed packages.

2. Have children design their own seed packages in rough draft before creating them on the seed package paper.

3. When both the front and back of the package have been designed, they can be pasted together with a flap at the top to create a seed package.

4. Display the packages on a bulletin board with a title that reads *The _____ Seed Company.*

by Robynne Eagan

My Dad Is a "Reel" Catch!

Materials

    6-12" (15-30 cm) stick or dowel
    6-12" (15-30 cm) length of string or heavy gauge fishing line
    round ring
    paper clip
    tagboard
    fine-tipped markers or colored pencils
    sandpaper
    odorless varnish or shellac
    paintbrush

Let's Make It

1. Have children find their own "fishing poles"—lengths of stick or dowel. Children can strip the bark from their sticks and use sandpaper to make them smooth.
2. With adult assistance, children can paint varnish on their poles in an outdoor area. Be sure to use varnish only with supervision, in an outdoor area. Children should leave the area as soon as they complete their task. Leave the poles to dry thoroughly.
3. Have each child measure and cut a length of fishing line. Tie one end of the line to the pole. A dab of glue can be used to keep the line firmly in place.
4. Attach a paper clip, ring, or similar fitting to the end of the line. This can be decorated to look like a fishing lure if desired.
5. Children can draw and cut fish from tagboard. Remember, fish come in all shapes and sizes!
6. Have children copy the following message on one side of their fish.

> Happy Father's Day, Daddy
> You're a reel catch!
> Love, _____

7. Have each child punch a hole near the fish mouth and attach a paper clip that can be hooked to the "fishing hook."

Mother's Day Painted Pots

Materials

    terra-cotta planting pots (any size)
    acrylic paints
    paintbrushes or sponges
    clear acrylic sealer
    card
    hole punch
    ribbon

Let's Make It

1. If using old pots, clean and dry them thoroughly before painting.
2. Have children paint the pots in their own creative way. Demonstrate various methods of painting. Paintbrushes can be used to paint dots, stripes, or other designs. Toothbrushes can be rubbed to create splatter designs. Sponge shapes might be dipped in paint to create prints. Small fingers and hands can be dipped in paint and pressed on the pot to make personal prints.
3. When the paint has dried, take the pots to an outdoor area, away from children, and spray with acrylic sealer. Allow to dry thoroughly.
4. Have children fill pots with flower seeds or flowering plants.
5. Each child can decorate a card and then punch a hole in it. Ribbon can be threaded through the hole and tied around the pot. (Print this message on the card.)

> My mom is very special
> in so many ways.
> My love for her is like this plant—
> it grows every day.
>
> Love, _____

Fireworks Extravaganza in a Bottle

Mark the Fourth of July or Canada Day with this celebration in a bottle!

Materials

    clear plastic bottle (water bottles work well)
    glitter
    colored beads
    food coloring (one color per bottle)
    pouring instruments (cup with spout or funnel)
    eyedropper

Let's Make It

1. Have children fill the water bottles about three-fourths full of water.
2. Use the eyedropper to add the coloring in each bottle.
3. Add glitter of all shapes and sizes for a dazzling effect.
4. Add colorful beads for sound and more whirling colors.
5. When complete, the lid should be tightly sealed.
6. Shake the bottle for an instant celebration!

May Day Flower Seeds

What's inside that little seed?

Materials

    packages of flower seeds
    paste
    fine-tipped markers or colored pencils
    tagboard

Let's Make It

1. Have children pour the seeds from the packages and paste them to the center of the tagboard.
2. Display the seed packages for children to see. Have children draw the flowers that will grow from the seeds in the space around the seeds.
3. Repeat the process with several types of flower seeds.
4. Label and display the finished projects.

Try This

- Consider using these flowers: pansies, impatiens, bellflowers, poppies, coneflowers, zinnias, delphiniums, cosmos, petunias.
- Try the project using vegetable or tree seeds.

Magical Fireworks in the Night

Materials

    8 1/2" x 11" (22 x 28 cm) white paper
    vibrant crayon colors
    one black crayon for each student
    pen with cap, end of paintbrush, or other pointy instrument

Let's Make It

1. Have students color over the entire surface of their paper. Colored area may be drawings, scribbles, or abstract pictures, as long as the entire surface is colored with crayon. No white spots allowed!
2. When the page is completely colored, children will cover the entire colorful surface with black crayon. They will turn their pages into night. Some children find this a very difficult task!
3. Now children will create fireworks in their night sky! Have children scratch away some of the black crayon with the pointy instrument. This will reveal the hidden color beneath.
4. Create a Fourth of July or Canada Day display board. Make a black background. Add the children's artwork and then decorate the border of your display board with national flags.

Blooming Math Trees

Spring is in bloom and so is your classroom as your students make math trees that not only look fresh and bright but also teach kids about equivalent equations.

First begin with a quick 10-minute warm-up lesson to review the terms *equivalent* and *equation.* Ask your students to think of all the possible combinations to reach the sum or difference of. For example, 8 + 4 = 12, but so does 6 + 6 and 14 - 2 and 2 + 2 + 3 + 5. On poster paper or the chalkboard, chart all the possible combinations that the children give you and then explain that they have just given you many "equivalent equations."

Now that the children realize they can use the four major operations and any combinations of them, they should be quite eager to go on and on to find as many equivalents as they can. But tell your students that instead of just writing these equations down on paper, you would like them to grow a beautiful spring garden and forest of equivalents right in the classroom!

You may want your students to work in pairs or groups for this activity, or they could work independently.

First give each child or group of children a tree trunk with a number in the middle of it. For younger children, the numbers can range from 4-10, and for older children the numbers can be as high as is appropriate for their age and ability.

Explain that they will receive cut-outs of leaves or bright-colored blossoms, and on each leaf or blossom they are to write one equation that will equal the number on their tree trunk. The object, of course, is to have the children think of as many equations or different ways to arrive at their given number as they can.

When the students have made at least 10 different equation leaves or blossoms, the trunks can be displayed on a bulletin board or wall, and then the children can paste or tape on the appropriate "foliage."

Some or all of the children can be "checkers" who make sure each tree's leaf and blossom equations are accurate.

That is all there is to blooming math. The only problem you may have is getting your students to stop growing equations. There always seems to be just one more!

by Joanne Coughlin

Here are some leaf, blossom, and tree trunk patterns to use in your classroom.

Springtime on the Farm

Many baby animals were born on Grandpa Walker's farm this spring—five lambs, four calves, and a colt. Mitzie, the mother cat, is hiding her new kittens. They are not in the shed, the garage, or under the back porch. You will know where she hid them when you finish the picture. Color the squares as follows.

1 =	Red
2 =	Black
3 =	Gray
4 =	Blue
5 =	Green

4	4	4	4	4	3	4	4	4	4	4	4	4	4	4	4	4	4	4	4	4	4	4	4	4	4	4	4	4	4
4	4	4	4	3	3	3	4	4	4	4	4	4	4	4	4	4	4	4	4	4	4	4	4	4	4	4	4	4	4
4	4	4	4	1	1	1	4	4	4	4	4	4	4	4	4	4	4	4	4	4	4	4	4	4	4	4	4	4	4
4	4	4	4	1	1	1	4	4	4	4	4	4	4	4	4	4	4	4	4	4	4	4	4	4	4	4	4	4	4
4	4	4	4	1	1	1	4	3	3	3	3	3	3	3	3	3	3	3	4	4	4	4	4	4	4	4	4	4	4
4	4	4	4	1	1	1	3	3	3	3	3	3	3	3	3	3	3	3	3	1	3	4	4	4	4	4	4	4	4
4	4	4	4	1	1	3	3	3	3	3	3	3	3	3	3	3	3	3	1	1	1	3	4	4	4	4	4	4	4
4	4	4	4	1	3	3	3	3	3	3	3	3	3	3	3	3	3	1	2	2	2	1	3	4	4	4	4	4	4
4	4	4	4	3	3	3	3	3	3	3	3	3	3	3	3	1	1	2	2	2	1	3	4	4	4	4	4	4	4
4	4	4	3	3	3	3	3	3	3	3	3	3	3	3	1	1	1	1	1	1	1	1	1	3	4	4	4	4	4
4	4	3	3	3	3	3	3	3	3	3	3	3	3	1	1	1	1	1	1	1	1	1	1	1	3	4	4	4	4
4	3	3	3	3	3	3	3	3	3	3	3	3	1	1	1	1	1	1	1	1	1	1	1	1	1	3	4	4	4
4	4	1	1	1	1	1	1	1	1	1	1	1	1	1	1	1	1	1	1	1	1	1	1	1	1	1	4	4	4
4	4	1	1	2	2	1	2	2	1	2	2	1	1	1	1	1	1	1	1	1	1	1	1	1	1	1	1	4	4
4	4	1	1	2	2	1	2	2	1	2	2	1	1	1	1	1	1	2	2	2	2	1	1	1	1	1	1	4	4
4	4	1	1	2	2	1	2	2	1	2	2	1	1	1	1	1	1	2	2	2	2	1	1	1	1	1	1	4	4
4	4	1	1	1	1	1	1	1	1	1	1	1	1	1	1	1	1	2	2	2	2	1	1	1	1	1	1	4	4
4	4	1	1	1	1	1	1	1	1	1	1	1	1	1	1	1	1	2	2	2	2	1	1	1	1	1	1	4	4
5	5	5	5	5	5	5	5	5	5	5	5	5	5	5	5	5	5	5	5	5	5	5	5	5	5	5	5	5	5

by Martha J. Morrison

Let It Rain, Let It Rain

Do you sometimes dread a rainy day? Well, don't! Here are dozens of ideas for rainy day learning experiences, and they are fun, too! After discussing rain, how it is formed, and what it is, try some of these rainy day activities and let it rain!

Science

Collect a newspaper, a piece of plastic, and a piece of fabric. Set them out in the rain. After a few minutes, inspect the three materials. Discuss the children's observations. Use the terms *absorb* and *repel*. Make a classroom list of materials that repel and those that absorb. If students are undecided about a material, test it in the rain.

Make three tight balls of newspaper. Place one in a department store paper bag, one in a gift bag, and one in a plastic grocery bag. Ask the students to predict which newspaper balls will stay dry. Set the bags outside on a rack for about 10 minutes. Check and discuss the results.

Fill two plastic cups—one with tap water and one with rainwater. Discuss visual observations. Smell the two cups and compare. Tap water may smell of chlorine. Add a few drops of each to slides and observe under a microscope.

Collect rainwater. Set out a plastic, paper, and foil or coated bag. Have students predict which will hold water. Add a cup of rainwater to each and observe. Do the experiment over a sink or tub.

Collect two flat pans of rainwater. Set one inside in a sunny window and the other outside in a protected area. Observe both containers of water for a week or two. Have students keep a daily log recording their observations. At the end of the observation period, read the logs. Look at a sampling of water from each container under a microscope to detect any living organisms. Compare the two slides.

Give each child a plastic or foam cup to set in an open area. After catching rain, have them taste the water and then each give one word telling how it tastes. Write the adjectives on a classroom chart. Discuss the fact that many people throughout the world depend on rainwater for some or all of their water needs such as drinking, bathing, and cooking.

by Jean Stangl

Math

Measure rainfall by placing three different containers in an open place. After a good rainfall, bring in the containers. Have children estimate which container has the most water in it. Pour the rainwater into three separate measuring cups to check their estimates. Discuss the results.

Empty the containers and set them out again. Place one in the open, one under a tree, and one under a drain spout. Have students predict which container will catch the most rain. Set a timer for 10 or 15 minutes and then check the containers. Discuss the results.

Which weighs the most—a cup of rainwater or a cup of milk? Add rainwater to one-third cup of powdered milk to make one cup of milk. Stir well. Measure one cup of rainwater. Have children make their decisions. Weigh the two on a balance scale.

Art

Give each student a piece of white construction paper. Sprinkle two or three colors of powdered paint on the paper. Have them take turns holding the paper just outside the door to catch raindrops. Look for similarities in their raindrop art patterns.

Collect and use rainwater to mix with powdered paint.

Freeze rainwater into ice cubes. Sprinkle powdered paint onto a piece of butcher paper and use the ice cubes to make rainy designs.

Motor Skills

Collect rainwater. Do this activity under a covered patio or cover the floor with a sheet of plastic. Set up an obstacle course using containers such as a round pan, flat pan, bucket, bottle, and cup. Add a small amount of rainwater to each. Give directions to small groups such as "jump over the round pan"; "hop around the bucket"; and "walk on tiptoes between the two cups."

Language/Writing

Have each child write a short paragraph telling why we need rain.

Share picture books about rain such as:
Where Does the Butterfly Go When It Rains? by Niki Weiss, Greenwillow, 1989.
Rain Makes Applesauce by Julian Scheer, Holiday, 1964.
Peter Spier's Rain by Peter Spier, Doubleday, 1982.
Rain! Rain! by Carol Greene, Children's Press, 1982.
Rainy Day Rhymes by Gail Radley, Houghton Mifflin, 1992.

Have students write down words that rhyme with *rain, drop,* and *wet.* Then have them write a rain poem. Share poems with the class.

After the rain, be sure to let your students check the sky for a rainbow!

Name _____

Spring Fun

Here's a game to play by yourself or with a group. Write a rhyming word in each blank. Color the page.

1. Winter snows are all now past.
   Hooray for spring! It's come at _____.

2. The world is full of daffodils
   That cover valleys, yards, and _____.

3. Men shed their winter coats and vests,
   While joyous songbirds build their _____.

4. Blossoms burst on apple trees,
   Attracting busy honey _____.

5. Lambs frolic in the fields new-green,
   Where colts and calves are also _____.

6. Sometimes it pours rain for hours,
   But "April showers bring May _____."

7. We wish that we weren't here in school,
   But could be swimming in some _____.

8. People order lots of seeds
   And hope their gardens won't grow _____.

9. Farmers work with plows and hoes.
   People dress in bright new _____.

10. Three cheers for bat and glove and ball—
    For spring's the grandest time of _____.

by Bonnie Compton Hanson

Seasonal Science

March can seem like the longest month of the year as we eagerly await the first signs of spring. Luckily, however, it is also Peanut Month, which will help dissolve the doldrums of classroom science activities. Peanuts are seeds, seeds that we eat, and are harvested from underground. Peanut vines are fascinating plants, and the children will be delighted as they dig into the soil to harvest their crop. Share the fun of learning about this unusual plant with the following activities and projects.

In the Beginning . . .

Activity

Have each child shell a peanut, peel off the red skin, then split it in half. Ask them to observe and describe what they find inside. They should find something that appears to be a tiny bump with little fingers. This is the embryo, or baby plant. The fingers are actually leaves, and the rest of the seed is actually food the plant will need to begin growing. Growth will not begin, however, until the seed is provided with water. Let children perform a simple experiment to demonstrate the effect water has on seeds. Place $1/4$ cup shelled, raw peanuts into a jar or small bowl. Pour $1/4$ cup water over the peanuts. Cover the jar or bowl (to prevent evaporation) and allow it to sit overnight. The following day, remove the peanuts and measure the remaining water. There should now be less than the original $1/4$ cup of water, as the seeds have already begun to absorb water in an effort to dissolve the stored food so the plant can begin to grow.

Project

Provide children with 3" x 12" strips of paper. Have them use rulers and pencils to measure and mark off four 3" sections across their strips. Beginning at the left-hand side, have them glue and label the parts of a peanut. Section one will be the shell, section two the skin, section three a shelled and peeled whole peanut, and section four will be both halves of a split peanut with the embryo and stored food labeled.

by Marie E. Cecchini

What Goes Down

Peanuts Need Food; Peanuts Are Food

Activity

Most children understand that plant roots are found underground. Some may even realize that gravity plays a part in the direction of root growth. You can demonstrate this using a self-sealing sandwich bag, a paper towel, and three or four peanuts. Fold the paper towel to fit into the bag, dampen it, then slide it into the bag. Place the peanut seeds on the paper towel and seal the bag. Hang the bag in a window or other warm place and wait for the seeds to sprout. Observe which way the roots are growing (down); then give the bag a quarter turn and rehang it. Wait two or three more days and observe the roots again. Keep giving the bag a quarter turn every two to three days and watch the roots create a design as they continue to react to the force of gravity.

Project

Provide children with paper, markers, glue, and peanuts in the shell. Have them draw pictures of a peanut plant, stem and leaves above ground and roots below on their papers. When the drawings are complete, let them glue real peanuts on their plant drawings below the soil surface.

Activity

Once again, observe the seeds that have sprouted. Note that the peanut halves have opened and turned green. These are the seed leaves. The baby plant is between them. Demonstrate the importance of seed leaves to the plant with a simple experiment. Choose two of the sprouted seeds to plant in soil in separate pots. Remove the seed leaves from one with scissors. Now, plant and water the seed sprouts. Observe the plants daily and note what happens. What happens to the seed leaves on the first seedling? What happens to the seedling with no seed leaves? New plants need the stored food in the seed leaves until they grow real leaves and can make their own food. As the plant uses the seed leaf food, the seed leaf shrivels, and eventually falls off the stem.

Project

Just as the peanut plant needs food to grow, the harvested peanuts become food for animals and people who need peanut protein to build body muscles. Have children compare creamy and chunky peanut butter. What senses can they use to help them explore the peanut butter? Next, let them make their own peanut butter by placing about 4 cups of peanuts, $1/2$ T. of vegetable oil, and a dash of salt into a blender or food processor. Grind/Blend until the mixture is smooth. Taste test all three peanut butters. Which do individual children prefer? Graph the results.

Cold Won't Grow

Activity

Demonstrate how temperature also affects seed growth. You will need two self-sealing plastic sandwich bags, paper towels, peanuts and water. Fold a paper towel to fit into a bag. Dampen the towel, slide it into the bag, and set three or four peanuts onto the wet towel. Prepare the second bag in the same manner. Set one bag in a warm place, such as a sunny windowsill, and the other in a refrigerator. Check both bags daily and note any changes that have taken place in the seeds. After about a week, note which seeds have sprouted and which have not. What conclusions can children draw from the results?

Project

Observe the sprouted seeds closely and name the plant parts. Have children fold a sheet of paper into quarters, and number the sections 1 through 4. Help them determine the four phases of plant growth (seed, roots, stem and leaves, peanuts); then have them draw, color, and label their own peanut sequence stories. Provide children with small containers, soil, and peanuts. Have them plant and water peanut seeds. When the seeds have sprouted, have children bring them home to report or plant outdoors. Peanuts can be harvested after about four months.

Peanut Plant

Peanut Butter Lovers' Day

March 1

Celebrate Peanut Butter Lovers' Day with our positively perfect peanut activities!

Who was America's greatest peanut expert? It was George Washington Carver, of course! This famous scientist found more than 300 uses for peanuts. Find out more about this amazing scientist and his many important discoveries by reading *A Pocketful of Goobers: A Story About George Washington Carver* by Barbara Mitchell (Carolrhoda Books, 1989).

by Mary Ellen Switzer

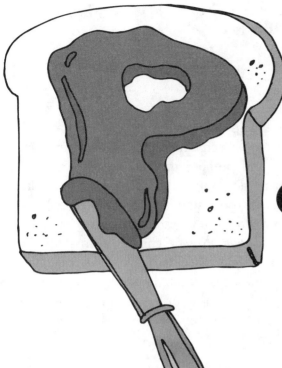

Be a Reporter

Extra! Extra! Read all about it! Have your students become reporters for the *Goober Gazette*. Ask them to write a newspaper article about a farmer who grows a giant-sized peanut.

Discuss the important elements of writing a news article. Tell them that a news article will answer the five Ws: Who? What? Where? When? and Why?

Explain that the most important ideas of the news story appear in the beginning of the article. Less important facts and details are reported later in the article.

Peanut Butter Jar Activities

March is Peanut Butter Lovers' Month. Celebrate this special month with the peanutty-est activities below.

1. You're the artist! Design a badge for Peanut Butter Lovers' Month.

2. Make a list of all the words you can think of using the letters in *peanut butter.*

3. Be an inventor! Design a new robot who can make a jar of peanut butter in just one minute. Draw a picture of your robot and label the parts.

4. Write an advertisement to tell the world about your amazing new robot.

5. Put wheels on a peanut and create The Great Peanut Racer. Draw a picture of your design.

6. Pretend you and your friends made the biggest peanut butter and jelly sandwich in the world. Who would eat your sandwich? Draw a picture of what it would look like.

7. Write an autobiography about Pauline Peanut.

8. It's story time! Write a story about the day all the peanuts turned purple.

Larry Legume's Story Starters

Calling all authors! Let's write a story about peanuts. Use the following story starters to help you with your story.

Abracadabra! I can't believe my eyes. The magician just changed me into a tiny peanut and . . .

It all happened when I was visiting the zoo. I was feeding an elephant some peanuts when suddenly . . .

As I rowed the boat ashore, I saw a sign that read: Welcome to Peanut Island.

Hello, my name is Patty Peanut—the world's first talking peanut! Being a peanut who can talk is very exciting. Let me tell you about my latest adventure.

Help! The Great Goober Cookie Company needs your help! The secret recipe for their prize-winning peanut butter cookies has disappeared. Write a story telling how you solved the mystery.

Lucky Pudding

Materials

measuring cup and spoons
pistachio instant pudding
small jars with tops (or cups)
spoons
milk

Preparations

- Decorate a container (big enough to hold pudding) with shamrocks, and so on. Label it *Lucky Powder*.
- Put dried pudding in container.
- Copy recipe on chart paper for students to record.

On St. Patrick's Day

Tell children a story about being visited by a leprechaun (make the story as wild as you want). Tell them he left this magic powder with gold nuggets (pistachio nuts) in it. Have students copy the recipe. Then help students follow the recipe. They will notice the MAGIC when the white powder turns green and gets thick! You might want them to write a story to go with their experience.

Recipe for Lucky Irish Pudding

1 baby food or other small jar with lid or paper cups
1 tablespoon Lucky Powder
1/4 cup milk

1. Put the powder and milk in the jar.
2. Put the lid on tight!
3. Shake the jar 50 times!
4. Wait five minutes.
5. Open jar and EAT!

Follow-Up

Discuss the changes that happened. Brainstorm a list of "before" and "after" descriptive words. Mix up the directions and use this as a sequencing exercise. States of matter could be another exercise to extend the activity at other grade levels. Solid (powder), plus liquid (milk) equals colloid (a substance that is neither a solid nor liquid). Other colloids include: gelatin, oobleck, flubber, gels.

230   **by Barbara Crosby**

Leprechaun Footprints

Materials

green paint (liquid or powder tempera, or poster paint)
tray or flat-bottomed container with short sides
(cookie tray, pie tin or other suitable tray) for paint
tray for blotting (lined with damp paper towels or lint free
   moistened cloth towels)
white mural paper
wash basin
soap and towels

Setup

Roll the mural paper across long tables or on the floor.
Tape it in place.
Set up the paint tray beside the mural.
Fill one tray with green paint and the other
with damp towels for blotting excess
paint from hands.
Fill a basin with warm water and set
up soap, washcloth and towel or
paper towels for easy access, or you
will have a green room!

Let's Make It

1. Accommodate only as many children as you can supervise at the mural at any one time.

2. Demonstrate how to make a leprechaun's footprint. Make a fist, thumb-side up. Gently place the bottom of the fist in the paint and blot on the blotter. Press the painted portion of the hand onto the mural paper to make a foot. Depending upon how much paint is on the hand, a few footprints can be made at a time. Put your thumb in the paint and make the imprint of the big toe above the foot and then dip a smaller finger in the paint (and blotter) to make the remaining toes.

3. Each child can make a trail across the mural to make it look as if a leprechaun walked across the page.

4. Don't forget to wash up!

Book Buddy Leprechauns

The third graders in Room 15 at Valley View Elementary are book buddies to the afternoon kindergarten class. For St. Patrick's Day, they planned something special. Playing leprechauns, they hid bags of foil-wrapped chocolate coins addressed to their little buddies.

Now the time is almost up and four children have not found their "pots of gold." **But they haven't looked everywhere.** One treasure's on top of the slide. Another is hidden by the tree. The third is inside the sandbox. And the last treasure is under the steps of the playhouse.

From the clues below, can you help them find their treasures?

Use the chart to help you. Write *no* in the appropriate box when you eliminate a possibility. Write *yes* in the appropriate box when you find someone's "pot of gold."

Clues

1. Emma looked in the sandbox, playhouse, and slide.

2. Haley does not like getting sand in her shoes.

3. Ryan won't go near the playhouse. He thinks it's only for girls.

4. Cameron's afraid of heights.

Hint: There can be only one "yes" in each row and column. The rest have to be "no." So once you have a "yes," the rest are "no."

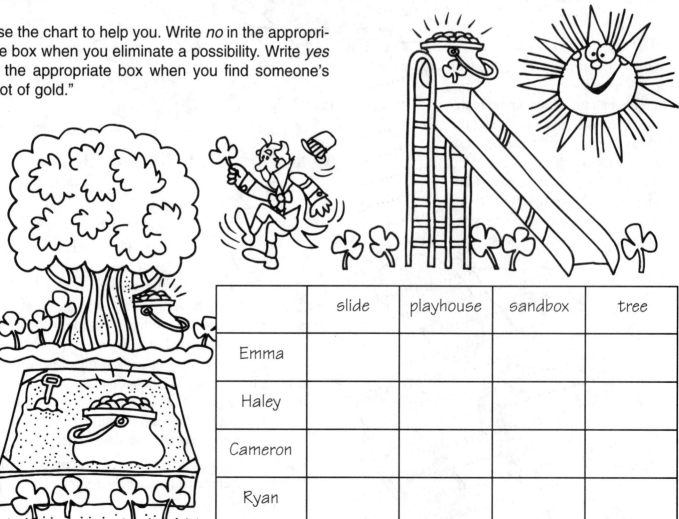

	slide	playhouse	sandbox	tree
Emma				
Haley				
Cameron				
Ryan				

Answers: Emma—tree; Haley—sandbox; Cameron—slide; Ryan—playhouse

by Nancy Vaughn

A PERSIAN NEW YEAR'S CELEBRATION

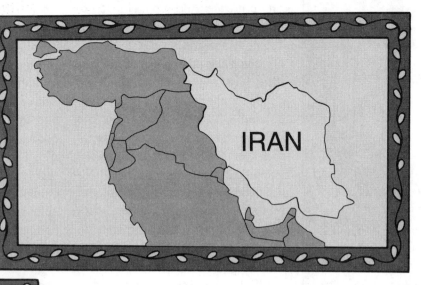

IRAN

BY MARIA T. OLIA

On March 21st, the first day of spring, Iranian American families celebrate the Persian New Year, *Noruz*. On this day Iranians will have a New Year's feast with their families and friends. They will exchange gifts, sing songs, and read Persian stories and poetry to ring in the New Year. It is important that Noruz be festive so that the day's happiness continues throughout the coming year.

Noruz is the most important Persian holiday of the year and all Iranians—Muslim, Christian, and Jewish celebrate it. Iranian families prepare for Noruz by giving the house a spring cleaning, called *khoneh tehkoni* or literally, "shaking down the house." At this time of year Iranian homes smell sweet from the baking of New Year's pastries such as *halvah*, a saffron-scented pudding, cardamom cookies called *goushe fil* (elephant ears!) and *rolette*, a cake filled with rose-water flavored cream.

Iranian children know that Noruz is when they sprout the *sabzi*. Two weeks before, Noruz children soak lentils or wheat berries in a bowl of water until they germinate. Then the water is drained and the bowl of sprouted seeds is placed on a sunny windowsill. It is the job of the children to water the sprouts so that they grow green and tall for the family's *haft-sinn* table.

A week before Noruz, every Iranian family sets up the *haft-sinn* table in their home. On the *haft-sinn* (seven Ss) table Iranian families place seven symbols of spring that begin with the letter S in Farsi (the language of Iranians). The *sabzi*, or sprouts, symbolize the greening of spring. A hyacinth plant, *sonbol* is placed on the table for its sweet smell. Apples, *sib*, symbolize beauty, and the fruit of the lotus tree, *senjed*, signifies love. Garlic *seer* stands for good health. A flask of vinegar *serkeh* represents old age

and patience. And a small plate of sumac, a russet-colored ground spice, symbolizes sunset.

On the table there are also candles; one for each child in the house, a mirror, a bowl of brightly colored eggs, and some coins. The coins represent prosperity. Parents give their children lots of chocolate coins to eat during the Noruz holiday! The eggs symbolize spring and rebirth. Finally, every Iranian child's favorite part of the *haft-sinn* is placed on the table, a goldfish swimming in a bowl of water. The goldfish represents Pisces, the astrological sign of spring.

During the last night of the year, Iranian families light the candles so that their ancestors can see the *haft-sinn* table and the happiness of the family reflected in the mirror.

On Noruz morning everyone in the house awakens early. On the children's beds, the parents have laid out new clothes. On this day all clothes must be new for good luck, even socks and underwear!

The Iranian New Year begins when the sun crosses the equator—the spring equinox. Day and night are equal, 12 hours each. According to a Persian legend, the world rests on one of the horns of a ram. At the exact moment of the spring equinox, the ram moves Earth from one horn to the other. On Noruz, Iranian children play a popular New Year's game. They place one of the decorated eggs from the *haft-sinn* on the mirror. The children watch care-fully to see if the egg moves on the mirror when the ram moves Earth from one horn to the other. Some children are very patient and see the egg move on the mirror every year!

On Noruz day Iranians feast with their families and friends. Traditional Iranian New Year's foods are eaten on this day. Iranians always eat fish and rice, noodle soup, and a spinach and parsley omelet. Eating fish brings good luck. Iranian families eat noodles because the tangled strands represent life's choices. The green omelet represents rebirth and spring. Iranians also eat lots of candies and pastries so that the coming year is a "sweet" one. After dinner Iranian families talk, tell stories, and read poetry. Parents, grandparents, aunts and uncles end the party by giving gifts of new, freshly minted money to all the children.

The New Year's celebration lasts 13 days. During this time Iranians visit the homes of family and friends to drink tea and eat pastries and fruit. Noruz is a very busy time for Iranian children and their families!

On the thirteenth day of Noruz, Iranians celebrate *Sizdeh Bedar* the "Getting Rid of Thirteen" day. Thirteen is considered an unlucky number in Iranian culture. Iranians also believe that the *sabzi* from the *haft-sinn* table contains the future bad luck of a family. For this reason it is believed that if you touch the *sabzi* of another family, their bad luck will be transferred to you! During this final day of the Noruz holiday, Iranian families have picnics in the countryside. They bring the sprouts from the *haft-sinn* table and throw them and any bad luck for the coming year in a river or lake. In this way they complete the cycle of the end of one year and the beginning of another. At the *Sizdeh Bedar* picnic Iranian children eat and play and talk about the fun they had celebrating their New Year with family and friends!

SPROUTING NORUZ SABZI

Children can make a plate of each kind of seed. Record and compare each seed's germination and growth.

You will need

> saucer or shallow bowl
> seeds: lentil, wheat berry, mung bean
> paper towel

1. In a saucer or shallow bowl, place a single layer of seeds.
2. Add enough water to the bowl to just cover the seeds.
3. Place a damp paper towel on top of the seeds.
4. Put the bowl of seeds in a shady spot for 2 to 3 days or until the seeds begin to sprout.
5. Check daily to make sure the seeds are damp. If necessary, sprinkle with more water.
6. After the seeds have sprouted, remove the paper towel and place the bowl of sprouted seeds on a windowsill to grow.
7. Do not allow the seeds to dry out! Spray or sprinkle with water daily.

by Maria T. Olia

NEW YEAR'S BAGS

Let children make special bags of goodies for one another to celebrate Persian New Year. Give each child a small paper lunch bag, a hard-boiled egg, a small candle, some chocolate coins, and some goldfish crackers. Also provide crayons, markers, scissors, glue, construction paper, and decorative stickers.

Have each child decorate a bag and an egg for another child in the class. (You may want to assign names, but if so encourage the children to keep them secret.) Each child should also design a Happy New Year greeting card to go in the bag of goodies. When the bags are completed, the children should fill them with the treats and hand deliver them to the ones for whom they were made with a smile and a Happy New Year wish.

by Mary Tucker

A 13-DAY CELEBRATION

The Persian New Year celebration lasts 13 days! Plan your own 13-day New Year's celebration. Ask children how they would celebrate. What special foods would they eat? What games would they play? What special symbols would they have (such as eggs symbolizing spring and rebirth in the Persian New Year celebration)? What special decorations would they use to decorate the room? Would they plan to do something different each of the 13 days?

Write their ideas on the board; then vote on them. If possible, set aside a day to have this celebration, allowing half an hour to represent each day. Ask parents to bring food. Let the children decorate the room and have a great time!

by Mary Tucker

April Is
National Humor Month!

Join the fun! April is National Humor Month, so tickle your funny bones with these hilarious books and activities.

Pancake Pie
by Sven Nordqvist
William Morrow & Company, 1984

You are cordially invited to a wild birthday adventure you'll never forget! A farmer named Festus is planning to celebrate his cat's birthday with a special pancake pie, but everything seems to be going wrong. Can he retrieve a lost key and outwit a mad bull in time to bake his famous birthday pie?

- Design your own pancake pie that everyone will love. Draw a picture of your pie and give directions for making it.

- Pretend that you made the biggest pancake in the world. Write a news story telling about your famous pancake. Remember the five Ws of a news story: Who? What? Where? When? Why?

Cinderella Bigfoot
by Mike Thaler
illustrated by Jared Lee
Scholastic, 1997

Tired of the same old fairy tales? There's a new Cinderella story on the bookshelves that's sure to entertain you. Meet Cinderella Bigfoot and her three beautiful stepsisters Weeny, Whiny and Moe. When Cinderella is not invited to the royal ball, her Dairy Godmother (a cow!) quickly comes to her rescue with a beautiful gown and a sparkling pair of size 87 glass sneakers. Will the handsome prince ask Cinderella Bigfoot to dance at the ball?

- Help Cinderella Bigfoot design a "missing" poster for her lost size 87 glass sneaker. Draw a picture of the glass sneaker, and write a description of the shoe on your poster.

- If you enjoyed this "fractured" fairy tale, other books in the series include: *Hanzel and Pretzel, The Princess and the Pea-Ano & Schmoe White and the Seven Dorfs.*

by Mary Ellen Switzer

Laugh It Up!

For more grins and giggles during National Humor Month, don't miss these sensational selections:

Read *Bug Off!* by Cathi Hepworth (G.P. Putnam's Sons, 1998). This wonderful book is "buzzing" with vocabulary words and pictures relating to insects. Each big word contains the name of a creepy-crawly, such as Fr**ant**ic. After reading this book, select your favorite insect. Be an insect "detective" and find out more information about your selection. Write a "Who Am I?" riddle about the insect, using some of the facts you have learned as clues.

Read *The Greedy Triangle* by Marilyn Burns (Scholastic, 1994). Choose one of the following shapes: triangle, quadrilateral, pentagon, hexagon, heptagon, or octagon. Design a cartoon character of that shape and write a funny story about your new creation.

Belly Laughs! Food Jokes and Riddles
by Charles Keller
Simon & Schuster Books for Young Readers, 1990

*Old Turtle's 90 Knock-Knocks,
Jokes, and Riddles*
by Leonard Kessler
Greenwillow Books, 1991

Tongue Twisters
by Charles Keller
Simon & Schuster Books for Young Readers, 1989

The Silliest Joke Book Ever
by Victoria Hartman
Lothrop, Lee & Shepard Books, 1993

Why the Chicken Crossed the Road

by David Macaulay
Houghton Mifflin Company, 1987

It all started when one innocent chicken scurried across a country road. This simple act soon sets off the wildest series of events ever, including a stampede, a train wreck, a bandit's escape, and a gushing flood.

- What was your favorite part of this story? Draw a picture showing that event.

- Be an author! Write your own cause and effect story about a pig that causes a series of humorous events.

National Poetry Month

April is National Poetry Month. This public celebration values great literature and invites everyone to take part, whether in school, a library, a bookstore, or at home. Thousands of organizations have participated in the annual festivals. Sales of poetry books increased and teachers and librarians noted an increased interest in poetry among students. The Academy of American Poets, based in New York City, has put together this celebration along with numerous sponsors. Across the country, bookstores, libraries, schools, and literary centers will participate in National Poetry Month. You can visit the Academy through its poetry web site (http://www.poets.org) to see a variety of poems, biographies, photographs, and recordings of poets reading their work. Also, contact the Academy to obtain information on how to receive posters and celebration materials.

The Academy of American Poets
584 Broadway, Suite 1208, New York, NY 10012-3250
TEL: (212) 274-0343   FAX: (212) 274-9427

Celebrate National Poetry Month in your classroom.

1. Read poems to your class. You can start with rhyming words as in Mother Goose rhymes, traditional children's poetry, and very funny favorites in Shel Silverstein's books *Where the Sidewalk Ends* and *A Light in the Attic*.

2. Have your students create original poems and then illustrate their work. Hang these in the classroom, halls, or library.

3. Ask students to read their poems over your public address system each day.

4. Ask local businesses to display posters of your students' poems and illustrations in their store windows.

5. Organize a contest for the most poems written in a specified time. Present a trophy or prize (maybe a famous book of poems).

6. Make a videotape of your students reciting their original poems.

by Tania K. Cowling

Fun Formats

Discuss the spring season with your students. Talk about the changes that are seen outdoors and celebrations that occur during this time. Teach these poem formats and have students experiment with them.

Haiku
(unrhymed Japanese verse consisting of 17 syllables)
First line = 5 syllables
Second line = 7 syllables
Third line = 5 syllables

Example:
Spring is showery
It brings the flowers to me
Colors of nature.

Cinquain
noun
3 "-ing" verbs
a thought
a synonym for the noun in line 1

Example:
Flower
Sprouting, Growing, Blooming
A colorful work of nature
Blossom

Five Senses
Example:
Spring is warm and bright.
It tastes like fresh fruit.
It sounds like songbirds singing.
It smells like fragrant flowers.
It looks like a rainbow of colors.
It makes me feel happy.

Name
Example:
Sunflowers of yellow and brown
Peonies of pink, red, and white
Roses with velvet red petals
Iris of vibrant purple
Nature at its best
Growing in the spring

Concrete

The verse creates a picture.

A caterpillar works hard at spinning his cocoon and after a while he becomes a BUTTERFLY.

Spring means we plan our gardens and plant the seeds, seeds, seeds, seeds, seeds.

Poetic Books to Read

Children of Long Ago by Lessie Jones Little. New York: Philomel Books, 1988.

Hand Rhymes by Marc Brown. New York: E.P. Dutton, 1985.

Honey, I Love and Other Love Poems by Eloise Greenfield. New York: Harper & Row Publishers, 1978.

Old Mother Hubbard and Her Dog by Lisa Amoroso. New York: Alfred A. Knopf, 1987.

Out and About by Shirley Hughes. New York: Lothrop, Lee & Shepard Books, 1988.

Read Aloud Rhymes for the Very Young selected by Jack Prelutsky. New York: Alfred A. Knopf, 1986.

Sing a Song of Popcorn edited by Beatrice deRegniers. New York: Scholastic, 1988.

Tomie dePaola's Mother Goose by Tomie dePaola. New York: G.P. Putnam's Sons, 1985.

Hats Off to *Easter!*

Hop down the bunny trail with these "eggs"citing springtime activities.

For spring ideas galore, don't miss *Easter Fun, Great Things to Make and Do* by Deri Robins and Maggie Downer (Kingfisher, 1996). Create that perfect Easter bonnet or a special springtime kite. Whip up a batch of candy nests or some tasty Easter rolls. Learn to make colorful papier-mâché eggs or a paper bird.

Enjoy more holiday crafts and activities in *Easter Fun Activity Book* by Judith Stamper (Troll, 1997). Conduct some amazing science "eggs"periments or have an outdoor spring scavenger hunt. Make your own Peter Rabbit puppets and create a cute popcorn bunny sculpture, using the easy-to-follow directions in the book.

Everyone loves a mystery, and your class is sure to enjoy *Peter Cottontail and the Easter Bunny Imposter* by Suzanne Smith (Ideals Children's Books, 1997). Peter Cottontail wakes up on Easter morning to a big surprise—all of his eggs are missing! Seems like one of Peter's helpers has been impersonating him. Can Peter solve the mystery in time for the big holiday?

Delight your children with *Mousekin's Easter Basket* by Edna Miller (Simon & Schuster Books for Young Readers, 1986). It's springtime again and Mousekin is searching for the perfect new home. During his search, he discovers many signs of spring—wildflowers, a basket of colorful eggs, children on an Easter egg hunt, and a beautiful white rabbit. The tiny mouse even finds a new home—an abandoned bird's nest.

by Mary Ellen Switzer

Hats Off to Writing!

Calling all authors! Use one of these sensational writing ideas to create your own springtime story.

Congratulations! While taking a springtime hike, you find the world's largest egg. Tell what happens next.

One day you see some strange rabbit tracks in your yard. You follow the tracks and . . .

It's a bird . . . it's a plane . . . it's the Easter Bunny! The Easter Bunny has a new plan to deliver this year's eggs. He's decided to travel around in a helicopter. Write a story about his adventure when a sudden storm occurs.

Just imagine that your chocolate Easter bunny could talk. Write a story about this magical event.

Be a detective! The Easter Bunny's secret chocolate egg recipe is missing. Write a crime report telling how his animal friends help him recover it.

I couldn't believe my eyes! This was the strangest spring flower I'd ever seen. Finish the story.

Surprise! You get a new bunny for Easter. What would you name your new pet? Write a "Dear Diary" entry telling about your first day together.

Just for fun! Pretend the Easter Bunny visits your classroom. Tell what happens.

TLC10198 Copyright © Teaching & Learning Company, Carthage, IL 62321-0010

What's Different?

Some children are enjoying an Easter egg hunt in the park. Look carefully at the two pictures. There are at least eight differences in them. Can you find them? Circle each difference you find.

Go, Ruby Rabbit

An Easter Adventure

Ruby Rabbit, Ruby Rabbit,
What's your little plan?
You want to be an Easter Bunny.
Well, I bet you can!

Ruby thought of how they always
Chose the rabbit BOYS
To be the Easter Bunnies,
Bringing Easter eggs and toys.

Early Sunday morning
They'd be testing bunnies out.
She thought that she was pretty fast
And strong, without a doubt!

But Ruby had a friend,
Her name was Sue the Kangaroo.
She really was a leaper,
Yes, a bounder! That was Sue!

Ruby knew that Sue could teach her,
Show her how to bound.
Help her pass the bunny test,
When Sunday came around.

Off she went to visit Sue,
A-hop, a-hop a-hop!
"Show me how to be a BOUNDER,
Not a bunny FLOP!"

"Jump into my pocket
And I'll take you for a ride.
You'll really get the HANG of it
By sitting there inside."

by Irene Livingston

"And after you're accustomed
To the way I leap so high,
You'll try it on your own, my dear,
And then you'll REALLY FLY."

So off they went together
And her heart began to flip.
A-boing, A-boing, A-boing, A-
    boing.
Oh, what a thrilling trip!

They hopped and leaped and
    bounded,
'Till at last she got the feel
Of how it felt to leap so high.
And now, to leap for real!

"Come on," said Sue. "You're ready
    now.
You've leaped with me enough.
I'll stand and watch and off you
    go.
It's time to do your stuff!"

Ruby took a giant hop
And landed on her tail.
"It isn't working," Ruby said,
And then began to WAIL!

And off she hopped. Her bunny
    heart
Was broken right in two.
"I want to be an Easter Bunny.
What am I to do?"

Sunday morning came around
And Ruby had the blues.
"I guess I'll go there anyway,
For what have I to lose?"

All the rabbits gathered.
Not a single other girl!
"I HAVE to win! For BUNNY
    GiRLS!"
Her mind was in a whirl.

At last, her turn. She had to hold
A basket full of eggs,
And HOP with them. Then sud-
    denly,
A lightness in her legs!

All through her bunny body then
The floaty lightness spread,
Up through her arms and shoul-
    ders
'Till it swirled inside her head!

She felt herself within the pocket
Bounding off with Sue.
She grabbed the basket in her
    hand
And feather-light, she flew!

A-boing, A-boing, A-boing, A-
    boing!
She hardly saw the ground.
The bunnies clapped and cheered
    and yelled
To see our Ruby bound.

No one there could go like Ruby!
Ruby won the prize:
The biggest, brightest Easter eggs!
She stood with shining eyes.

She's now an Easter Bunny.
So remember, when you see
A furry, long-eared little guy,
That HE could be a SHE!

Jasmine and Ritu's First-Ever Easter Eve Extravaganza!

Jasmine and Ritu were lying on their wooden porch making Easter cards.

"How many days until Easter?" Ritu asked Jasmine.

"Four," Jasmine said.

Ritu counted on her fingers. "That means only three days until Easter Eve!" she shouted.

"There's no such thing as Easter Eve," said Jasmine.

"Why not?" Ritu asked. "There's Christmas Eve."

Jasmine thought. "I don't know. I guess nobody ever thought of it before."

"Well now that we've discovered it, we'd better do something about it." Ritu tapped her pencil against her card.

"I know!" said Ritu. "Let's have an Easter Eve party! We can make these cards into invitations."

"Great idea," said Jasmine. She printed a few lines on a card, then showed it to Ritu.

It read:

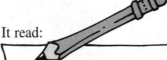

> Please come to Jasmine and Ritu's FIRST-EVER EASTER EVE EXTRAVAGANZA!
> Crafts, games, songs, and treats included.
> Party to be held at Jasmine and Ritu's wooden porch on Easter Eve.
> Come early for lots of fun.
> P.S. Bring a friend.

Jasmine and Ritu spent the next two days planning and decorating for their Easter Eve Extravaganza. They kept very busy. Getting ready for an extravaganza was lots of fun—and hard work, too.

Finally Easter Eve arrived.

The porch was decorated with Colorful Daisy Rabbits (which Ritu had made), Dandelion Chicks (Jasmine made those), and 10 purple Surprise Eggs (made by Jasmine and Ritu together).

Every guest brought a friend. Dong brought Sarah. Cody brought Jaspreet. Tara brought Julie. And Amanda brought her little brother, Jayson.

"Okay. Everyone is here," said Jasmine. "Let's play Put the Egg in the Easter Basket."

"I'll be first," said Sarah. Ritu blind-folded her. Jasmine spun Sarah around three times. Sarah missed the Easter basket and put the egg in the flowerpot. Everyone laughed. The egg was put in a chair, a drawer, and in Julie's pocket. Ritu laughed so hard she had tears running down her cheeks.

After the game, Ritu spread out a long roll of craft paper. "Everybody pick one jar of paint and a brush. Let's make a picture of spring!"

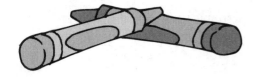

by Carol Jane Hort

Sarah painted five teeny, white bunnies. Dong painted little pink eyes on them. Ritu made a brown nest. Julie painted a brood of fuzzy yellow chicks. Jasmine made the green grass. Tara painted orange lilies. Jaspreet painted purple crocuses. Amanda painted big, blue raindrops. And Cody painted a big, brown mud puddle. Jayson played in a big, brown mud puddle.

Jasmine helped Amanda clean up Jayson. Everyone else helped Ritu pin up the artwork.

"It's time for the Easter Eve feast!" called Jasmine.

Ritu showed everyone how to make brown or white yummy Easter Bunny faces. She used pita bread, cream cheese, peanut butter, vegetable sticks, and dried fruit. Then Jasmine showed them how to make bowls by carefully peeling whole leaves off a head of lettuce. Everyone filled their lettuce bowls with tiny sliced celery boomerangs, baby carrot cubes, and jelly beans. They pretended to be Easter rabbits while they feasted on the snacks. Ritu ate the most jelly beans. Jayson used his lettuce bowl as a hat.

When the feast was finished, Ritu brought out the markers. Each guest colored one hard-boiled egg. While they worked, they sang:

One little, two little, three little Easter eggs,
Four little, five little, six little Easter eggs,
Seven little, eight little, nine little Easter eggs,
Ten little Easter Eve eggs!

And:
Happy, Happy Easter Eve,
Never, never, never leave.

Crafts and games and treats and sun,
Please don't end all our great fun.
Happy, Happy Easter Eve,
Never, never, never leave.

And:
We wish you a Happy Easter,
We wish you a Happy Easter,
We wish you a Happy Easter,
And a great Easter Eve!

The 10 colored eggs were carefully hidden for the next day's Easter egg hunt. Then Jasmine and Ritu's old and new friends started to say good-bye.

"Wait," said Ritu. "One more surprise before you go."

Jasmine and Ritu handed out the purple surprise eggs.

"Hold your egg over your head," said Ritu. "On the count of three, SQUEEZE for a big surprise. One, two, THREE!"

Everyone squeezed. Down floated a shower of pink, purple, and yellow confetti. Everyone laughed.

Finally, the guests had to leave.

"Great party," said Dong.

"It was fun," said Sarah.

"Cool games," said Cody.

"And wild decorations," said Jaspreet.

"Thank you for the snacks," said Amanda.

"We never even knew there was an Easter Eve," said Tara.

"See you tomorrow for the egg hunt," said Julie.

Jasmine and Ritu left the decorations up for Easter Sunday and went inside.

"That was a great Extravaganza," said Ritu. "It's a good thing we discovered Easter Eve."

"Yeah," said Jasmine, flopping onto the sofa. "Maybe next we could discover the 12 days of Valentine's, or October 32nd, or You're Welcome Day."

Ritu smiled. "But first comes Easter Tuesday."

Jasmine and Ritu's Surprise Eggs

For each student you will need:

• one blown egg*, dyed or decorated
• paper funnel
• confetti (make with colorful paper and a hole punch)
• clear tape

Directions:

1. Use the funnel to fill the egg with confetti.
2. Place a piece of clear tape over the hole in the egg to stop the confetti from falling out.
3. Take the students outside for a shower of color. Have them hold their eggs over their heads and squeeze!

*To blow eggs, use a knitting needle or ice pick to make a hole, about 1/2" in diameter, in one end of the egg. Shake out the egg. Wash the shell with cool water. Let it dry thoroughly.

Ritu's Yummy Easter Bunny Faces

For each student you will need:

• one pita bread (bagels work well, too)
• peanut butter (for a brown bunny) or cream cheese (for a white bunny)
• purple grapes or raisins (for brown) or fresh or dried cranberries (for white)
• celery
• two carrot sticks

Directions:

1. Cut two slits in the top of the pita bread. Insert one carrot stick in each hole to make the "ears." (If you are using bagels, stick ears on after step 2.)
2. Spread the pita with peanut butter or cream cheese. This is the "fur."
3. Use the fruit to give the bunny eyes and a nose.
4. Slice some very thin lengths of celery. If you can get it to peel into curls, that's even better. Position a few pieces on either side of the bunny's nose for the "whiskers."
5. The students may enjoy their nutritious yummy Easter Bunny face.

Ritu's Colorful Daisy Rabbits

Give each student a white daisy. Have them pick off the petals, leaving two on the top for ears. Next, put about $1/3$ cup of water and a few drops of food coloring in a jar. Have the students put their daisy rabbits in the jar. Check them after an hour. The daisy rabbits will "drink" some colored water, making the petal ears change color. Use different-colored dyes for variety.

Jasmine's Dandelion Chicks

Have the students pick large dandelions. Glue on orange diamond shapes for beaks and black circles for eyes. Sticker cut-outs or thickened paint works well, too. To save mess and maximize imaginations, simply have the students pinch a beak shape into the dandelion face.

For Creative Writing or Discussion
"How would you party?"

Having a party is a great way to get together with friends and celebrate anything! If you could plan your own special party, what would it be like? What would you celebrate? Use your imagination to come up with an all-new occasion. What would be special about it? What decorations would you use to show your theme? Think of some activities for you and your friends to do at the party. In what ways do these activities celebrate your theme? Have fun!

Lunch Bag Easter Basket

Here's an Easter basket made from a paper lunch bag that is both easy and inexpensive to make.

Materials: paper lunch bag (brown or white), scissors, glue, crayons or markers, string (optional), pre-cut patterns the size of the lunch bag

Directions:
Close the lunch bag, having folds at the bottom (A) and top (B). Place pattern on bag. Just above fold (B) start tracing solid lines. Cut on solid lines. (You will be cutting double.) One side will be the front of the bunny, the other side the back. Color a face and bow tie, and glue string whiskers on the front side. Glue a cotton ball tail on the back side. Glue or tape tips of ears together to form the handle.

Basket can be filled with "grass" and lightweight candies or crackers.

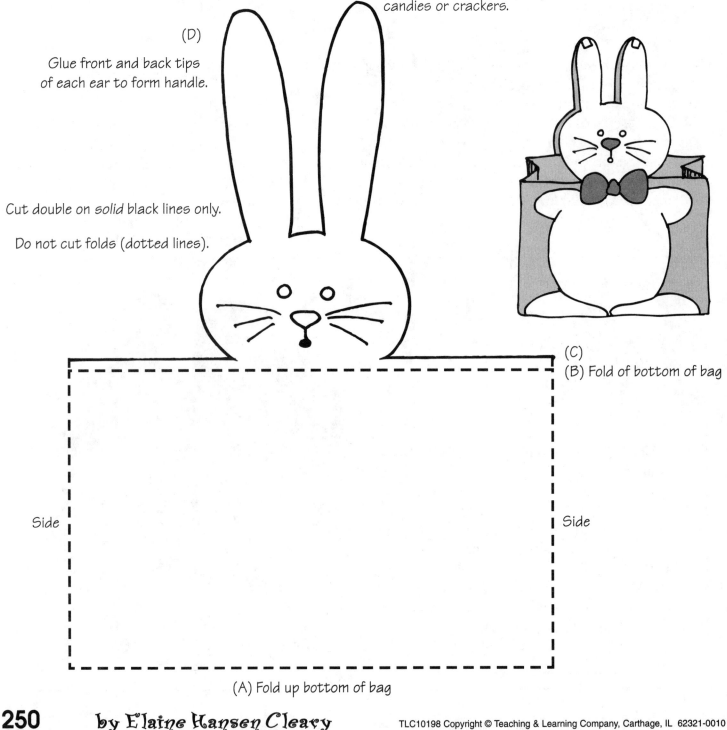

(D)

Glue front and back tips of each ear to form handle.

Cut double on *solid black lines only*.

Do not cut folds (dotted lines).

(C)
(B) Fold of bottom of bag

Side

Side

(A) Fold up bottom of bag

by Elaine Hansen Cleary

Easter
Bulletin Boards

Here is a creative story starter for your April bulletin board. Begin by having students copy the story below. Have each student fill in the blanks to describe his or her magic-egg creature.

Inside the (adjective) magic egg was a (adjective) (noun 1). It was (color adjective) and (size adjective). The (noun 1) liked to (action verb) and eat (noun 2) and (noun 3).

I thought it was (adjective) and very (adjective).

Then have each student trace the pattern on wallpaper scraps and cut out the egg shape. "Crack" the egg by cutting a zigzag pattern down the center. Fasten the two halves in the middle on the side with a brass fastener.

Have students draw and color their magic egg creatures on construction paper and glue them onto one side of the cracked eggs. Staple the egg to the top of each story.

by Ann E. Scheiblin

Read . . . the story of the magic egg.

Celebrate EARTH DAY

As we celebrate Earth Day, we become acutely aware of the many natural necessities we take so much for granted. As you discuss Earth Day with your class and take part in related activities, help them remember that taking care of our natural resources is a daily, lifelong process. Talk about ways you can celebrate Earth Day every day, right in the classroom, then follow through.

Brown Bag Posters

Have children cut brown grocery bags apart to form large rectangles. Provide markers or crayons and ask children to draw pictures of plants and/or animals on one rectangle, creating a poster. Let them frame the drawings by using magazine pictures of plants and animals, or by tracing and cutting plant and animal shapes from scrap paper. Display the posters within the classroom and throughout the school.

Earth Day Flags

Cut smaller rectangles from brown grocery bags for this activity. After you've discussed Earth Day and some of the ways people can work together to make Earth cleaner, have children create pictures on the rectangles depicting ways they feel they can help. Encourage them to develop appropriate slogans for their flags. Write the slogans on their flags. Tape or staple each flag to a paper towel tube. Then lead them an Earth Day parade, waving the flags and playing some of nature's instruments, such as sticks or rocks for banging and scraping, and gourds for shaking.

by Marie E. Cecchini

Planting

As you talk about planting seeds and plant growth, incorporate Earth Day values. Make use of plastic containers not accepted by your local recycling center and decorate them with stickers. Plant sunflower, pumpkin, or vegetable seeds, then have the children take their seedlings home to transplant. Talk about ways to make use of sunflower blossoms, pumpkins, and vegetables. Ideas might include saving some seeds to plant next year, roasting a sunflower or pumpkin seed snack, carving jack-o'-lanterns, making pumpkin pies, and eating the vegetables.

To roast seeds, wash and dry seeds. Spread them on a cookie sheet, sprinkle lightly with cooking oil and salt. Roast in a moderate oven (350°-375°F) until browned, stirring occasionally. Very helpful hint: It only takes a few minutes to brown them. If you leave them in too long, they will pop all over the oven like popcorn!

Racing Raindrops

For this game, you will need two droppers and one cookie sheet. The children work in pairs and each person places one drop of water on one side of the cookie sheet. Gently tilt the end of the cookie sheet up, and watch the raindrops race.

Plate Slide

Let the children take turns sliding an aluminum pie plate across the floor, then measure and record the distance each plate traveled. Have them try this a second time, starting their plates at the top of a ramp. Compare the ramp-aided distance with the flat distance. What conclusions can they draw?

Earth Day Bowling

Divide your class into two teams. Let children set up several empty two-liter soda bottles as bowling pins. Use empty aluminum cans as bowling balls (crimp or tape any rough edges). Have them take turns rolling the "ball." Keep track of the number of pins knocked down. Add their scores at the end of the game. Store the game in a cardboard box so the children can play independently. When the game no longer serves its purpose, recycle all the game parts.

A School Garden

Ask parents or local stores to donate packets of flower seeds and/or bulbs. Check with your school supervisor for permission to plant a flower garden. Work together as a class to plant and care for a garden the whole school can enjoy. Label the rows of seeds as they are planted. You may also want to record some of the results such as which kinds of seeds sprout faster.

Global Coverage

Provide children with butcher paper, natural sponges, and tempera paint in blue and green. Have children sponge paint blue "water" sections and green "land" sections all over the paper, as if it were a world map. When the paint is dry, use this paper as a tablecloth on which to set prepared plates of food.

Nature Search

Divide your class into several teams. Provide each team with a paper bag and a list of items to collect such as a smooth rock, four blades of grass, a leaf with three points, a purple flower, and so on. Set a time limit for collecting. At the end of the allotted time, the team that returns with the most items collected from the list wins.

School Yard Cleanup

Provide the children with appropriate-sized trash bags. Supervise them as they peruse the school grounds for litter. Younger children may need to go in small groups headed by parent volunteers. Deliver all the bags to the trash pick-up area and be sure everyone washes their hands!

Plant a Class Tree

Check with local nurseries to see if one would be willing to donate a small sapling for an Earth Day project. Also, call your local newspaper and let them know about your special project. They may be able to get your class picture in the next edition. Be sure to obtain permission from your school supervisor regarding all aspects of this project.

Cookie World

Purchase, or have the children bake large, plain cookies (one per child). Use food colors in blue and green to tint white icing. Provide the children with craft stick spreaders and let them create their own cookie "worlds."

THE EARTH DAY PLEDGE

Celebrate and honor our home, planet Earth, on Earth Day. You need not go any further than your backyard to discover and celebrate the marvels and mysteries of Earth.

I pledge to respect and care for the Earth on Earth Day and every day.

I will help to keep the Earth clean by _____

_____

I will help to keep the air clean by _____

_____

I will help to keep the water clean by _____

_____

My favorite things in nature are _____

_____

I am thankful for _____

_____

I will always care for the Earth because _____

_____

_____

Signed _____

by Robynne Eagan

BIODEGRADABLE B♲B

Characters

Nate Newspaper
Peggy Plastic
Candace Can
Benny Bottle
Bob (a banana peel)
George
Jack
Sylvia
Denice
other children

by Jane Tesh

Playing time:
10 minutes

Time: present

Setting: the town landfill

At rise: *Nate Newspaper, Peggy Plastic, Candace Can, and Benny Bottle are sitting sadly together in the landfill, surrounded by other articles of trash.*

Nate: *(Sighs heavily)* Another day in the town landfill. *(All sigh)*

Peggy: Another boring day!

Candace: I can't believe I'm still here.

Benny: Face the facts, Candace. We'll be here forever.

Candace: There must be something we can do. I feel so useless.

Peggy: Benny's right. There's nothing we can do. We're just trash someone threw away. *(Sighs)* Nobody wants an old plastic jug like me.

Benny: Or an old bottle like me.

Candace: Or a can.

Nate: What about newspapers? We're thrown away every day. *(There is a loud roaring sound.)* Look out, everyone! It's the bulldozer again! *(All lean to the right and move closer together, saying "Oof! Ouch! Watch it!" Bob, a banana peel, comes sliding in and lands on top of Benny.)*

Benny: Oh, no! More garbage! *(They untangle themselves. Bob is indignant.)*

Bob: Hey! Who are you calling garbage? I happen to be a very important biodegradable banana peel. *(Offers his hand.)* Bob's the name. I'll soon be part of the soil, adding nutrients and all that stuff.

Benny: Don't bet on it.

Bob: What do you mean? Isn't that why all of you are here?

Peggy: Tell him, Nate.

Nate: Pal, I've been here for months, and I haven't even begun to biodegrade.

Bob: *(Shocked)* Months!

Nate: And get this, some newspaper buddies of mine have been here for 30 years, and you can still read them!

Bob: *(Amazed)* What?

Nate: It's true. There's all kinds of stuff in here that's as good as new, especially the cans, bottles, and plastic containers like Candace, Benny, and Peggy.

Bob: Wait a second! I thought garbage was thrown into these big landfills to biodegrade.

Benny: Like Egyptian mummies.

Bob: Wow!

Peggy: And look at me. I'm plastic. I'll never biodegrade. I'll be plastic forever.

Benny: Same here. Glass stays glass.

Candace: And me! Aluminum is aluminum.

Bob: Then what are you doing down here? You should be doing something useful.

Nate: Like what?

Bob: I don't know. But anything would be better than being trapped in this place. *(Looks around and shudders.)* Mummies! Ugh! *(Paces for a moment while the others watch anxiously. Snaps fingers.)* I know! Let's break out!

Peggy: Break out? You mean leave?

Bob: Sure! Come on, let's get out of here!

Benny: Bob, we can't.

Bob: Of course we can. I'm lean and slippery. Just follow me!

Candace: *(To Nate)* What do you think, Nate?

Nate: Sounds like front page news to me. Let's do it!

Candace: Well, I'd pop my top to get out of here. Count me in.

Peggy: Me, too. How about you, Benny?

Benny: You're not leaving me behind!

Nate: Okay, Bob, lead the way! *(All exit.)*

Scene 2: *A roadside. The little band of brave litter walks along, looking in all directions.)* No one's following us.

Peggy: I think we made it.

Benny: Now what, Bob?

Bob: Well, goodness, I don't know. I thought I'd find a shady place to sit down and, you know, rot.

Candace: But we can't do that! *(Children enter, carrying sacks and plastic garbage bags. Bob and the others react with horror.)*

Benny: Oh, no! We'll be carried back to the landfill!

Nate: Quick! Lie down. Maybe they won't see us. *(All lie down and stay very still. The children spot them and come running.)*

George: Over here! There's some more trash!

Jack: Great! Another aluminum can. *(Pulls Candace to her feet.)*

Sylvia: A good glass bottle. *(Pulls Benny to his feet.)*

Denice: Terrific! More newspapers. *(Pulls Nate to his feet.)*

Nate: *(To Benny)* I don't understand. What's going on?

George: Good work, gang! We'll have a big pile of stuff to recycle.

Nate: Recycle! Did you hear that? We're getting another chance! We're going to be useful!

Sylvia: *(Pulls Peggy to her feet)* George, I know glass and aluminum cans be melted and used again, but what about this plastic container?

George: Oh yes. Plastic can be used over and over. That container may become part of a new ski jacket or material for a new building.

Peggy: Wow! I can't wait!

Jack: And did you know that the energy saved from one aluminum can could operate a 75-watt light bulb for eight hours?

Candace: That's me! I can do that!

Denice: And we can save as many as 500,000 trees by recycling newspapers like this one.

Nate: I'd love to save some trees!

Jack: *(Pulls Bob to his feet)* Denice, what about this banana peel?

Denice: Oh, you can leave that, Jack. It'll become part of the soil. It's biodegradable.

Bob: *(To the others, smugly)* Told you.

George: Let's get these things back to the recycling center. *(Children start off with the recyclable articles, who wave good-bye to Bob.)*

Nate: So long, Bob!

Peggy: Thanks for the rescue!

Candace: Now we can do something useful in the world!

Benny: I'll be coming around again, Bob!

Bob: *(Sits down and relaxes, his hands behind his head)* Ahhh, back to nature!

All: Recycle everything you can—
Plastic, paper, cans, and glass.
It's up to all of us on Earth
To make our planet last!

Earth Day Trash Garden

Activity

Find a secluded place on the playground and have the students dig to loosen the soil. Clean out a small trash container and place the contents on the ground next to the spot. Have students name the items; then predict what would happen to each if it were "planted" in the garden. Bury the items in the trash garden, keep it moist, then dig the items up once a week to check the results. Discuss the word *biodegradable*. Compare your previous list with the present results to discover which items are biodegradable. After several weeks, remove items that are not biodegradable.

Project

Provide students with eggshells to use as biodegradable planters. Have them gently fill the shells with soil; then add one or two seeds. Maintain the shell gardens in an egg carton, watering with a spoon or an eyedropper. Once the seeds have sprouted, the seedlings can be planted by gently crushing the eggshell before placing it in the ground.

by Marie E. Cecchini

EARTH Games

Let your kids' appreciation for nature blossom forth on Earth Day. When spring fever leads to restless wiggles, round up your class for some wacky Earth Games. Play works best outdoors, but most games can be adapted for indoor fun if the weather doesn't cooperate.

Grass Pull

And in the green corner—grass! Not only does it hold dirt in place, but birds like its soft strength for nest-building. Have each player choose a long blade of grass. The first player forms a loop out of the blade, holding the ends between thumb and index finger of one hand. The second player pushes a blade through the loop made by player 1, and makes a loop in the same manner. Both players pull against each other's blades. One will eventually break. The winner takes the opponent's broken pieces and moves on to face the next player. The game continues until everyone has played. If both blades break at the same time, neither player may play again and the blade pieces are forfeited. The winner is the player whose blade remains intact and has accumulated the most pieces of broken grass. (For indoor play: Cut fresh blades just prior to playing or they'll become limp and dry.)

Tumbleweed

When the wind blows, tumbleweeds roll across open land and roads until they get caught on fences or against buildings. Dry and leafless, tumbleweeds break off at the ground, losing their connection to the Earth's moisture. Have each player practice a forward roll, imitating a tumbleweed. Kids who cannot tumble may curl up in a ball and roll sideways. Divide players into two teams. Call out "Blow, wind, BLOW!" and blow out. At that signal, the first player on each team tumbles once and runs to the back of the line. The next players tumble, and so on down the line. The first team to complete their tumbles yells, "Tumbleweed!" To play again, rearrange teams so that everyone has a chance to be on a winning team. (For indoor play: A mat or large comforter works well for tumbling.)

by Jacqueline Horsfall

Costume Cleanup

Help keep the Earth looking lean, mean and green. Using rubber bands or twisties, tie off the arms and legs of an old Halloween costume. Organize a "litter bug" hunt where kids scout out trash to "stuff" the costume. Fill arms and legs with soda cans; place paper trash in the body cavity. (For extra sanitary protection, provide plastic baggies to wear over hands.) Back in the classroom, cut off the costume's extremities and recycle cans and bottles. Close up the remainder of the costume, prop it up on the dumpster—and top it with a scary mask! (Outdoor activ   ity only.)

Squirrel in the Tree

Have you ever heard a squirrel chattering away up in a tree? Besides being noisy critters, they're incredibly smart, able to locate hidden stashes of food and break into bird feeders with ease. Have one player (squirrel) stand in the center of a circle of kids (hollow of a tree). Holding hands and circling the squirrel, the group chants:

Squirrel, squirrel,
Up in a tree,
Tries to get out
But can't break FREE!

On the word *free,* the squirrel tries to escape the hollow in any way possible: running, crawling, burrowing under the legs, or breaking through arms. The "tree" circle tries to prevent the squirrel from escaping. The escaped squirrel chooses a new squirrel to take its place in the hollow, and the game continues until everyone has a turn as squirrel. Some of your squirrels will show themselves to be as quick and bright as real squirrels —they'll dash out of the hollow before the chant ends! (For indoor play: A wide-open space is needed.)

Dear Mother Nature

Dear Mother Nature,
Our pledge to you
Is to care for your Earth
'Cause it's our Earth, too.

We pledge to pick up
Any litter we see
And help people remember
To keep water clean.

We'll do all we can
To recycle, reuse.
We know that resources
Are not to abuse.

by Marie E. Cecchini

JOHN JAMES AUDUBON

Naturalist, Ornithologist and Artist
Created intricate drawings, studies and paintings of birds.
Birth date: April 26, 1785

BIRD NESTS (Cooking)

Melt 1 1/2 tablespoons of margarine over medium heat. Stir in 6 ounces of large marshmallows until melted. Add 3 cups of crispy rice cereal and 1/4 to 1/2 cup of coconut. Stir until well coated and mixed. Form large spoonfuls of the mixture into small nests. Allow the nests to cool and dry. Place several jelly beans in each nest before serving. Chow mein noodles may be used in place of cereal.

LITERATURE

Incorporate books about birds into the classroom. Add them to the classroom library or reading space and read them aloud for story time. Don't forget other areas of the classroom when introducing books—place a book about birds in the science area, on a classroom windowsill, in a dramatic play pet store center, on a shelf with stuffed animals, or in a basket of books for outdoor reading. Try some of these books about birds:

Owl Babies by Martin Waddell, Candlestick Press, 1996.
About Birds: A Guide for Children by John Sill, Peachtree Publishers, 1991.
The Best Beak in Boonaroo Bay by Narell Oliver, Fulcrum Pub., 1995.

If possible, include in the classroom library and throughout the classroom several books that show the work of Audubon.
John James Audubon's Birds of America (watercolors)
A Bird Guide by John James Audubon (Richard Hooper Pough)

An encyclopedia volume about birds and bird identification field guides would also be valuable classroom additions.

BROKEN EGGS (Math)

Cut 10 to 12 egg shapes from poster board or construction paper. Cut each egg apart in the middle, using a zigzag, pointed cut. Write a numeral from 1-10 or 1-12 on each half. On the back of the egg halves, draw a corresponding number of dots or small feathers that add up to the written numeral. For example, write the numeral three on two adjoining halves; on the back, place two dots on one half and one dot on the other. Mix the egg halves. Children sort the eggs, finding the matching numerals and counting the dots on the back to check their work.

A LETTER TO THE AUDUBON SOCIETY (Language)

Involve children in a letter-writing experience and compose a letter to the National Audubon Society. Begin with a statement about your purpose in writing: as an extension of the classroom recognition of April 26, the birthday of John James Audubon. Encourage children to contribute to a list of the day's or week's activities. Add a page on which children can sign their names and make bird drawings. Children's ideas and words about Audubon can also be dictated and recorded. As you write, discuss proper letter-writing form. Record the mailing date on a calendar. The address is National Audubon Society, 950 Third Ave., New York City, NY 10022-2793.

BIRD DRAWING (Art)

Look at Audubon's drawings and paintings of birds. Talk about drawing birds in the wild. Re-create a forest, field, or meadow in the classroom by hanging colored pictures of birds throughout the area. Vary the positions, placing the pictures high, low, and at eye level on walls, furniture, and doors. Supply a box of visors and props such as cameras, binoculars, and viewers. Binoculars and bird viewers can be constructed from cardboard paper towel tubes. Provide clipboards, paper, and colored pencils for children to use as they move about the classroom. Encourage the young naturalists to observe, study, and draw the birds they see. A similar drawing experience may be facilitated outdoors.

FLYING FEATHERS (Game)

Use real feathers for this game or cut feathers from paper and felt. Children blow the feathers up into the air and try to keep them afloat. Hands may not be used. Keep the feathers flying just by blowing.

EARLY BIRD CATCHES THE WORM (Motor)

Turn plastic scissors into hungry birds for this fine motor exercise. Glue two wiggly eyes or small felt circles on one side of a pom-pom (golf ball size). Glue several multicolored feathers on the top of the pom-pom. Attach a 6" chenille stem to the bottom of the pom-pom with glue. Use the stem to wrap the pom-pom bird around the scissors at the point where the scissors are joined. Make nests by drawing an oval on a piece of brown construction paper. Spread glue inside each oval and sprinkle straw or grass clippings on the glue. Next cut different colors of chenille stems into various lengths. Bend, twist, and curl the stems to make worms. Place the worms on a green piece of construction paper. Children hold the scissors sideways with the pom-pom bird at the top; the scissor ends become the bird's beak. They move and manipulate the scissors to pick up the worms from the green paper "grass" and move them to the brown paper "nests."

SING LIKE THE BIRDS (Music)

Make bird whistles before music time. Cut a 1" x 7" strip of lightweight paper for each child. Children fold the strip in half to create a 1" x 3 1/2" piece, and then fold up 1" on each end. They cut a 1" long triangle in the folded end.

To play the bird whistle, children hold the folded end flaps loosely between the thumb and finger of one hand, placing the whistle against their lips. Then they blow hard between the flaps. The air flowing through the triangular notch makes bird music. Use instrumental background music as children play the bird whistles. Add other "bird noises" to this fun music time: inflate balloons and stretch the necks as the air escapes, use assorted plastic whistles, and tap on tuning forks.

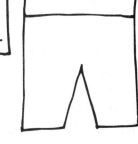

The First of May

A May Day Play

Characters:
    Old Man Winter
    Helper 1
    Helper 2
    Madam Spring
    Daisies
    Tulips
    Marigolds
    Violets

Setting: In the park.

At Curtain Rise: (*Old man winter sits to one side of stage on bench, asleep and snoring loudly. Helpers 1 and 2 enter, carrying Maypole. They go to center stage and set to work putting it up, hammering with wooden hammers. Old Man Winter awakens.*)

Old Man Winter: (*Stretching and yawning.*) Oh! Oh! What is going on here? What is all the noise about? (*Helpers go on hammering. Old Man Winter shakes his fist at helpers.*) I say there, you two! Stop that noise! Stop it at once! Who are you anyway?

Helpers: (*Helpers stop hammering and point to Old Man Winter. They speak together.*) Who are YOU, old man?

Old Man Winter: Why, I am Old Man Winter, of course. (*Helpers start to giggle.*) Who are you? And what are you laughing about?

Helper 1: Old Man Winter!

Helper 2: He says he's Old Man Winter! (*Helpers run off, laughing.*)

Old Man Winter: (*Out loud to himself.*) I wonder why those two were laughing? I *am* Old Man Winter. (*yawns*) I wonder how long I was asleep?

Madam Spring: (*She looks at Old Man Winter.*) My helpers tell me that you say you are Old Man Winter. Is that true?

Old Man Winter: Yes! Indeed it is! And what a wonderful winter we are having! Lots of snow, cold winds, and ice storms. With all that work I was quite worn out, so I took a little nap. But who are you?

Madam Spring: I am Madam Spring. And you must have taken a BIG nap. Do you know what day this is?

Old Man Winter: Why, er, no. Not exactly. I believe it is someday in February. Isn't it?

by Mary Prescott Moya

Madam Spring: (laughing) Oh my, no! Just a minute. I'll show you. (Runs off and comes back in carrying a large calendar. On it, printed in large letters, is May 1.) Look!

Old Man Winter: (Jumps up in surprise.) Oh dear! Oh dear! I'd better go back to my land of ice and snow! Good-bye! Good-bye! (Hurries off.)

Madam Spring: (Calling out.) Come, pretty springtime flowers! It is time for our dance. Come, Daisies. Come, Tulips! Come, Marigolds! Come, Violets! (Flowers run on stage. Helpers enter, too. All take hold of streamers on Maypole and dance around it, singing.)

The First of May! Oh spring day!
Old Man Winter has gone away.
Around the Maypole we dance and sing
To welcome happy, happy spring!

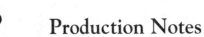

Production Notes

Play time: 10 minutes

Costumes: Old Man Winter is bundled up in winter clothing and wears a fur cap. Madam Spring wears a crown of flowers.

Props: Maypole may be made from a lamp stand, hat tree, or broom handle fastened into a cardboard box stand. It is decorated with streamers made out of colored crepe paper; wooden hammers; large calendar.

Setting: In the park. There is one bench.

The Maypole Song

Mary Prescott Moya

The first of May, oh gay spring day. Old man winter has gone a - way. A - round the May pole we dance and sing to wel - come hap - py, hap - py spring.

The WARMTH of the Sun

ACTIVITY

Spring has arrived and the sun stays with us for longer periods each day. Share some fun with the sun for Sun Day in the first week of May. Try an ice cube experiment to determine how the temperature of the sun's rays varies as the rays pass through different colors. Collect four or five jars and cover each with a different color of construction paper. Be sure to include black and white. Place the same number of ice cubes in each jar and set the jars in a sunny window. Have the students observe which set of ice cubes melts faster. A variation of this would be to fill each jar with the same amount of water; then place the jars in a sunny window. After half an hour or so, have the students use thermometers to check the temperature of the water in each jar. Help students conclude that darker colors absorb sunlight, thereby creating higher temperatures, while lighter colors reflect it. If this is the case, can they determine what color of clothing would be more appropriate for summer?

PROJECT

On a bright, sunny day, have your students create theme solar prints. Have them bring in items that belong to a specific category, such as kitchen utensils, workbench tools, garden tools, office supplies, leaves, doilies, and so on. Let them arrange the items on large sheets of dark-colored paper outside in direct sunlight. Check the projects periodically until print shapes can be distinguished. Return them to the classroom for a bulletin board display. Have the students title their works of art.

by Marie E. Cecchini

Fitness Fun

Building the basics of fundamental physical skills in young children can improve their agility, eye-foot and eye-hand coordination, as well as add to their enjoyment and success in future sports endeavors. Basic skills to develop in young children include galloping, balancing, running, hopping, jumping, skipping, throwing, catching, and kicking. Help children begin to learn, move, and grow with the following activities.

Stepping-Stone Path

Use large, hollow blocks to create a path that leads to story time. Place the blocks along the floor, leaving space between each, in a meandering path formation. Have each child step onto and down from all of the blocks on the path, then sit quietly in the story area.

Color Find

Reinforcing colors through movement can make this activity more fun. Have children sit together as a group. Choose one child to stand and listen as you give directions such as "Run to find something green," "Gallop to find something brown," and so on. When he or she finds the object, the child stops, names the object and color, then returns to the group using the same physical movement. Variation: Place number, letter, or color cards across the chalkboard tray. Seat children a distance from the board. Again, give each child specific directions for retrieving a certain card and returning to his or her seat with it.

　　　　　by Marie E. Cecchini　　**269**

Exercise Class

Let children use carpet squares as exercise mats and hold your own exercise class once or twice a week. Simple exercises could include bending to the left/right, touching toes, stretching to the sky, running/marching in place, and pretending to jump rope. You may want to develop a sequential exercise routine to do consistently, so you can put music to it just like a "real" exercise class. Add some fun to this activity by giving children a homework assignment of inventing an exercise of their own. Suggest sample ideas such as finger wiggles, knee bends, shoulder lifts, and so on. Allow individual children to share their exercises with the class when they are ready.

Feel the Beat

Combine your exercise program with a simple science lesson on how the human heart works. Talk with children about the human heart. Demonstrate its size by having them each make a fist. Have them feel the left side of their chest cavities to locate the beat of their hearts. Discuss how this muscle works to pump blood throughout the body. Next, show them where to find the veins in their wrists and briefly discuss the relationship of the heart to the veins. Have them place their index and middle fingers over these veins to locate their pulses. Experiment to discover whether the heart works harder (pumps faster) when the body is resting or moving. Help them take a pulse count for a 15-second interval while resting, then again after running in place for a minute. Record the numbers and encourage them to interpret the results.

Bubble Action

For this activity, you will need purchased or homemade bubble solution and wands to form bubbles. Homemade bubble mixture can be made by combining water liquid dish detergent an a few drops of glycerine, which is available at drug stores. Add a sufficient amount of detergent to produce bubbles. Wands can be made by bending pipe cleaners or wire. Divide the class into two teams and have them take the materials outside on a nice day. The teams will alternate turns as bubble blowers and bubble chasers, while the teacher is the action caller. To play, the teacher names an action such as running, skipping, or galloping, then the blowers produce bubbles which the chasers must go after using the designated motion.

Exercise Marathon

Similar to an obstacle course, this activity requires children to pass through several exercise stations. Set up and demonstrate a variety of stations. At the ball toss, each child will toss a ball up and catch it a specified number of times. The high jump involves jumping over a cardboard box. The balancing act might be walking across a board or around a tire; and for crawling under, over, and through, you might utilize a table, a cushion, and a cardboard box. Encourage the children to pass through the maze of stations as often as they wish, leaving some space and time between individuals so the participants will not feel rushed.

Balloon Bounce

Tie several sets of plastic rings from soda six-packs together to form a net, then tie each end of the net to a chair. Provide the children with an air-filled balloon and let them take turns bouncing the balloon over the net. Place a few children on either side of the net and count how many times the balloon can cross the net without touching the floor.

Balloon Dance

Provide each child with an air-filled balloon and permanent markers. Have them use the markers to create faces on the balloons. Help them to tape tissue paper or crepe paper streamers around the base of their balloons. Let the children use their balloon people for dancing partners as you play a variety of musical selections. Remind children that dance is also a form of exercise.

Note: All activities involving balloons require direct adult supervision.

Tree Ball

This outdoor activity will help the children develop eye-hand coordination. Use a rope to suspend a sponge ball, or a plastic bag stuffed with crumpled newspaper, from a tree branch. Let the children take turns hitting the ball with a paddle, stick, or wrapping paper tube. Encourage them to hit it in different ways, such as hard, soft, with both hands, right or left hand only, from a squatting position, and so on.

TINY AND FAST

Tina was worried. She wanted to win. She went to sleep every night dreaming about crossing the finish line first. She had been practicing every day, but whenever she saw Fast Freddie, she was afraid she didn't stand a chance.

Her parents called her Tiny Tina. She was not only the baby of the family, she was the smallest person in her class.

Tomorrow was Outdoor Events Day. All kinds of races were going to be run on the track at school. Tina's teacher had told her she was to run the megathon run, the longest and hardest race of all.

But so was Freddie. Freddie was the biggest boy in the class. And everybody called him Fast Freddie. He could run and jump and play ball as well as the kids in the third grade, who were much older.

Tina tried to think good thoughts. And she kept right on doing everything she could to make sure she did her best on race day.

Dad said a body without food is like a car without gas—it won't go very far. So Tina made sure to eat a good breakfast, lunch, and dinner so she had plenty of fuel to run on.

Fast Freddie didn't. Tina drank many glasses of water during the day so she could go a long way without getting tired.

Fast Freddie didn't.

Instead of running the day before the race, Tina did other things, to rest her legs.

Fast Freddie didn't.

Tina was careful to go to bed early the night before the race.

Fast Freddie didn't.

The day of the big race, Tina arrived early so she could stretch.

Fast Freddie didn't.

At the start of the race Fast Freddie burst out in front with his usual speed.

Tina didn't. She started out slow and settled into a strong, steady pace.

At the water station halfway through the race, Fast Freddie zipped right past without even a sip. When Tina reached the water station, she took a cup of water and kept going slow and steady.

Near the end of the race, the curves were sharp and the hills were steep.

Fast Freddie started to run out of gas. His mouth was dry. His legs were stiff. He was tired.

So far ahead, I have plenty of time to rest and still win, he thought. So he leaned against a tree and closed his eyes.

Tiny Tina didn't even notice him sleeping there as she trotted past. She was feeling very excited about being near the end. All of a sudden, she seemed to not be tired at all. Even the hills and curves weren't so bad.

As Tina ran the last leg of the race, she searched for Fast Freddie, but he didn't seem to be anywhere in sight. At least, not until she crossed the finish line, then she saw him . . . 20 yards behind her! Tiny Tina won the race!

Fast Freddie didn't.

by Debra Atkinson

WINNING POWER

To run and jump and dance and play,
Eat like a winner every day!

Spaghetti, noodles, bread, and rice
For energy to burn on ice.

Apples, peaches, apricots
For dribbling, passing, taking shots.

Turkey, ham, chicken, fish—
Muscles grow with foods like this.

Yogurt, pudding, milk, and cheese—
Bones and teeth need some of these.

To carrots, corn, and baby peas
Say, "May I have more, please?"

Practice this type of routine
And you'll be on the winning team!

Activity

Read "Tiny and Fast" with your students, then use the following questions to lead a discussion.

1. Who prepared most for the race?

2. What kind of things did Tina do to prepare for the race?

3. Did you know that 70% of your body is water? Where do you think most of that water is stored—muscle, bone, or fat? (muscle)

4. Why do you think Tina stretched before the race?

5. Encourage your students to draw illustrations of the important "winning" ways Tina prepared for the race: positive thinking; good nutrition; plenty of water; rest; training/practice; and stretching.

by Debra Atkinson

Balancing Act

May Is Physical Fitness Month

There are many different skills involved in various sports, such as running fast (speed), running far (endurance), strength, and agility. Here's a skill that students might not have thought about: balance. Without it, we'd spend a lot of time falling down and getting up again. Each body has a natural sense of balance, but that can be improved upon, like any skill, with practice. Have students take the following "tests" to see how well-balanced they are now.

Flamingo Balance

1. Have students wear tennis shoes and stand on a hard, flat surface.
2. Have them put the sole of one foot on the inside of the opposite knee, so they're standing like a flamingo or a stork.
3. Have students close their eyes and see how long they can maintain their balance. Count slowly or use a clock to time them.

The longer students can keep their balance, the better their *static* balance. Students might like to know—divers and gymnasts use static balance.

Flamingo Hop

1. Have students wear socks and stand on a hard surface.
2. Tell them to place the sole of one foot on the inside of the opposite knee again, with eyes open this time.
3. Direct students to hop, turning a quarter turn every five seconds. See how long they can maintain their balance doing this.

Dynamic balance means the body must respond to constant movement. Students might like to know—downhill skiers and surfers need a high degree of dynamic balance.

by Debra Atkinson

Workout with Simon Sez

May Is Physical Fitness Month

Get ready for a workout with Simon Sez
with just a slight twist, in the rules, that is.
For Simon may not always say,
but we're gonna do it anyway!

READY! . . .

Simon says to march in place.
Put that smile back on your face.
Come on now, pick up the pace.
Simon says, "Let's run a race!"
        (run around the room)

Back in place, jump like a frog.
Jump right through that hollow log.
Now turn that jump into a jog.
Simon says, "Let's work those quads!"

Now, Simon says to take a breath,
From time to time you've got to rest.
Another one, puff out that chest.
Get ready, everybody, it's time to stretch!

Touch your toes, your knees, and thighs.
Twist your waist from side to side.
Reach your arms up to the sky.
Now clap your hands, c'mon, don't be shy!

Now bring your arms just halfway down.
Spin those airplane wings around.
Ready for takeoff, don't look down!
Simon says, "Let's fly around town!"
        ("fly" around the room)

Back in place, arms at your side.
Breathe in and out, like the ocean tide.
Altogether now, wave good-bye.
Simon says, "You've exercised!"

by Diane Z. Shore

275

Holiday Sing-Alongs

by Mabel Duch

Cinco de Mayo

To the tune of
"Do You Know the Muffin Man?"

Do you know the story of,
  The story of,
  The story of,
Do you know the story of
This great and happy day?

Yes, I know that brave Juarez,
  Brave Juarez,
  Brave Juarez,
Yes, I know that brave Juarez
Chased the French away.

The French, they had no right to rule,
  No right to rule,
  No right to rule,
The French, they had no right to rule
Our lovely Mexico.

Our soldiers and the people said,
  The people said,
  The people said,
Our soldiers and the people said
The French have got to go.

So Juarez formed an army troop,
  An army troop,
  An army troop.
So Juarez formed an army troop
To chase the French away.

That's why we like to celebrate,
  Celebrate,
  Celebrate,
That's why we like to celebrate
On the fifth of May.

Cinco de Mayo (May 5) commemorates the day that Benito Pablo Juarez led his makeshift army against the well-trained French invaders at Pueblo. Unfortunately, it was not the end of the French invasion, but it was the beginning of the end.

Many consider Cinco de Mayo the most important fiesta day in Mexico. Its celebration features flower-filled parades and mock battles, but children can enjoy a piñata at almost any festival.

Piñata Materials

- two large paper sacks, one inside the other
- strong strapping tape and adhesive-backed colored plastic tape
- tempera paint and paint-brushes, scissors and tacky glue
- colored tissue paper and flower pattern

Procedure

Fill the inside sack with candy, gum, and toys. Fold the ends over and tape down with strapping tape. Cover with colored tape. Decorate with paint and tissue paper flowers (see directions below). Flowers are an important part of a Cinco de Mayo celebration.

Tissue Paper Flowers

Place the flower pattern on three sheets of tissue paper. Trace lightly with a pencil and cut out all three flower shapes together. Lay the tissue paper cut-outs on top of another, overlapping the petals. Twist the cut-outs in the middle to form a small stem. When gluing stems to the piñata, bend them sideways. If flower forms are not fastened together after gluing stem, add a drop of glue.

Make one or more piñatas. If you make several, use somewhat smaller bags. Children can work together on the piñata or piñatas. Remind them that any paint must be dry before gluing flowers.

When the piñata is finished, tape a loop to the top, folded section. Use the strapping tape and cover with colored tape.

Have a piñata parade and take the piñata or piñatas to the game area. Encourage children to wear bright clothing. Girls can make flowers to wear in their hair. As they march, have children sing the Cinco de Mayo song. Very young children may sing the first two verses.

Review the piñata rules when you reach the game area. Allow each blindfolded child to take a designated number of swings at the piñata. Keep the onlookers well away from the stick. A "magic" circle drawn around the area may help. If the child swinging the stick gets too close to the edge of the circle, have a "magic word" to stop him or her. Then gently lead the child back to the proper place.

Paper plate Piñata

Fold a 9" paper plate in half and open back up. Glue long strips of crepe paper or ribbons to the center of the paper plate. Fold the plate in half and staple along the edges, stapling a yarn "handle" about 4" up from the center on either side as illustrated. Glue pattern piece to the center of the folded plate and fill with treats as shown.

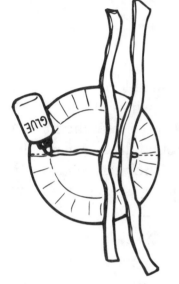

by Veronica Terrill

National TRANSPORTATION Week

Mark Transportation Week by taking a closer look at how we get places. National Transportation Week includes the third Friday in May. A unit on transportation builds on your students' natural curiosity and fascination with vehicles. Transportation can be as simple as walking across the room or as exotic as rocketing into space.

Try these activities and observe, classify, and identify the many modes of transportation.

BODY TRAVEL (Creative Movement)

Pretend you and your children are going on a trip. First ride your bicycles. Lie on the floor and pedal with your legs up in the air. While pedaling, decide where you want to go on your trip. Suddenly, you hear a train whistle. "Let's hop aboard!" Up on your feet, place your left hand on the shoulder of the person ahead of you. Now, with your right hand, rotate your entire arm in a circle, like the locomotion of a train's wheel. Move around the room, "chug-a-chug-a-choo-choo." After your train trip, "toot" the whistle. Everyone is off the train. For your return trip, take an airplane ride. "Zoom" around the room, arms extended. Circle the airfield, drop your landing gear, and make a smooth landing. Wow, what a fun trip!

WOODEN GLIDER

Give each child two wooden tongue depressors to make this airplane. Paint the sticks with bright colors. When they are dry, glue them (one on top of another) onto blue construction paper. With chalk, color in billowy clouds. You can even glue cotton onto the clouds for texture. Explain to the children that glider airplanes float in the air without motors.

by Tania Cowling

ORIGINAL POEM

Your students can write original poems using this five-step formula.

1. size and shape of the vehicle
2. color of the vehicle
3. purpose of the vehicle
4. where you would like to go in this vehicle
5. name of person who drives this vehicle

Example:

Small
Red and black
Goes fast and wins trophies
On the race track
Race car driver

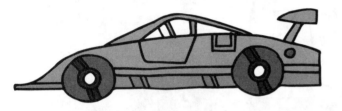

TRAVEL COLLAGE

Using old magazines, cut out pictures of cars, trains, boats, airplanes, motorcycles, trucks, rockets, and bicycles. Glue these randomly on paper to create a travel collage. Ask the following questions and let the students decide which vehicle is the correct answer.

1. Which one travels on tracks?
2. Which one takes people on vacation in the air?
3. Which one do we park in the garage?
4. Which one travels on the ocean?
5. Which one carries food to the grocery store?
6. Which one is like a bicycle with a motor?
7. Which one could take us to the moon?

SHAPE TRAIN

Help your students cut out rectangular train shapes from construction paper or wallpaper scraps. Glue these boxcars into place on a white sheet of paper. Wheels can be drawn with markers, or cut-out circles can be glued on. To stamp wheels, use an old wooden spool. Dip the spool end into paint and stamp down on the paper. Another wheel idea is to glue on pasta that is shaped like wagon wheels. Your train project will have shape, color, and texture.

Check out this web site on the internet with photos of various railroad stations across the country.
http://trainweb.com/photos/index.htm

LICENSE PLATES

Collect a variety of old license plates. Compare state pictures and colors. Let the children explore these plates on a table and even do "license plate rubbings." Place a sheet of paper on top of the plate. Using the side of a crayon, rub across the top of the metal license plate. Display the artistic replicas.

280

WHEEL PAINTING

Gather a few small toy cars (also include tractors, motorcycles, and trucks). Pour tempera paints in shallow containers. Provide a large sheet of paper and let the children dip the wheels of the vehicle into the paint and "drive" across the paper, back and forth with lots of colors. Add sound effects and create a "zoom-zoom" painting!

RED LIGHT, GREEN LIGHT

One child pretends to be the traffic light. This child turns his back to the rest of the class while they line up at the other end of the room. When the traffic light says "green light," the children take steps closer to him. Then the traffic light says "red light" and quickly turns around to see if anyone is moving. At this time, all children should be in a "freeze" position. Any child who is caught moving is sent back to the starting line. The game continues until the first child touches the traffic light. This lucky child becomes the new traffic light.

TUNA BOATS

Prepare tuna fish spread in the classroom. Let the children place some of this spread inside a small dinner roll. From a slice of American cheese, cut a triangle. Place the sail (cheese triangle) into the boat (tuna roll) with a toothpick. First sing a round of "Row, Row, Row Your Boat," then enjoy this fun lunch.

LITERATURE

Freight Train by Donald Cres, Beach Tree Books, 1996.
The Little Engine That Could by Watty Piper, Grosset & Dunlap, 1978.
Boats by Anne Rockwell, E.P. Dutton, 1993.
Cars and Tucks and Things That Go by Richard Scarry, Golden Press, 1997.

MUSIC

Gather 'round and sing these traditional traveling songs:
   "Down by the Station"
   "The Bus Song" (The Wheels on the Bus)
   "Row, Row, Row Your Boat"
   "I've Been Working on the Railroad"
   "Bumping Up and Down" (In My Little Red Wagon)
   "Wabash Cannonball"

Summer Sensations

Summer is here! Get your class in the summertime mood by reading *The Twelve Days of Summer* by Elizabeth Lee O'Donnell (New York: William Morrow and Company, Inc., 1991). Your students will enjoy the lively verse as a little girl shares her first 12 days of summer down by the seashore. Ask your students to choose their favorite sea creatures from the book and create picture books with facts and pictures about the animals. They may use encyclopedias and reference books to help them with their research.

Discover the many noises of the summer season in *The Summer Noisy Book* by Margaret Wise Brown (HarperCollins Publishers, 1951). Share the sounds that a dog named Muffin hears as he travels through the countryside on a summer day. After reading the story, have your class make a list of sounds they might hear on a trip to the beach.

How I Spent My Summer Vacation
by Mark Teague
New York: Crown Publishers, 1995

A boy gets more than he bargains for when he heads west for his summer vacation. When he gets kidnapped by a group of cowboys, he decides to hit the dusty trail with them and becomes a cowhand. After learning a few handy cowboy tricks, he soon performs his greatest feat—stopping a cattle stampede!

- The Bar M Ranch needs your help! Write a "help wanted" advertisement for a cowhand to work at the ranch. What qualifications do you think a cowhand needs?

- Ride 'em cowboy! Write a story about how you stopped a cattle stampede.

- Pecos Bill, move over! Create a new western tall tale hero. What does your new hero look like? Tell about this hero's greatest adventure.

Let's Go Swimming
by Shigeo Watanabe
illustrated by Yasuo Ohtomo
New York: Philomel Books, 1990

Splash! Head for a day at the swimming pool with Bear and his father. Although Bear is afraid of the big pool at first, his father's patience and reassurance pays off.

- Be an artist! Design a poster with rules and pictures about swimming pool safety.

- Congratulations! You were just chosen "Junior Lifeguard for the Day." Tell about your unforgettable experience.

- Design a new pool toy that would be an instant summertime hit. Draw a picture of your amazing toy. Now decide what you would name it.

by Mary Ellen Switzer

Book nook

My Mom Made Me Go to Camp

by Judy Delton
illustrated by Lisa McCue
New York: Bantam Little Rooster, 1990

Poor Archie! He doesn't want to go to camp, but his mother sends him anyway. When he "saves" the children in his tent from a flying bat, he becomes a hero. Camp soon becomes a lot better!

- Draw a picture of a backpack. Now draw some things you would pack for summer camp.

- Dear Mom! Write a postcard that Archie might send his mother telling her about camp.

- Off to camp we go! Plan a summer camp that all your friends will rave about. What games would you play? What food would be served? Design an ad with pictures and information about your camp.

Arthur's Family Vacation

by Marc Brown
New York: Little, Brown & Co., 1993

When rain threatens to dampen Arthur's family vacation, he decides to take everyone on some fun-filled "field trips." Thanks to Arthur's careful planning, the family manages to have a wonderful time despite the inclement weather.

- Vacation fun! Make a list of four activities you would enjoy doing on a rainy day.

- What rainy day activity do you like best? Tell why.

- Design a new board game that you and your family could play during vacation on a rainy day. What would you call your game? Draw a picture of the gameboard. Write the directions for playing your game.

Curious George at the Beach

by Marjorie Rey & Alan J. Shalleck
Boston: Houghton Mifflin Co., 1988

Come on along for an unforgettable day at the beach with Curious George. That inquisitive monkey soon disrupts a volleyball game but later manages to rescue a boy who almost falls off the pier.

- Hooray for Curious George! Design a special trophy for that quick-thinking hero—Curious George.

- Draw a picture of your favorite part of the story.

- Just pretend! Imagine that Curious George visits your classroom for the day. Tell what happens.

All About Mothers

Mothers are my kind of people,
They come in each possible size.
They know when you're telling a story . . .
They just have to look in your eyes.

They see when you're pinching your brother,
They know if you're sneaking a snack.
Their eyes can be reading a paper
But somehow, they see out the back!

Their hearing is just as amazing.
You don't have to be in their sight—
They hear when you crumble a cookie
And know if you cry in the night.

A mother can smell like a tiger
If you use after-shave or perfume.
She'll know if you didn't use toothpaste
The minute you walk in the room.

Mothers forget you were naughty
As soon as you do something right.
They praise you and say you're terrific,
Then kiss you and hug you real tight.

Mothers will say you are clever
And handsome and pretty and smart.
Mothers have ears, eyes, and noses,
But really, they're mostly all heart!

by M. Donnaleen Howitt

Mother's Day Is on the Way

In springtime, teachers often scramble for a suitable yet simple Mother's Day project. Once again, the sense of smell can lead you to a winning project. Vanilla candy can be a pretty and welcome gift when you package it in colored plastic wrap, tied with purple and pink ribbons. I like to use pre-packaged white chocolate bark and molds such as cherubs and hearts. Melt the mixture in a microwave and then let the children ladle it into the molds. These candies turn out beautifully with very little work, and the children feel like they have created something fancy for their mothers. The scent of vanilla makes this a particularly pleasant gift.

by Dr. Linda Karges-Bone

Water Weight

Activity

Have your students ever had this experience? They stick one hand into a pool or lake to test the water temperature and, finding it warm, they jump in, only to find it much colder than expected. Help them discover what causes this with a simple experiment. First, fill a mayonnaise jar about 2/3 full with cold water. Next, tie a length of string around the neck of a baby food jar, fill this jar with hot water, and add a few drops of food coloring. Use the string to gently lower the jar of colored (warm) water into the jar of cold water and observe what takes place. Your students should observe the warm water bubbling out of the small jar and rising to the top of the cold water in the large jar. Help them to conclude that warm water is lighter than cold, therefore it will rise to the top. How can they relate this discovery to their warm water/cold water experience at the lake or pool?

Project

Experiment with color and water to make great sun catcher gifts for Mother's Day.

Have students use their fingertips to dot coffee filters with colored water. Set these aside to dry while you help the students cut out the inner sections of plastic lids, creating circular frames. Students can cut their coffee filters to fit their plastic rims, then glue the filters in place. Add a yarn loop to the back for hanging. Create similar sun catchers by helping students melt crayon or wax shavings between two squares of waxed paper. Frame these with cardboard, decorate the frames with marker, and add a ribbon loop for hanging.

A Special Thanks on **Mother's Day**

Mother's Day Songs

Tune: "Bingo"

There are two words I love to use.
   (put up two fingers on one hand)
I use them every day, oh:
T-h-a-n-k   *(point to the lettered fingers)*
T-h-a-n-k
T-h-a-n-k
Thank you very much!
   (point to both words)

Tune: "This Old Man"

Mother's Day, Mother's Day.
We will celebrate and say,
Mothers are special in every way.
Let's say "thank you" to our moms today.

Spoken: THANK YOU!

Puppet to Go with Mother's Day Song
Materials
   one garden glove
   magnetic letters *t, h, a, n, k, y, o,* and *u*
   assorted silk flowers to decorate glove
   hot glue gun and glue sticks or craft glue

Directions
1. Glue the *t* to the thumb (palm side), *h* to the pointer finger, *a* to the middle finger, *n* to the ring finger, and *k* to the pinky.

2. On the center of the palm glue *y-o-u*.

3. Place flowers around the glove and glue as desired.

Use the glove to point out the words *Thank you* when singing the song. The glove may be used with both songs.

286   by Mary Ruth Moore

Hanky Thank-You Game

As a follow-up to the song, use a permanent marker to write *thank you* on an old hanky. To introduce the importance of saying "thank you," drop the hanky in a child's lap and say "thank you" to that child, then tell what the child did that you appreciate. This child is then encouraged to find another child to say "thank you" to, and the game continues with each child having a turn to say "thank you" to someone.

You can also play Drop the Handkerchief with the children, dropping the "thank you" behind the children's backs. Emphasize that we must drop the words *thank you* many times every day in order to be polite.

Thank-You Note Writing

As a follow-up to the importance of saying "thank you" to mothers and to everyone, allow students to write thank-you notes to their mothers and someone else they would like to thank. Sing the thank you songs as the writing begins.

Thank You!

T is for the trust to Mom I'll give,

H is for our home where we live.

A is for always, she's always there.

N is for nice, she really cares.

K is for kind, in word and deed.

Y is for young, Mom's young at heart.

O is for the one who meets my needs.

U is for understanding from the start.

Thank you, Mom!

Thank-You Bulletin Board

Materials
- buttons
- lace, material scraps, ribbon
- construction paper
- large bulletin board letters to spell *thank you*
- chart with the above poem written on it or, write the poem on the background paper

Around the board, have students place their own handmade portraits of their moms. Have an assortment of real buttons to glue on dresses or as earrings. Lace, ribbon, and material scraps will add variety to their pictures.

Mother's Day Tribute

Use this story as an example for the children to follow to fill in their own Mother's Day descriptive story. It will be a good exercise in similes. Encourage them to be creative in their ideas and Mom will be very pleased and entertained!

Name _____

I think my mom is great!

She is the cat's meow _____ and the icing on the cake _____ !

This is how I would describe my Mom:

My mom has _____ hair, the same color as _____.

Her eyes are _____, just like _____.

My mom is _____ like _____.

She has a nose that she says is _____, just like _____.

Her smile makes me feel very _____, like _____.

My mom likes to _____; I like _____.

_____ is her favorite color, like _____.

My mom is very smart and knows a lot about _____.

Her favorite food is _____ and mine is _____.

My mom is wonderful! My favorite time with her is when _____.

_____.

Love, _____

by Sheila M. Hausbeck

Pop-Out Mother's Day Card (Front)

fold →

1. Use reproducible sheets for the front and inside of cards.
2. Use construction paper or lightweight cardboard for the cards. Color the pictures.
3. Use construction paper or lightweight cardboard for "pop-outs."
4. Paste "pop-outs" on cards on the places marked with Xs.

by Sister M. Yvonne Moran

Pop-Out Mother's Day Card (Inside)

fold →

Dear Mom,

I give you these flowers.
I want them all to say—

Happy Mother's Day!

Pop-Out Father's Day Card (Front)

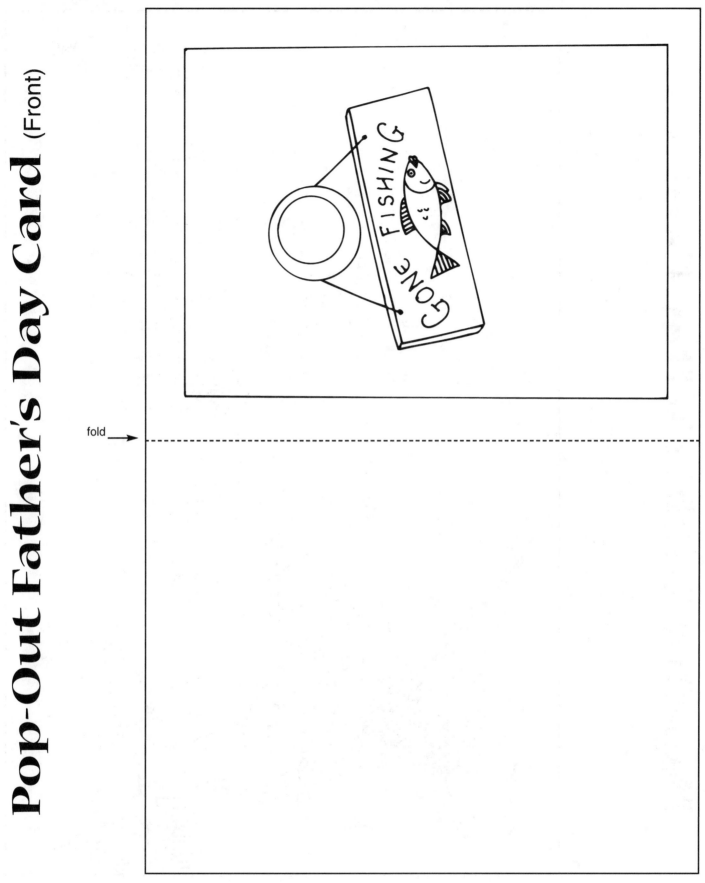

fold →

1. Use reproducible sheets for the front and inside of cards.
2. Use construction paper or lightweight cardboard for the cards. Color the pictures.
3. Use construction paper or lightweight cardboard for "pop-outs."
4. Paste "pop-outs" on cards on the places marked with Xs.

by Sister M. Yvonne Moran

Pop-Out Father's Day Card (Inside)

Dear Dad,

Have fun on Father's Day.
This is my wish—
I hope you can go to your favorite spot
And catch a great big FISH.

Happy Father's Day!

Fold on dotted lines.

Father

Fold on dotted lines.

Mother

1. Use construction paper or lightweight cardboard for the cards. Color the pictures.
2. Use construction paper or lightweight cardboard for "pop-outs." Color the "pop-outs."
3. Paste "pop-outs" on cards on the places marked with Xs.
4. A piece of string may be used for the fishing line. Glue each end of the string to the paper.

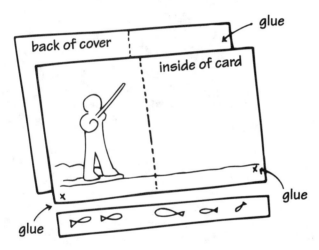

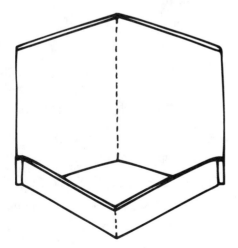

Fold on dotted lines.

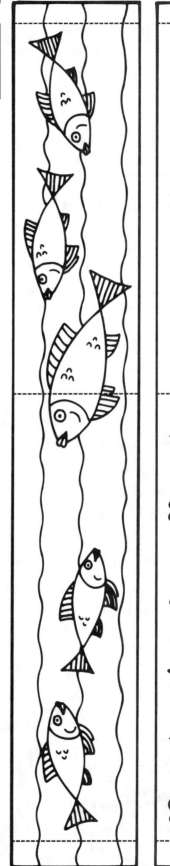

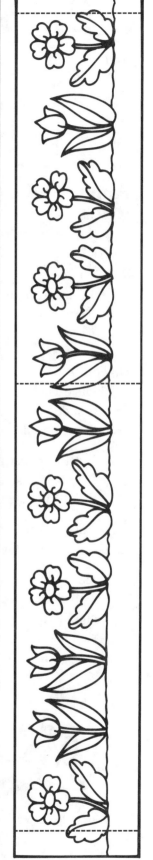

293

For a Dear Dad

Even though the school year is nearly over, let's not forget to make a special surprise for Dad on Father's Day. Any one of the following gift projects is sure to be something your students will enjoy making—and Dad will love to receive it on his special day!

Family Photo Bookmark

Materials

construction paper
photographs
clear adhesive paper
   (2" clear packing tape can be substituted)
decorative edging shears
glue
felt tip pens
ruler

Directions

1. Have each child bring in several family photos that do not need to be returned. Instruct children to cut people and pets from these photos.

2. Cut the construction paper into 2" x 7" strips, then let the students glue their photo cut-outs to the strips. Allow to dry.

3. Cover each photo strip with clear adhesive. Smooth out any bubbles with the side of a ruler.

4. Have children trim the edges of their bookmarks with decorative edging shears. Next, have each child write a message for Dad on the back and sign his or her name.

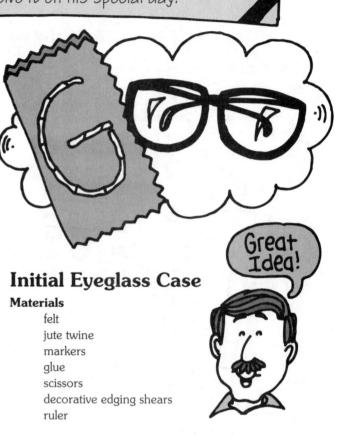

Initial Eyeglass Case

Materials

felt
jute twine
markers
glue
scissors
decorative edging shears
ruler

Directions

1. Use the edging shears to cut a 7" felt square for each child.

2. Show children how to fold the square in half, then glue the long side and one short side together to form the glass case.

3. Have students use a marker to print their father's first initial on the front of the case.

4. Have students trace the initial with glue, then help them cut pieces of twine and set them in the glue. Allow glue to dry.

by Marie E. Cecchini

Designer Hankies

Materials

  men's handkerchiefs
  permanent markers
  corrugated cardboard
  stapler
  utility knife (adult use)

Directions

1. Use the utility knife to cut several large squares of corrugated cardboard.

2. Staple a handkerchief to each of the cardboard squares. This will keep the fabric taut while students decorate the handkerchiefs.

3. Let students use permanent markers to create their own Father's Day designs on their handkerchiefs.

Pot of Gold Change Dish

Materials

  baker's clay
  gold acrylic paint or white tempera
    mixed with gold glitter
  paint brushes

Directions

1. Prepare baker's clay by mixing 4 cups flour and 1 cup salt with $1 1/2$ cups water. Knead the mixture until smooth, adding a small amount of water if the clay is too stiff.

2. Have children mold the clay into small pinch pots. Allow pots to air dry, or bake them at 300°F for about one hour.

3. Let children paint their pots with gold acrylic paint (a little goes a long way), or use a mixture of white tempera and gold glitter.

Dad's Delight Snack Mix

Possible Ingredients

  popped corn
  nuts
  dry cereal
  croutons
  pretzels
  sunflower seeds
  chocolate chips
  raisins
  shredded coconut
  mini marshmallows
  sandwich-size plastic bags
  ribbon

Directions

1. Set out the ingredients in individual bowls. Place a serving spoon or small scoop in each bowl.

2. Provide each child with a small plastic bag. Instruct children to create their own special snack mix for Father's Day.

3. Seal each bag with a twist tie and a ribbon bow. Note: You may want to ask parents to donate the items for this project.

Dads

Mothers are OK for hugging,
But Dads are for holding you high . . .
Up to a branch on an oak tree,
Up when a bump makes you cry.

Up when the waves are too scary,
Up when a dog barks too loud,
Up when parades go down Main Street—
Up to see over the crowd.

Up when your bike is all wobbly,
Up when you can't reach the bar,
Up when your legs won't keep walking,
Up when you wish on a star.

Mothers are just fine for cuddling,
And Grandmas are good when you cry.
Grandpas like telling you stories,
But Dads are for holding you high.

by M. Donnaleen Howitt

296

Arbor Day

What is the biggest, most spectacular, green plant of all?
Why the tree, of course. Celebrate this wonderful plant on Arbor Day.

PLANT A TREE

Start a new tradition in your school—plant a tree on Arbor Day.

Directions

1. Choose a location for your tree. How high can the tree grow in that location. Will it be shady or sunny? Will other plants or trees interfere with its growth? Don't plant too close to a building, power line, or another tree.
2. Choose a tree. Select a tree that is well-suited for your school yard and climate. Have your group research through books, internet, or visiting a local garden center. Think about how the tree will look in the future. Is it well-suited for the location where you are planting it?
3. Plant it! Dig a hole that is twice the width and twice the depth of the tree's root ball. Set the tree in the center of the hole. Add soil and compost, if needed, to the bottom of the hole to bring the base of the tree to the soil line. Fill the hole around the tree with original soil mixed with compost. Sprinkle the soil with water and pack lightly. Sprinkle a layer of mulch around the tree and water well. Water the tree as needed to keep the soil moist until the tree has taken root.

BY ROBYNNE EAGAN

THE GIFT OF A TREE

Help children to think about trees in a special way. Encourage students to plant a tree on a special day in their lives—maybe this year's Arbor Day celebration. Talk about the planting of a tree as a wonderful way to mark a special day or an important event—like a birth, a birthday, Mother's Day, Father's Day, an anniversary, graduation, as a memorial, or to mark the day you move into a new home. Trees make special, environment-friendly gifts that help us to mark important events—and the passage of time after that event. Have photos taken beside the special tree and in the same spot every year that follows.

Watch how your gift to the Earth grows over time!

Trees are part of the plant category called woody-stemmed plants. Plants in this category have a thick or thin bark called a woody stem.

MEET A TREE

Take away one sense to enhance the others.

You Need
blindfold for each child
"seeing" volunteers

Directions

1. Have volunteers blindfold children and lead them to "meet a tree." Encourage children to use all of their senses to get to know their tree. Have them feel, smell, measure with their bodies. What can they discover without using their eyes? Do their fingers reach around the trunk? What about their arms? Are there leaves growing on the tree? Is there any moss? How does the bark feel? Can the child reach any branches? Is it hot or cool under the tree? Does the tree have a smell?
2. Have volunteers move children away from their trees and mark the spot discreetly with the child's name. Once children are a distance from the tree, blindfolds can be removed.
3. Ask "seeing" children to try to find "their" trees.
4. Have children join together as a group to discuss their discoveries about their trees. What led them to their trees? What made it difficult to identify their trees?

Tree Bark Rubbings

Have you ever investigated bark?

Bark is a fascinating part of a tree. It keeps a tree alive. It can be smooth, rough, shiny, or dull. There is an inner layer of bark called the cambium and an outer layer generally referred to as bark that surrounds the tree like a coat. It protects the tree from insects, animals, fungi, weather, and fire. Each species of tree has its own unique bark. Investigate for yourself.

You Need
construction paper
crayons with wrappers removed

Directions
1. Hold the construction paper over the bark.
2. Rub the side of a crayon gently back and forth across the paper until you have created an impression of the bark.
3. Compare the various impressions.

Tree Flowers

Can you find the flowers on an evergreen tree? You might be able to see them, but maybe you don't recognize them as flowers! The flower of the evergreen tree is called the cone.

There are both male and female "flowers" or cones. Small, yellow male cones give off pollen in early spring and then drop off the trees. These are usually difficult to spot. Can you find any of these cones?

When we think of a pinecone, we usually think of the large, woody female seed cone. These cones take two seasons to mature into the woody cones that we recognize as pinecones. In the first spring, the cone opens long enough to allow pollen grains to adhere to a sticky fluid. Within 15 months, pollination is complete and the seeds develop. The cone becomes woody and opens up, releasing hundreds of winged seeds. Can you find any of these? The squirrels usually do! Squirrels love to take the cones from a tree and eat the seeds!

Take a Closer Look

Children can get a fresh perspective on trees by taking a closer look. All that is needed is a simple magnifying glass. Have children zoom in on leaves, branches, bark, mosses, flowers, cones, and insect holes. They might find out that there is more to a tree than meets the naked eye!

Celebrate Summer

With the coming of summer comes the end of a school year. A year of friendships, learning, and special camaraderie should be celebrated.

Circle of Friends

You Need
large area of pavement
large box of colored chalk
group of children

Directions
1. Have friends form a circle and then lie down, fanning out from the center to form a circle of friends.
2. Pair each child with the one next to him or her.
3. Have partners use the chalk to trace around each other on the pavement. The child's name should be written beneath the tracing.
4. When both partners have been traced, children stand and form the circle again, standing by their own images.
5. Have children rotate to the next spot in the circle. Allow children 30 seconds to add color and detail to the body tracings in front of them.
6. Continue in this manner—rotating one space at a time—for intervals of 30 seconds until children have rotated back to their own tracing.
7. Stand back and enjoy the circle of friends. Take a photo for the future!

Summer Sky Watch

Invite children to wear their sunglasses and kick off their shoes for a study of the sky.

Have students lie on their backs in the middle of a lush summer field and turn their eyes skyward. What do they see? What do they hear? How would they describe the colors? Watch for airplanes, birds, dragonflies, blowing leaves or dust, and clouds, of course.

Why is the sky blue?
This question is sure to be inspired by this activity! Our atmosphere is composed of many air molecules—primarily nitrogen and oxygen. Nitrogen and oxygen reflect blue, violet, and green bands of sunlight but allow the other colors to pass through. When we look to the sky, we see only the scattered bands of reflected blue, violet, and green combining together to form shades of blue.

On July 1, 1867, a few northern British colonies united into a federation called Canada. Since then the country has grown to include 10 provinces and three territories. It is now the second largest country in the world. The maple leaf and the beaver are two of the primary symbols of Canada. Every year across the country people have parades, picnics, special concerts, events, and fireworks to celebrate the peaceful birth of Canada.

Canada Day

July 1

Canada Flag

The Canadian flag has a red maple leaf in the middle with two red bars on either side.

Materials
white paper for flags
red construction paper
paste
red poster paint
maple leaves

Teacher Preparation
- Cut out rectangular red strips of paper.
- Gather large maple leaves.

Directions
Give each child a rectangular sheet of paper. Instruct them to paste a red bar on each of the shorter sides. Dip maple leaf into red paint and press the vein side onto the middle of the white paper. Or, apply red paint to leaf using a paint roller.

Helpful Hint
If there are no maple leaves where you live, cut out a maple leaf from stiff sponges.

Beaver Lodge

Materials
twigs
mud or wet sand
seaweed or leaves
dry sand

Teacher Preparation
- Talk about beaver dams and show pictures.
- Take children to the beach or anywhere near water.
- Gather twigs, leaves, or sea weed.

Directions
Have children dig a round hole. Place twigs across the top of the hole securing them in the wet sand or mud. Place seaweed or leaves on top. Sprinkle dry sand on top.

by Devorah Stone

Paper Quilts

Materials
large white paper
different colored construction paper
crayons and felt tip markers
paste

Teacher Preparation
• Cut construction paper into squares.
• Show children pictures and symbols of Canada.

Directions
Instruct each student to decorate a small square with a symbol of Canada. Examples: Canada goose, beaver, hockey stick, skates, loon, maple leaf, moose, and so on. Paste all the squares together into one quilt.

Bannock

Bannock is a truly Canadian bread based on Scottish flat breads. Explorers and traders baked this bread all across Western Canada. Native people made this bread their own. It tastes great alone or with jam.

Ingredients
1 cup white flour	1 cup whole wheat flour
1/2 tsp. salt	1 T. baking powder
2 T. sugar	2 T. shortening or lard
3/4 cup water	

Utensils
large bowl
pastry blender, forks, or whisk
small rolling pins
cookie pan, frying pan, or barbeque grill

Directions
Mix dry ingredients. Cut in vegetable shortening or lard, with pastry blender, dull plastic knives, or a whisk until it's in fine crumbs. Have one student mix dough while the another sprinkles water on the mixture a little at a time. Turn dough out onto floured board. Knead dough 10 times. Divide dough and let children roll it out to about 1/2" thick. Bake at 450°F for 10 to 15 minutes. (You can also pan fry with butter or grill until golden brown on both sides.)

Helpful Hints: 1) Instead of mixing dry ingredients, shake them. Provide a tight plastic container and have the students take turns shaking it.
2) Punch a few small holes in a small yogurt container and use it for sprinkling water.

The Parade

I watch Old Glory passing by,
The marchers hold the banner high.
I say the pledge, that's what I do
As I salute Red, White, and Blue.

The music plays, I sing along.
My heart loves that star-spangled song!
I'm proud to watch the banner blow,
I sing the notes both high and low.

I watch Old Glory passing by.
I stand up tall, my head's held high.
Oh Stars and Stripes that fly above,
I wish you peace. I wish you love.

by Jacqueline Schiff

A Tribute to the Red, White, and Blue

Be True to the Red, White, and Blue

Ask children to give their nicknames. Tell them that the American flag has four nicknames: "Old Glory"; "The Red, White and Blue"; "The Star-Spangled Banner"; and "The Stars and Stripes."

Tell children you will play a recording of a famous patriotic song called "The Star-Spangled Banner." It was written by a man named Francis Scott Key. "The Star-Spangled Banner" is our national anthem.

It is the song of the United States of America. First read the words to the song as children color pictures of sky, mountains, fields of grain, and fruits of nature.

After playing the recording (preferably a vocal arrangement), read the children the poem, "The Parade." Choose some children to play the marchers. Give them miniature flags. Have the other children pretend to be the parade spectators.

Play a tape of parade music. As the marchers march around the room carrying their flags, the spectators hold their hands over their hearts. When the music stops, the marchers stand in place holding their banners high.

Lead the children playing the spectators in saluting the flags and reciting the Pledge of Allegiance.

by Jacqueline Schiff

Holiday Sing-Alongs

by Mabel Duch

Holiday Marching Song

*To the tune of
"Row, Row, Row Your Boat"*

Beat, beat, beat your drums
With beats both quick and strong,
Joyfully, joyfully, joyfully, joyfully
As you march along.

March, march, march, my friends,
Singing all the way,
Joyfully, joyfully, joyfully, joyfully
It's Independence Day!*

Wave, wave, wave your flags,
Wave and sing with glee,
Joyfully, joyfully, joyfully, joyfully
"We're glad our country's free!"

* Canadian children should substitute "It is
Canada Day!" for this line. If used for another
patriotic holiday, they should sing "Canada,
hooray!" If used in the United Sates for Flag Day,
Memorial Day, or Veterans Day, children should
substitute "Hooray for the U.S.A!"

Background

Independence Day, commonly called The Fourth of
July, celebrates the signing of the Declaration of
Independence on July 4, 1776.

The Declaration told the English that the 13 colonies
wanted to be free, but they still had to fight for their
freedom.

Canada Day, formerly Dominion Day, is celebrated
every year on July 1. It commemorates July 1, 1867,
when New Brunswick, Nova Scotia, Quebec, and
Ontario formed the Dominion of Canada. Other
provinces joined later.

Discussion

1. What is freedom?
2. When we say a country is *free,* what do we
   mean?
3. What are the advantages of living in a free
   country?

Activities

Practice the song until the children know it well. Then have them use flags and drums while they march and sing the song.

Drums can be made from coffee cans. Cover with white paper and decorate with colored adhesive tape. Use unsharpened pencils as drumsticks.

Have children bring small flags from home. Or enlarge a flag picture and make copies for the children to color. Leave enough space at the left to wrap around and tape to a dowel.

Let your children enjoy sharing their holiday marching song with others by marching and singing around the school or neighborhood.

The flag on the right has been the flag of the United States of America since 1960, after Hawaii joined the Union. Every time a new state joins, a star is added to the flag. What will the flag look like if another state joins?

The 13 stripes represent the 13 original colonies. At one time, a stripe was added for each new state. But the flag was getting too big, so the flag was changed back to 13 stripes. Can you imagine a flag with a stripe for every state?

The flag on the right has been Canada's flag since 1965. It was the first Canadian flag not bearing a British symbol. The maple leaf is a national symbol of Canada, as is the beaver.

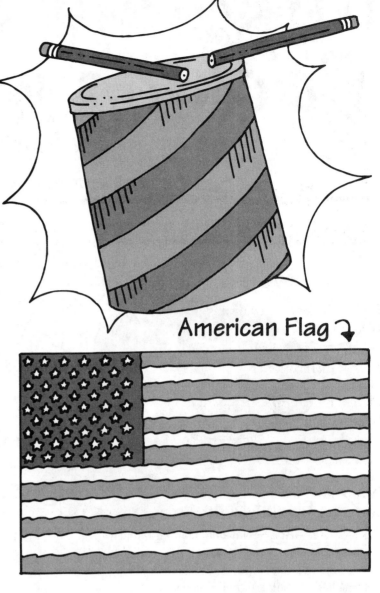

American Flag ⤵

Canadian Flag ⤵

Cooking with Kids

What fun your class will have developing and devouring these Epicurean delights for spring and summer.

Cool Fondue

Ingredients

applesauce	cinnamon
vanilla yogurt	ground cloves
fresh fruit pieces	nutmeg

Combine equal amounts of applesauce and yogurt. Mix well. For each cup of applesauce used, stir in 1 tsp. of cinnamon and 1/4 tsp. of ground cloves. Sprinkle the top with nutmeg. To eat, dip pieces of fresh fruit into the mixture. Toothpicks are optional.

Biscuit Bugs

April—National Garden Month

Ingredients

refrigerator biscuit dough
raisins, frozen corn and/or peas
cheese bits
olive slices

Have children shape a piece of dough into a garden insect. They might roll and coil the dough for a snail, roll for a caterpillar or worm, pat into a ball for a lady-bug, and so on. Provide them with the additives listed above or other choices for adding eyes, spots, legs, or other features. Then bake the biscuit creatures.

Crunchy Raisin Salad

May

Ingredients

| 2 lbs. carrots, shredded | 1 cup raisins |
| 3/4 cup celery, chopped | 2 cups vanilla yogurt |

Toss the shredded carrots, raisins, and chopped celery together in a large bowl. Stir in the yogurt. Chill before serving.

by Marie E. Cecchini

Banana Tacos

May 5—Cinco de Mayo

Ingredients

instant banana pudding	milk
banana slices	taco shells

Prepare the pudding with milk as directed on the package. Chill. Spoon pudding into taco shells, then push banana slices into the pudding.

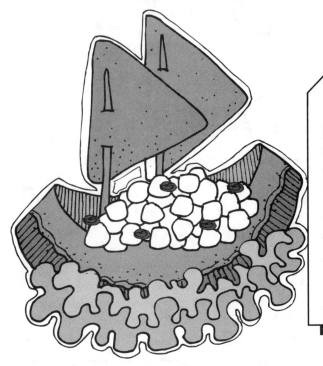

Melon Boats

Summer/Beach

Ingredients

melon slices	cheese slices
cottage cheese	leaf lettuce
raisins	toothpicks

Place a lettuce leaf on a plate. Set a melon slice onto the lettuce. Spoon cottage cheese into the center of the melon. Add raisins to the cottage cheese to represent people. Break cheese slices into two triangles. Slide one toothpick into each cheese triangle sail. Place one sail at either end of the melon boat.

Clowning Around

Summer/Circus

Ingredients

bread slices	raisins
peanut butter	cherries, halved
cream cheese	strawberry slices
shredded carrots	blueberries

Cut or tear one bread slice into a circle. Spread cream cheese over the circle and place it on a plate. Create a clown face by adding raisin eyes, a cherry half nose, strawberry slice cheeks, a blueberry mouth, and shredded carrot hair. Cut or tear a second bread slice into a triangle. Spread peanut butter over the triangle. Place this at the top of the clown face for a hat. Add a cherry half pom-pom to the top of the hat.

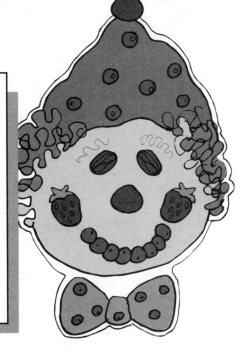

Chocolate Soda Creams

March—American Chocolate Week

Ingredients

chocolate syrup	milk
ice cream (vanilla or chocolate)	club soda
whipped cream	chocolate candy pieces

Have each child place 2 T. of chocolate syrup and 1/4 c. of milk in a glass and stir. Add a scoop of ice cream, then pour in club soda until the glass is almost full. Top with whipped cream and a candy piece.

Peanut Butter Fondue

March 1—Peanut Butter Lovers' Day

Ingredients

1 c. creamy peanut butter	1 c. light cream
1/2 c. honey	

fruit chunks—apples, peaches, pears, bananas, etc.

Measure peanut butter into a fondue pot or saucepan. Blend in the cream and honey. Heat over low heat, stirring constantly until the mixture starts to boil. Reduce heat to warm. Have children prepare the fruit. Have children spear fruit with forks and dip into mixture.

Crunchy Peanut Treats

March—Peanut Month

Ingredients

1/2 c. peanut butter	1/2 c. peanuts
3 c. chow mein noodles	
1 c. butterscotch or chocolate pieces	

Stir and melt candy pieces with peanut butter over a double boiler until smooth. Remove the mixture from heat and stir in peanuts and chow mein noodles. Mix well to coat. Drop by spoonfuls onto waxed paper and refrigerate until set, about 30 minutes.

Holiday newsletter

With summer right around the corner, many parents wonder what they can and should do to maintain their children's academic skills, as well as help them prepare for the next grade level. In an effort to answer these queries, a recent poll was taken at my daughter's school. Every single teacher responding to the survey listed reading as their number one recommendation. Some of their ideas were to read to and with your child, and to listen to your child read. Ask your children questions about their reading (characters, story line, and so on). Get your child a library card and then use it. Incorporate books, newspapers, magazines, traffic signs, bus schedules, cereal boxes, milk cartons, grocery lists, and TV listings into your home reading program. This will help answer their questions as to why they need to learn to read. It gives meaning to the idea of reading. Another way to demonstrate the importance of reading is to let the children see you use reading skills for such things as shopping or errand lists, recipes, mail, and so on. Children will be better motivated to read if they understand the need. Reading is the key element in all subject areas. Encourage your children to use and improve their reading skills.

by Marie E. Cecchini

Simple Science

Celebrate Earth Day by recycling an old tire and a trash can lid into a simple birdbath. First, nestle the trash can lid into the hole in the tire to keep it steady. If you do not have an old tire, some loose gravel, sand, or dirt will work as well. Next, surround the trash can lid with several stones to make perches for the birds. Fill the bath daily with fresh water, and clean it weekly with a hose and rag to prevent slimey buildup. Encourage your child to observe bird bathers. How do they bathe with no hands? Borrow a bird book from the library to help identify some of your visitors. Help your child keep a journal of the birds spotted, drawing pictures of each, and writing each bird's name. How many varieties does your birdbath attract?

On the Move

Physical activities provide children with an opportunity to move and explore how their body parts work together. Outdoor games can improve agility and stamina, and group games can promote cooperation. Flying disc exercises can incorporate all of the above, as well as encourage creative game playing. A flying disc can be store bought, or you can use a paper plate or even a hat. After a simple toss and catch, challenge your child to discover new ways to share the disc. Can you roll or kick it to your partner? Can you toss it behind your back, under one leg, or through both legs? Try playing toss and catch with both players facing away from one another. Does it work if you bat it with your hand? Can you toss and catch more than one disc at a time? The possibilities are endless.

Creative Kitchen

Try this creamy confection on toast, bagels, crackers, or rolls. You will need an 8-oz. package of softened cream cheese, 1/2 cup of powdered sugar, and 1/2 cup of mashed strawberries. At this time of year, many rural areas offer "pick your own" strawberries at local farms. Make it a family affair by doing just that. To make the strawberry cream cheese, simply combine the ingredients above in a bowl or blender, then use a wire whisk to blend until the mixture is smooth. This should be refrigerated until ready to be used. Try adding a drop or two of blue food color, then spread on a white bagel or cracker for a special July 4th treat.

Communication Station

Encourage children to begin a new collection, or help them organize an established one. Rocks, dried flowers, and dead bugs (for the squeamish, remember this is the child's collection) can be mounted in shoe box lids. Let children add labels, then look up information in a reference book and discuss some of the characteristics of each item. Create a scrapbook about the child's favorite famous person. Include magazine and newspaper pictures and articles. Date each article and prompt your child to tell why this person is so special.

You can also take photographs of your child enjoying several summer activities, such as swimming, gardening, or day trips. Have your child use these photos to design a personal keepsake book. Encourage the child to write a caption for each photo, and then add a few comments about the activity (for instance: Was it fun? Who else was there? What was the best/worst part?).

Collections are a learning experience, rich in language, that provide many happy memories to share.

Poetry in Motion

Creating a summer activity box can help your family ease through the summer slumps. Help your child cover an old shoe box with summer designs, then cut a slot in the box top. Together, brainstorm a list of things to do. These can be quiet, active, or zany ideas. Help your child write each idea on an index card or piece of note paper, using a blue marker or ballpoint pen. Let your child push each idea card through the slot. Copy the "Slump Busters" poem, share it with your child, then glue it to the side of the box. Whenever the summer slumps threaten,

remove the lid, and have your child draw a card (eyes closed). Add new ideas throughout the season.

Slump Busters
From Memorial Day to Labor Day
Whatever will we do?
Think you're stumped? Just pick a card.
Then read the words in blue.
Now you have a great idea
For something fun and new!

From the Art Cart

Having children create their own handmade gifts is a wonderful way to help them remember that gift giving is about thoughtfulness, not dollars. During the summer months, Mother's Day and Father's Day provide perfect opportunities to reinforce this idea. Plaster of Paris paperweights are simple, yet allow for individual creative expression, and can be used by both parents. First, prepare the plaster of Paris (available from craft or art supply stores) according to package directions (two parts plaster to one part water). Have the child shape a handful of plaster as desired, then decorate with household items by pressing the items into the plaster. For Mother's Day, these might include artificial flowers, decorative buttons, pebbles, and shells. For Father's Day, golf tees, nuts, screws, nails, washers, or bolts might be used. No fishhooks, please! Allow the paperweights to dry on newspaper for several days, then glue pieces of felt to the bottom to protect table or desktops.

Holiday Newsletter

Even though summer offers youngsters time to relax from the rigors of school, learning is an ongoing process not to be completely abandoned. Here are a few ideas for keeping in touch with your children and keeping your children in touch with learning during their school break: 1. Read with your child as often as you can and let your child see you reading newspapers, magazines, and so on. Encourage your child to read for fun. Check out local libraries and yard sales for books. 2. Make time to talk with your child about things he or she finds important. Never underestimate the value of praise and encouragement. A little goes a long way. 3. Write notes to your child regarding phone messages or neglected chores. Encourage your child to leave notes for you, also. 4. Provide your child with a place and materials for working on any special projects he or she may dream up. 5. Finally, try to monitor television viewing and remind your child that nutritious meals/snacks and plenty of rest are still important. Enjoy a happy, healthy summer!

Simple Science

Thoughts of summer bring to mind beaches, salt water, and boats. Here is a seaside experiment your child can try right at home. Let your child mold an aluminum foil boat, or use a small aluminum pie plate. Fill a dishpan or sink with water and have your child estimate how many pennies or paper clips the boat will hold before it sinks. Then have your child float the boat on the water and drop one penny or paper clip into the boat at a time, until it sinks. How close was the estimate? Now, dissolve several tablespoons of salt in the water and repeat the experiment. Again, estimate and compare the results. Adding salt to the water increases its density, therefore the boat should hold more before sinking the second time the experiment is performed.

On the Move

May is National Physical Fitness Month, so it is time to get moving. Have your child retrieve a clean sock from the laundry. Fill the foot of the sock with rice or dried beans, or simply drop a ball into the toe, then tie a knot above this filler. Use this new toy to play catch with a friend or even yourself by swinging it up into the air and catching it before it hits the ground. Toss it over the branch of a tree or through a hoop suspended from the branch. Set up a distance throwing competition with friends or family members. You might also suspend the filled sock from a tree branch so your child can hit it with a bat, racket, or other balls. And children always love the thrill of target practice, so make use of empty soda bottles or cans and try to knock them over with the loaded sock. Making movement fun is not as difficult as you think.

Creative Kitchen

Measure, mix, and chill a no-bake raisin snack for the summer.

Peanut Butter-Raisin Grahams

1 c. peanut butter
1/4 c. raisins
1/3 c. powdered milk
1/4 c. graham cracker crumbs
1/4 c. honey
1/2 c. flaked coconut
1/4 c. sesame seeds

Combine all of the ingredients in a large bowl, reserving some of the coconut. Roll the mixture into small balls, then into coconut. Chill and store in the refrigerator.

by Marie E. Cecchini

309

Communication Station

A local newspaper is a great at-home source of language experiences for your child during the summer and throughout the year. Sharing thoughts on a local issue and discussing pertinent facts may interest your child in writing a brief letter to the editor. Comic strips or short columns can be cut apart by block or paragraph and serve as a puzzle. Can your child put the pieces back together so they make sense? Classified ads can be used to locate available pets or local yard sales. Entertainment sections offer ideas and information for planning family outings. You can also encourage reading through store sale information for a special item your child has been requesting, or have your child read through the coupon section for items on your shopping list. Making use of what is available and relevant to everyday living can help instill the desire to make use of language skills.

Poetry in Motion

Disposable cameras are inexpensive and can be a lot of fun. Purchase one or two for your child during Photo Month in May and encourage creative picture taking. After the pictures have been developed, your child may want to turn them into a collage, adding a self-composed verse to describe this work of art. An example of a verse might be, "Quick as a flash, In the wink of an eye, The lens of my camera, Lets nothing slip by." You and your child may also choose to mount and caption several photographs separately, or select one favorite to enlarge and place in a frame.

Mathworks

Math lessons are not limited to memorizing facts. The truth is, we use numbers every day. Opportunities to help your child become accustomed to and comfortable with using math naturally are all around us. Here are a few examples you might want to try. Children can help add up the cost of a meal out, practice telling time using mall or car clocks, and read prices on items or gasoline purchased. If your family frequents baseball or soccer games, or plays miniature golf, enlist your child to keep score. Have a yard sale and let your child keep track of the price of each item sold to total earnings when it is over. Set up a rain gauge and thermometer for your young weather person to check each day. Chart temperatures and rainfall. On your next trip to the grocery store, have your child use a calculator to keep a running tab of items you place into the cart, rounding off numbers up or down. There are many ways to demonstrate to your child how math works for us practically every time we turn around. Give it some thought and create math magic of your own at home.

From the Art Cart

Nothing beats the thoughtfulness of a homemade gift. Here are two simple gift projects for Mother's and Father's Day your child may want to try. Mom would love a garden bookmark to use with any summer reading material. Help your child cut a plastic strip from a clean milk jug. Let your child cut garden pictures from old magazines or seed packets. Place a piece of rolled cellophane tape on the back of each picture, then set the pictures on the plastic strip. Cover the entire strip with clear packing tape for a long-lasting page marker. A woodshop chime might be just the thing for Dad this Father's Day. Your child will need a narrow strip of wood, moulding, or a length of dowel; dental floss; and building nails. Tie one end of a length of dental floss below the head of a nail, then tie the opposite end of the floss to the wood strip. Repeat with each nail and hang the nails approximately the same length so they will chime. Create a hanger by tying opposite ends of a length of floss to the ends of the wood strip. Secure the floss to the wood with glue. When dry, hang to catch the breeze and listen to the jingle.

The Reading Room

Reading for enjoyment is relaxing any time of year. Make summer a special reading time. Unwind outdoors with a glass of lemonade, a chair or blanket, and a good book. Enjoy the warmth and green all around. Daydream. Books can take you anywhere.

American Too by Elisa Bartone, Lothrop, Lee & Shepard, 1996.

Biscuit by Alyssa Satin Capucilli, HarperCollins, 1997.

A Day at Damp Camp by George Ella Lyon, Orchard, 1996.

The Giant Carrot by Jan Peck, Dial Books for Young Readers, 1998.

In the Swim: Poems and Paintings by Douglas Florian, Harcourt Brace, 1997.

Mama's Perfect Present by Diane Goode, Dutton, 1996.

Projects for a Healthy Planet, Simple Environmental Experiments for Kids! by Shar Levine and Allison Grafton, John Wiley and Sons, 1992.

TLC10198 Copyright © Teaching & Learning Company, Carthage, IL 62321-0010

Happy Easter!

Something to Sing About!

Spring Is Here!

"Hoppin" in to show you

_____'s

Great Work!

_____ is

an

"Eggs"tra
Special Student!

_____
_____

Think Green

Happy St. Patrick's Day!

Hi There

Mother's Day!

Please Recycle!

Happy Earth Day!

Fiesta!

Have a Fun Summer!

Dads Are "Grrr"eat!

Happy Mother's Day

Keep Our Planet Clean

4th of July

The End of School

Spring

Brighten Your Day with a Book!

OUTSTANDING

Hi Sensational Summer!

Fun Facts

Sunny Bunny Award

Star Student

Egg-cellent

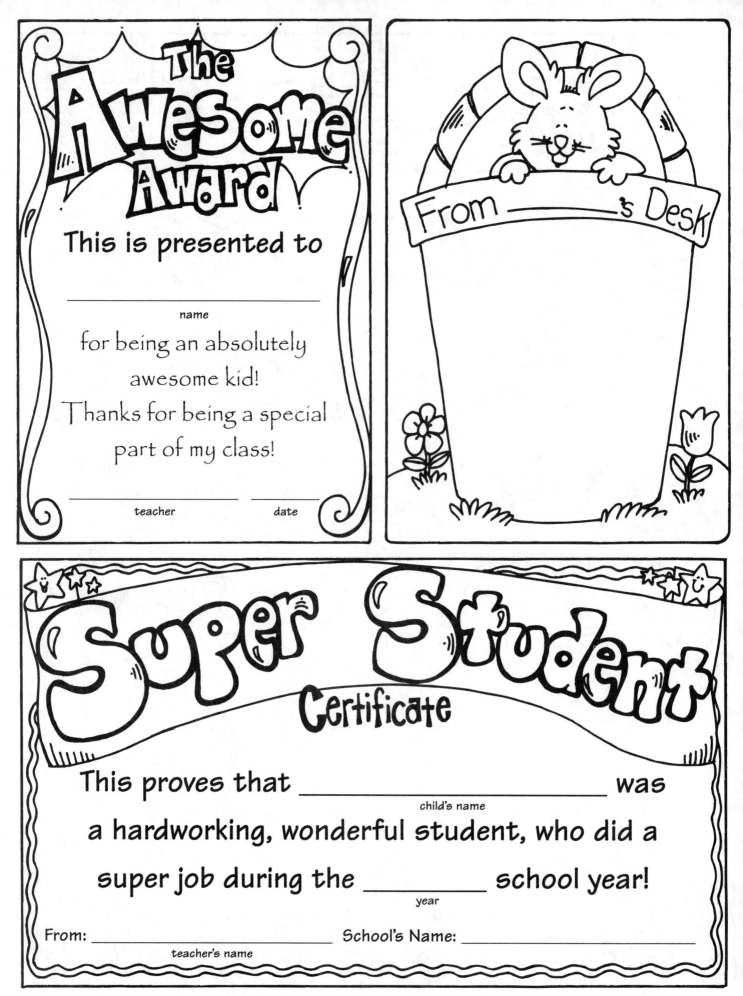

The Awesome Award

This is presented to

_____
name

for being an absolutely
awesome kid!
Thanks for being a special
part of my class!

_____
teacher   date

From _____'s Desk

Super Student
Certificate

This proves that _____ was
child's name

a hardworking, wonderful student, who did a

super job during the _____ school year!
year

From: _____   School's Name: _____
teacher's name

318

Clip Art for Summer